ORDER IN COURT
The Organisation of Verbal Interaction in Judicial Settings

OXFORD SOCIO-LEGAL STUDIES

General Editors: J. Maxwell Atkinson, Donald R. Harris, R. M. Hartwell

Oxford Socio-Legal Studies is a series of books and conference proceedings published by the Centre for Socio-Legal Studies, Wolfson College, Oxford (a research unit of the Social Science Research Council). The series is concerned generally with the relationship between law and society, and is designed to reflect the increasing interest in this field of lawyers, social scientists and historians.

Published simultaneously with this volume

Ross Cranston: REGULATING BUSINESS: LAW AND CONSUMER AGENCIES

David P. Farrington, Keith Hawkins, Sally M. Lloyd-Bostock (editors): PSYCHOLOGY, LAW AND LEGAL PROCESSES

Forthcoming titles

Donald R. Harris, Mavis Maclean and Hazel Genn: COMPENSATION AND SUPPORT FOR ILLNESS AND INJURY

Doreen J. McBarnet: CONVICTION: THE LAW, THE STATE AND THE CONSTRUCTION OF JUSTICE

Mavis Maclean and Hazel Genn: METHODOLOGICAL ISSUES IN SOCIAL SURVEYS

Alan Paterson: THE LAW LORDS

ORDER IN COURT

The Organisation of Verbal Interaction in Judicial Settings

J. Maxwell Atkinson

SSRC Centre for Socio-Legal Studies, Wolfson College, Oxford

Paul Drew

Department of Sociology, University of York

First published 1979 by
THE MACMILLAN PRESS LTD
London and Basingstoke
Associated companies in Delhi
Dublin Hong Kong Johannesburg Lagos
Melbourne New York Singapore Tokyo

Typeset by
VANTAGE PHOTOTYPESETTING CO. LTD
SOUTHAMPTON AND LONDON
Printed in Great Britain by
Billing & Sons Limited, Guildford, London and Worcester

British Library Cataloguing in Publication Data

Atkinson, J Maxwell
    Order in court. – (Oxford socio-legal studies)
    1. Conduct of court proceedings – England
    2. Oral communication
    I. Title   II. Drew, Paul   III. Series
    347'.42'05   KD7117

    ISBN 0–333–24431–1

Contents

Preface   vii

Acknowledgements   ix

1   Analysing Court Proceedings: Sociological and
    Ethnomethodological Approaches   1

2   Examination: A Comparison of the Turn-taking
    Organisations for Conversation and Examination   34

3   Opening a Hearing: Sequencing and the
    Accomplishment of Shared Attentiveness to
    Court Proceedings   82

4   The Management of an Accusation   105

5   The Production of Justifications and Excuses
    by Witnesses in Cross-Examination   136

6   The Data Base and Some Analytic Considerations   188

7   Postscript: Notes on Practical Implications
    and Possibilities   217

Notes   233

Appendix: Transcription Symbols   265

Bibliography   269

Index   273

Preface

Hearings in courts involve verbal exchanges which in many respects appear to be organised differently from talk in conversation. The distinctive character of talk in judicial settings is a recurrent theme in studies and discussions of court proceedings by sociologists, lawyers and others. It is frequently treated on the one hand as the source of the 'oppressive' nature of court-room interaction, and on the other as a means of ensuring the efficient and proper conduct of cases. In this book, we are also concerned with the organisation of talk in courts, and with how participants manage the business of courts within the constraints imposed by that organisation. We do not, however, propose to take sides in any debate between the critics and supporters of our legal system. Instead we attempt to describe formal, structural or sequential properties of aspects of the organisation of verbal interaction in courts, and to identify some systematic features of certain sequences, such as those involving blame allocation during the cross-examination of witnesses.

The detailed analyses of empirical materials presented in the middle parts of the book (Chapters 3–5) derive very much from recent work in ethnomethodology and conversational analysis. Chapter 1 is therefore designed not only to show the relationship between our analytic approach and those adopted in other research into court-room interaction, but also to outline the development of ethnomethodology's programmatic concerns and the general aims of conversational analysis. And in Chapter 2 we introduce the model of the organisation of turn-taking for conversation which has been elaborated by conversational analysts, with a view to specifying formal constraints that may operate in examination. The focus then shifts to analyses of the opening sequences in a Coroner's Court hearing (Chapter 3), and blame allocation sequences in a Tribunal of Inquiry (Chapters 4 and 5). In Chapter 6 some issues associated with the analysis of different types of data are considered, with particular reference to the expanded scope for further research that is provided by the availability of tape-recorded trials. A final postscript consists of a number of highly tentative speculations about possible implications that work of this sort may have for practical debates concerning the design and reform of court procedures (Chapter 7).

While we have co-operated closely in the preparation of this book, the chapters were written separately. Chapters 1, 3, 6 and 7 (by J.M.A.) result from work done as part of a more broadly conceived programme of multi-disciplinary research into the social organisation of judicial procedures, which is one of the projects currently being conducted at the SSRC Centre for Socio-Legal Studies. In developing the studies reported in these chapters, the encouragement and support of colleagues at the Centre have been greatly appreciated, and particular thanks are due to Donald Harris, Keith Hawkins, Doreen McBarnet and Christopher Whelan.

Chapters 2, 4 and 5 (by P.D.) have been very much revised from material originally written up as a Ph.D. thesis in sociology at the University of Lancaster.

We are grateful to Judy Davidson, Robert Dunstan, John Heritage, Anita Pomerantz, Rod Watson, Jeremy White and Tony Wootton for their detailed and helpful comments on earlier drafts of various chapters. While the final versions have benefited from their remarks, it should be emphasised that these colleagues may not agree with all that appears here, and we alone are responsible for what remains.

Transcripts of tape-recorded extracts from criminal trials in Massachusetts derive from a much larger corpus of such data collected under the auspices of a U.S. National Science Foundation Programme in Law and Language at Boston University, and we are indebted to Brenda Danet and Bruce Fraser for making copies of the tapes available to us. We are also grateful to Anita Pomerantz, Barbara Rawlings and Tony Wootton for many of the conversational extracts used in Chapter 2.

Maxwell Atkinson
Paul Drew

Acknowledgements

Parts of the earlier sections of Chapter 1 were originally included in a paper entitled 'Order in Court: Some Preliminary Issues and Analyses', in K. Kulcsar (ed.), *Proceedings of the I.S.A. Sociology of Law Research Group, 1976 Conference on the Sociology of Law and Legal Sciences*, Budapest: Hungarian Academy of Sciences, 1978. Chapter 3 is a slightly modified version of 'Sequencing in the Opening of a Court Hearing: Some Features of Turn Organization in a Multi-party Setting', which appeared in G. Psathas (ed.), *Studies in Language Use: Ethnomethodological Approaches*. Boston: Irvington, 1979. Chapter 4 is a revised version of 'Accusations: The Occasioned Use of Religious Geography in Describing Events', *Sociology*, 1978, Vol. 12, No. 1 (Special Issue on Language and Practical Reasoning).

We are grateful to the editors and publishers concerned for permission to include the revised materials in this present book.

1 Analysing Court Proceedings: Sociological and Ethnomethodological Approaches

I A NEGLECTED AREA IN SOCIO-LEGAL STUDIES

In a recent sociological study of pre-trial procedures, it was noted that 'in the revised sociology of law the procedures of the legal structure have been curiously ignored' (McBarnet, 1976, p. 172). This remark would appear to be particularly apt in relation to court procedures which, with a few notable exceptions (e.g. Garfinkel, 1956; Linton, 1965; Emerson, 1969; Carlen, 1974, 1975, 1976a, 1976b), have received relatively little detailed attention from social scientists. To an extent this can be seen to be perfectly consistent with the fact that, in purely quantitative terms (amount of time involved, manpower, etc.), court proceedings comprise a very small and diminishing proportion of the total volume of legal activity that takes place in advanced industrial societies. And it is also consistent with the way in which sociology's traditional concern with the problem of social order at the societal or macro- level of analysis implies a view of what goes on in courts as no more than one tiny element of the legal system, which in turn is only a part of the social structure as a whole.

But, while the comparative neglect of court procedures by sociologists in the past may be easy enough to understand, it might reasonably have been expected that more interest in them would have been generated as part of the revival of sociological research into legal issues referred to above. For this has been greatly influenced by other theoretical and methodological developments in sociology which have advocated or displayed a marked shift in focus away from apparently given social facts and structures towards more detailed empirical analyses of the social processes and interactions which constitute them. Such trends have been manifested in a range of widely acclaimed studies of the 'law in action', although it is noticeable that most of the best known of these (e.g. Sudnow, 1965; Skolnick, 1966; Cicourel, 1968; Ross, 1970) have concentrated primarily on social processes which take place at varying distances away from the courts themselves. Indeed, even in those studies which have been explicitly concerned with what goes on in court-rooms, analyses of actual hearings have tended to feature as only a part or phase of some more general process that is the main topic being investigated. Emerson (1969), and Carlen (1976a), for example, were both primarily concerned with the processes of justice administration in and around the particular courts they studied (American Juvenile and English Magistrates' Courts respectively), and both arguably relied at least as heavily on data gathered outside the actual court-rooms from officials and others as they did on data derived from the hearings themselves.

That sociologists of law have tended not to attempt detailed empirical analyses of court proceedings, but to regard them merely as part of some more general process, can in one sense be seen as a reflection of the discipline's long standing assumption that formal appearances or procedures are likely to be essentially misleading to the analyst, and that the 'reality' of any situation is available for discovery and documentation by probing 'behind the appearances'. Indeed, such a view has received specific amplification and support in the theoretical and methodological writings of symbolic interactionism, which have had considerable influence on recent developments in the sociology of law. Thus, from the dramaturgical model associated with the early works of Goffman (e.g. 1959), the lesson can readily be taken that what goes on 'back stage' is likely to be more interesting and important than what takes place on it. That studies of the law in action should extend far beyond the court-room walls is also consistent with some of the central ideas of labelling theory more generally for, while court decisions may be seen as crucially important symbolic points at which labels are formally and officially applied, they can also be viewed as no more than a passing moment in the extended sequences of interaction involved in the labelling process. Similarly, a fundamental idea in the research methodology which has been heralded as providing the key to such areas of social life, namely ethnography or participant observation, is that data should be collected from many different parts of the particular organisation being studied with a view to arriving at some sort of balance between the diverse and often conflicting versions of reality claimed to be oriented to by the subjects involved (e.g. several of the papers in Filstead, 1970).

Such methodological injunctions not only provide support for a broader research orientation which takes in court-room interaction as one phase among many, but it is probably also the case that the much recommended unstructured techniques of observation are less well suited to the analysis of formal court proceedings than they are to the study of interaction in other settings. Thus, while descriptions of relatively short sequences of interaction or isolated quotations from informants can be fairly easily recorded in the ethnographer's field notes at the end of the day, the data of court hearings are more resistant to such methods of reportage. Sequences of interaction in court are frequently very extended and a single trial may last for days or weeks, and the significance and relevance of some particular utterance, or sequence of utterances, may not become apparent until it is too late for it to be recorded. An obvious solution to this would be to keep a record of the whole proceedings, but social scientists seldom have the technical competence or the stamina to produce a verbatim transcript. The answer may then be to seek access to the official transcripts, or permission to tape-record the proceedings but, while this book argues strongly in favour of such data as an essential requirement for the rigorous empirical analysis of court-room interaction, even these pose very considerable problems for the researcher. The total collection of Scarman Tribunal transcripts on which Chapters 4−5 are based, for example, extends to scores of volumes containing many thousands of words. Similarly, just to listen once to tape recordings of a trial lasting forty hours would take a full working week, which would not, of course, allow time for anything other than the most casual analysis to be done. Nor is it simply a question of time, for there are a range of complex and difficult issues concerning what to listen for, which extracts to select for analytic attention, the grounds on which such selections are made, and how conclusions made about them are to be warranted. These are problems to which the approach adopted in this book has fairly clearly specifiable solutions, which will be dealt with in more detail in later sections. But other sociological approaches remain remarkably vague about how researchers might come to terms with such issues when confronted with the volume and type of data that is generated by court hearings.

In the absence of much in the way of precise guidance as to what to do in the face of such problems, one reaction is to shy away from a detailed examination of the data and to focus analyses on more general issues which can be illustrated or allegedly tested out with reference to selected examples. Clues as to what might be worth selecting are, of course, to be found in various sociological traditions, but symbolic interactionism and, more recently, Marxism have probably been the major influences to date, so that main emphasis of court-room studies has tended to be on what courts are claimed to do to defendants (e.g. intimidate, bewilder, oppress, alienate, label, stigmatise, etc.) rather than on the details of how they work. Indeed, the fact that courts work at all, and apparently do so rather smoothly, appears to have been regarded as a passing and essentially uninteresting matter of fact. Yet some model of social order and social interaction will inevitably be used by researchers in constructing descriptions and explanations of how court proceedings are experienced in different ways by the participants involved. In other words, existing theories of social order and action have to be invoked and applied as a resource in developing characterisations of court-room interaction and in making them intelligible for others. On the face of it, this may seem perfectly reasonable and unproblematic, but it does raise an important issue about the use of social scientific theories and methods for the study of some substantive area such as court proceedings, namely that the impression can all too readily be given that the knowledge so employed is firmly established, uncontested, definite and valid. It is, in other words, very easy to obscure the fact that there is still profound disagreement within the social sciences in general, and sociology in particular, about fundamental theoretical and methodological problems concerning the nature of social order, and how it is to be studied, described and explained.

One implication of this is that attempts to apply such 'scientific' knowledge to the study of some particular area of social life will be as sound (or otherwise) as the knowledge so employed, even though readers of research reports are not always alerted to the shakiness of the foundation on which a study may have been based. Frequently the preliminary or tentative character of a project is concealed by confident sounding conclusions about the 'real nature' or the 'essence' of some problem in the social world. And, in so far as the decision to embark on one type of research will of necessity have ruled out others, all studies will be more or less polemical about the merits and defects of alternative methodologies. Thus, in its attempts to adapt recent developments in the analysis of naturally occurring talk to the study of court proceedings, this book is clearly not written from a neutral standpoint. But the approach in question and the tradition from which it emerged have given rise to so much controversy within sociology that there is arguably a special need to preface even the preliminary studies which follow with an extended introduction to the logic and character of such work (Chapters 1 and 2).[1]

Before proceeding to this more general discussion, however, one feature of the orientation we adopt is worth noting in relation to the past neglect of court proceedings as a topic for sociological analysis. For while it may seem obvious enough that a systematic approach to the study of natural language use is a sensible and even essential starting point for the analysis of data consisting largely of extended verbal exchanges, it is perhaps less widely appreciated that, even in social science disciplines other than sociology, empirical research into language use is still a relatively recent development. The influence of ordinary language philosophy, however, coupled with technological innovations in audio- and video-recording, have stimulated an increasing interest in such research. Psychology has seen the growth of psycho-linguistics as an expanding field, in linguistics there has been some movement away from the traditionally predominant concern with grammar and syntax to- wards pragmatics and speech act theory, while in anthropology there has been the emergence of the ethnography of communication and componential analysis. Viewed in these terms, then, the development of ethnomethodology and conversational analysis by sociologists can be seen as a trend which is consistent with similar changes in emphasis taking place elsewhere. And, in so far as this multi-disciplinary con- vergence is a recent phenomenon the products of which are only just becoming available, it is hardly surprising that the organisation of verbal exchanges in courts has yet to be subjected to much in the way of detailed scrutiny.[2]

   Finally, it may be noted that law, or at least jurisprudence, has not remained isolated from this growing interest in language use, the major contribution of H. L. A. Hart (especially 1961) having been to update jurisprudence by locating it within the tradition of ordinary language philosophy. But law and philosophy are disciplines without a tradition of empirical research and, even though these recent developments can be read as proposing the study of speech practices as one way forward (particularly now that technology has rendered the invention of exam- ples for analytic attention a largely obsolete and redundant methodolog- ical practice), jurisprudence appears to have responded in more predict- able ways to the insights of Hart, preferring to remain faithful to its traditional abstract interest in the nature of rules, rights, obligations, etc. (e.g. Twining and Miers, 1977; Hacker and Raz, 1977).[3] Moreover, what empirical reaction has emerged from jurisprudence has tended to argue on behalf of an enthusiastically anticipated emergent sociology of law (e.g. Campbell, 1974) in which studies of language use appear to be accorded as low a priority as jurisprudence itself. In contrast with such recommendations, the sociological orientation adopted in the present

book may well have more in common with Hart's approach to legal
philosophy than with most currently available sociologies of law. With
these latter, it shares little more than an interest in empirical investigations of social and (by implication) legal order, but it differs fundamentally on how these might be done and particularly on the emphasis given
to an adequate understanding of language use as the *sine qua non* of any
such endeavour.

   The remainder of this chapter, then, consists of a general introduction
both to the logic of taking this position in relation to the analysis of court
proceedings and to some of the connections between mainstream sociology, ethnomethodology and conversational analysis. A more technical
introduction to the turn-taking system for conversation follows in
Chapter 2, which focuses also on the relationship between the organisation of conversation and cross-examination.

II   LANGUAGE USE AS TOPIC AND RESOURCE IN UNDERSTANDING COURT PROCEEDINGS

Whatever else may be said about court proceedings, the fact that talk is
an all pervasive and highly significant feature can hardly be seriously
doubted. As is noted in one of the leading treatises on the law of evidence,
'Perhaps the most important feature of an English trial, civil or criminal,
is its "orality".' (Cross, 1974:202). Yet it would seem strange to *any*
competent speaker of English were one to conclude from this that the
term 'trial' can therefore be equated with 'people talking'. For any such
person could presumably point out that it is clearly *not* 'ordinary talk'
that takes place in courts of law, and that there is a sharp distinction to be
drawn between the kinds of talk that characterise court proceedings and
those which are to be heard in various other contexts. Another complaint
about the conclusion which might be raised involves noting that the
word 'trial' can be used to refer to contexts where talk does not take
place, or at least is not a necessary feature of the setting (e.g. sporting
trials, trial examinations, etc.). And an objection available to anyone
familiar with the book from which the above quotation was taken would
be that such a conclusion is misleading or invalid because the statement
from which it was derived was quoted out of context.

   It is not intended here to expand on this list of charges, nor to plead
innocent to them or otherwise try to refute them. Rather they have been
introduced to illustrate two of the themes which are central to the
concerns of this book. The first has to do with the ways in which any

speaker of a natural language (i.e. any competent member) can, and continually does, analyse, categorise, evaluate and distinguish between different ways of talking in particular contexts.[4] And this reference to 'context' which, it will have been noted, featured in all three objections listed above, points to the second general theme. For the fact that talk and other social actions are situated in particular contexts has been a perennial problem for all who have ever tried to design some rule or definition for general application, and for those whose task it is to apply them to particular settings. Efforts to resolve such problems, furthermore, are not helped by the ease with which the notion of 'context', or features of specific ones, can be invoked in support of claims that there is something wrong with a rule, or that it does not apply in some particular case. Such issues are, of course, very well known to philosophers, lawyers and social scientists, and no attempt to embark on an exegesis of rival treatments of them is to be started here. Instead of confronting so complex a task, the main point to be considered below is the apparently simple and obvious one that these problems are also well known to other competent members, lay and professional. A neglected and potentially fruitful line of enquiry, therefore, is to examine how such knowledge comprises both the topic and resource in formalising, specifying and analysing court procedures. And central to this is the idea that the professional/expert orientation of lawyers and social scientists to such problems is grounded in their unexplicated everyday abilities to monitor and analyse talk.[5]

This point can be clarified in a preliminary way by considering what is, in comparison with more conventional sociological offerings, a rather less grandiose speculation about the origins of the law (and bureaucratic procedures more generally), namely that the recognition of certain problems associated with more mundane ways of talking may have had much to do with the emergence of law in the first place.[6] In other words, had the workings of more 'ordinary' reasoning procedures (as manifested in, for example, conversational practice) been found to be adequate for settling all manner of disputes, there would presumably have been no call for the design and development of the kinds of special procedures now embodied in the legal systems of different societies. But the open textured character of language (for a recent useful discussion of which, see Heritage, 1978) is such that the more familiar ways in which 'conversational' discourse is organised have proved themselves to be rather inadequate for the practical purposes of, among other things, resolving important disputes, settling matters of fact, allocating blame and responsibility, etc., and for deciding such matters with recognisable 'definiteness' and 'finality'. Yet even when steps are taken to remedy the situation by attempting to specify laws and procedures of implementation, enough of the 'troublesome' properties of ordinary talk remain to leave sufficient doubt, ambiguity and scope for competing interpretation to keep a large legal profession in business. That this is so, however, is hardly surprising if it is the case that properties of language use give rise to the problems and topics addressed by the law, cannot be avoided, and are also used either in attempts to remedy them (e.g. by establishing special/legal procedures), or in the process of deciding whether some particular problem or topic falls under the auspices of these special procedures.

Viewed in these terms, then, court procedures can be seen to provide one way of producing decisions which are recognisable to members, for practical purposes, as being more 'definite', 'binding', and 'final' than is often the case with those arrived at in the course of ordinary conversations.[7] The existence of special legal rules of evidence and procedure can thus be regarded as the product of continuing and determined efforts to find principled solutions to identifiable practical problems posed by ordinary discourse. Most rules of evidence are 'exclusionary' which means that they seek to prohibit the use in court of various conversational practices which may, in most everyday settings, be perfectly adequate and acceptable methods for discovering and deciding matters of fact, blame, responsibility, and so forth (e.g. statements of opinion, evidence of past conduct, hearsay, etc.). In other words, such rules of evidence can be seen to be oriented to specific features of mundane talk which are perceived as being in some way flawed or inadequate for certain purposes. In so far as they are designed to provide a remedy, or at least improve on these 'weaknesses', then, legal rules of procedure can be regarded as the result of a continuing analysis of problems associated with language use in 'non-legal' contexts.

Interestingly, however, attempts to specify rules of evidence and procedure, as well as the further ones for putting them into practice or recognising breaches of specific ones, are eventually confounded before arriving at anything like an ultimate solution by the very features of language use (and particularly its open-textured and context-dependent character) which occasioned the design of the rules in the first place. Thus, however thorough legal scholars are in their attempts to spell out the nature and scope of a rule, the demands of accuracy will sooner or later call for some confession such as 'everything depends on context', which Cross (1974, p. 200) makes in relation to the problem of how to recognise a 'leading question'. Similarly, the potential of exhaustive texts as effective aids to understanding legal procedures is sometimes a source of considerable pessimism to lawyers, as is exemplified in the following:

> The best way to learn how the courts work is to go and watch them . . . The rules which govern the process of law enforcement only become comprehensible when they are seen in action: in the abstract, they seem a hopelessly abstruse and confusing muddle.
>
> (Barnard, 1974, p. 1)

And, just as books on legal procedure may in such a way resort to commending the use of ordinary common sense practices (like going to look) as a resource for learning the professional ones, other common sense procedures may even be recommended as good legal practice. Practical manuals on advocacy, for example, may stress special care in how one talks in court and the need for lawyers to speak with clarity, simplicity, succinctness, etc. (e.g. Napley, 1970, p. 57), even though there are no explicit legal rules of procedure designed to achieve such ends.

Although there may in principle be no clear or absolute solution to the problem of how and where a precise line is to be drawn between legal and other styles of talking, there can be little doubt that in practice members are well able to identify and use such a contrast. It is obviously not necessary to be a trained professional lawyer to be able to recognise that there is something distinctive about the kinds of verbal exchanges that take place in courts of law as compared with conversations in more everyday settings, even though it might not be easy to provide an exhaustive specification of the similarities and differences involved. For all practical purposes there is a definite and objective contrast which is plain for all to see, and it is thus not only a fact or topic that is available for inspection, evaluation, preservation or alteration, but it is also a device which can be used as a resource for doing such interpretive work. That contrast can equally well be used to defend or criticise legal procedures. In support of legal procedures, for example, it can be proposed that the existence of such a contrast is a good and necessary thing on the grounds that, were mundane ways of talking left unattended to arrive at decisions on the sorts of matters dealt with by courts, all safeguards against the *ad hoc*, prejudicial, biased and haphazard resolution of disputes would be lost. In the very ways that they do provide for departures from everyday methods of reasoning, legal procedures are supposed to overcome, or at least mitigate, problems such as these, which might otherwise arise. With its specialised definitions of everyday conduct (e.g. crimes, torts, contracts, etc.) and of procedures for deciding whether they apply in particular instances, legal language is designed to provide for a higher degree of specificity and standardisation than ordinary discourse.[8] Without a recognition of the contrast between 'legal' and 'ordinary' procedures, and of the former's capacity to facilitate some sort of escape from some of the more troublesome features (and possible consequences) of the latter, it would be difficult to make sense both of the meaning of revered legal notions such as 'due process', and of the grounds on which their virtues are proclaimed.

The use of a contrast between the organisation of language use in courts and other areas of social life can equally well lead to quite opposite conclusions, which may be highly critical of legal procedures. Sociologists have tended for the most part to take such a line, though the thrust of their critiques differ according to the type of 'other' procedures with which the 'legal' ones are compared. Compared with those of science, for example, legal procedures can be found to be inferior or out of date:

> The legal process of examination, cross-examination and re-examination can hardly be rated highly as an instrument for ascertaining the facts of past history, at least no scientist would expect to extract the truth from opposite distortions ... No one can fail to be struck by the contrast between the high degree of sophistication attained by forensic science in the detection of crime and the pre-scientific character of the pre-trial process itself.
>
> (Wootton, 1963, pp. 33–4)

This contrast between legal and scientific procedures, which designates the latter as a more recently developed improvement on the former, implies that legal procedures are too like the everyday ones of common sense. It also shares with other pleas for a science of judicial proof a mistaken optimism about the extent to which science can be pressed into the service of deciding moral questions. Certainly science shares with the law a long history of trying to sharpen up and refine its linguistic apparatus. But, whereas the scientist does this in the interests of solving theoretical problems posed by the natural order of things, the lawyer engages in conceptual debate and refinement in order to reach practical solutions to problems of the social and moral order. But, as philosophers, historians and social scientists know only too well, such issues have remained enduringly resistant to 'scientific' methods and theoretical resolution. Indeed, were it the case, as Wootton implies, that a validated set of decontextualised objective and scientific procedures for 'ascertaining the facts of past history' are already available, then the main problems of many disciplines would by now have been solved in a single stroke. Moreover, even to envisage the discovery of such procedures as an attainable possibility involves assuming a social and moral order with little resemblance to the one we know. For the certainty with which such matters could then be resolved would leave little if any scope either for moral and political conflict or for even asking questions like those which have traditionally provided the central focus for philosophy, history, law and the social sciences.

Whereas Wootton and others may have contrasted legal procedures unfavourably with those of science, a more recent tendency has been for sociologists (e.g. Linton, 1965; Emerson, 1969; Carlen, 1974, 1975, 1976a, 1976b) to compare them with common sense everyday procedures, and to exhibit a marked preference for the latter. Such studies have been strongly influenced both by symbolic interactionism in general, and by the dramaturgical perspective of the early Goffman in particular. Accordingly, they involve attempts to see court proceedings 'from the actor's point of view' to locate the 'symbolic meanings' that the 'drama' and its features may have for them and what the consequences and causes of these might be. Generally speaking, defendants are described as being variously baffled, bullied, thwarted, misunderstood, coerced, oppressed, manipulated, etc., all of which can then be readily contrasted adversely with alternative claims about the propriety of legal procedures and the ideals of justice. These unpleasant experiences are depicted as being consequences of the activities and utterances of judicial and court officials and of the way the drama is organised. Such effects are often depicted as being intended by the perpetrators, and the suggestion is sometimes even made that the structure or ceremony itself can actually engage in intended activities:

> ... the ceremony seeks to impose upon the delinquent the role of wrongdoer and systematically to deny him power or the opportunity to express less than full commitment to this discredited role.
>
> (Emerson, 1969, pp. 172–73)

Given that Emerson has little to say about how such highly critical descriptions are to be empirically warranted, it is perhaps hardly surprising that the ceremonial metaphor gets overworked in this and similar studies.

Compared with Emerson, Carlen's work exhibits a somewhat more sophisticated appreciation of the problems relating to the ties between professional procedures and common sense everyday ones. In one paper, for example, she refers to Emerson's study as one of several 'metaphorical critiques', which have 'all used dramaturgical or game imagery in analysing court room interaction' (Carlen, 1976b, p. 48). But while the critiques in question (which include Garfinkel, 1956; Blumberg, 1967; Emerson, 1969), together with several 'largely reformative' English studies of court practice (which include Hood, 1962; Bottomley, 1970; Dell, 1970; King, 1972) are described as 'immense contributions', a common flaw is attributed to all of them in that:

> . . . (the investigators just listed) have tended to ignore or take for granted other equally consequential dimensions of social control: the coercive structures of dread, awe and uncertainty depicted by Camus and Kafka; the coercive structures of resentment, frustration and absurdity depicted by Lewis Carrol and N. F. Simpson. That the masterly descriptions of a Kafka or a Camus are unlikely to be bettered by sociologists is obvious. The idea, however, that such surrealism and psychic coercion properly belong to the French novel, rather than to the local magistrates' court in the high street is erroneous. In this paper, based on two years' observation of the Metropolitan magistrates' courts, I shall argue that the staging of magistrate's justice in itself infuses the proceedings with a surrealism which atrophies defendents' ability to participate in them.
>
> (Carlen, 1976b, p. 48)

What seems to be implied here is first that sociologists are in the same kind of enterprise as novelists, second that the former are the inferior competitors, and third that such phenomena as 'surrealism' and 'psychic coercion' are nevertheless available for observation and report by sociologists. And, given the second of these points, sociological attempts to explore structures articulated in novels start out with the rather pessimistic prospect of being no better than the original sources. Whether or not such ideas were intended, this passage can be read as an unusually precise and honest statement about where the logic of following through most varieties of interpretive sociology may lead. For they (like more traditional 'positivist' methods) are based on the assumption that sociologists have access to special methods for seeing and describing the social world, which are different in specifiable ways from those available to anyone else (including novelists), and that it is through the use of those methods that the purportedly superior accuracy, objectivity, etc. of their descriptions can be warranted. Attempts to produce convincing and widely acceptable demonstrations that this is indeed the case have, however, repeatedly failed, in spite of widespread knowledge and concern for the issue. Thus, there are good grounds for believing that an increased awareness of such problems as obstacles standing in the way of quantitative procedures in sociology has yet to be matched by as rapid a growth in the realisation that problems of at least the same order and magnitude may apply equally to the various qualitative/interpretive alternatives.

While these observations have been inferred from what seems to be implicit in much of Carlen's analysis, it is worth noting that her approach exhibits a more explicit awareness of the close ties between ordinary and professional procedures. It also involves a determined and original attempt to resolve such problems by giving prominence to the way in which ordinary common sense theories are continually referred to and used in the carrying out of legal procedures by all concerned in them. For example, the fact that game and dramatic metaphors are apparently routinely used by court officials to organise and make sense of court procedures is invoked by Carlen to provide the warrant for organising her own study around such metaphors. Thus, the distinction that can be made between one of the metaphors on the one hand (e.g. 'game', 'drama', etc.) and other available and plausible models on the other (e.g. 'due process', 'just' and 'fair' procedures, etc.), is used to develop a critical or ironic contrast between the official legal models and the alternative common sense metaphors. In other words, by displaying that multiple versions of 'what is really going on in court' are available, doubt can be cast on any single version that may be offered as *the* version, such as, for example, the official legal ones. Alternatively, by stressing the way in which officials regularly use common sense metaphors in the course of doing legal work, it can be implied that they regard such categories as 'games' or 'theatre' as a literal (or at least the most appropriate) description of 'what is really going on in court': whereupon, other categories can be invoked to show how inaccurate and unreasonable these now purportedly 'actual' procedures of the court officials are in comparison with other plausible and tenable versions of what is going on. One can, for example, point out that, while it may all be a game to the officials, the court hearing is a serious business for the defendants. And just as commonsensically available metaphors can be used to propose ironic contrasts and assert the impropriety of legal procedures, so the apparatus can be developed in support of more generalised and far-reaching suggestions via the introduction of one of sociology's favourite metaphors, namely the 'macro' social structure of capitalism:

> The court is not a theatre. It is an institutional setting charged with the maintenance and reproduction of existing forms of structural dominance. Court workers, unlike stage actors, have to account not only for the way they interpret their parts but also for the authorship and substance of the scripts. Aware of the written rules of law, court workers often claim that their script has been written elsewhere; proud of a judicial competence, court workers often claim that they write the script themselves; called to account for the mode and substance of their performance, court workers, using the imagery of the theatre, claim that they perennially tell a tale of possible justice. To conserve the rhetoric of justice in a capitalistic society such a tale is as necessary as it is implausible.   (Carlen, 1976a, p. 38)

These various critical remarks about the way the commonsensically available contrast between legal and other procedures has been used in previous studies are not intended to indicate that the contrast has no analytic interest or potential. Nor is it the contention that one's everyday members' competences, such as the ability to identify and use contrasts between ways of talking and interacting, should not be used in recognising what seems noticeably 'odd' or 'special' about court procedures. For, if it is accepted that there are no absolutely and unequivocally objective methods for warranting a single description as definitely and uniquely correct, independently of context, then it is difficult to imagine what procedures other than our member's everyday competences could be used for doing such descriptive work. Rather, the core of our critique of other studies is that, having been used to recognise those features of court-room interaction which appear 'odd' in contrast with features of interaction in some 'ordinary' setting, those same 'odd' features are used to establish or confirm the same contrast as a *fact* or *topic* for further analysis. In other words, the more instances of 'odd' procedures that can be identified by using the contrast as a resource, the more progressively 'confirmed' as a fact or topic does that contrast appear to become. In this way, a generalised commonsensically available description (i.e. the contrast between the 'legal' and the 'ordinary') is used as a resource in finding and analysing the instances of 'oddness'. Such instances then become a collection of 'factual evidence' subsequently usable in support of the view that the original contrast (or some metaphorical variant of it) now has the status of a scientifically discovered and thereby warranted 'finding'. The analytic problem subsequently becomes to explain, or make further generalised sense of that 'finding' (e.g. by looking for suitable metaphors), and the results of such efforts typically do little more than reproduce and emphasise the same contrasts that were originally used to notice the 'finding' in the first place. ✳

Further clarification of the above may be provided by considering the following passage:

> Interaction in 'natural' settings, between relative equals, proceeds according to norms that by and large protect the interactants from embarrassment, humiliation, and discrediting. The parties cooperate to protect both the encounter and the claims advanced by the other. (Goffman, 1959). In contrast, interaction in the court setting proceeds according to a set of norms characteristic of authority permeated relationships. Thus, during the court room hearing, court officials may disregard many of *the conventional norms of face to face interaction.* The hearing is conducted on the basis of 'transformation rules' (Goffman, 1961), which enable officials to act in ways that *in normal interaction* would constitute clear violations of appropriate rules of behaviour.
> (Emerson, 1969, p. 202 – our italics)

The main point to be noted about this is the way in which the contrast between the procedures of court-room interaction and ordinary interaction is presented. At the outset a rule is specified which is clearly tied into some specific context (settings between relative equals). Then we get a contrast between the first rule and a generalisation about the rules of court settings. By the time the first italics are reached, the contrast is no longer between *situated rules* appropriate in *particular contexts*, but between two (purportedly) generally applicable types of rule, with the references to 'conventional norms of interaction' and 'normal interaction' implying (a) that it is sensible to regard *all* situations which might be described as ones where 'normal interaction' is taking place as ones governed by some common set of rules, or in other words that they are in an important sense identical, and (b) that sociologists have been able to identify this collection of 'normal' rules with such definiteness that their findings can be safely used for inspecting court procedures. By holding the 'rules of normal interaction' to be constant across all such contexts, then, the impression is given that the analysis of court procedures can be done with reference to a sound, validated and objective body of knowledge about the structure of everyday 'normal interaction'. This is done despite profound disagreements within sociology and social psychology about which, if any, findings or theories can be regarded as generally acceptable. But, proceeding as if there were some consensus among experts opens the way for almost *any* possible rule to be extracted from *any* specific context other than court hearings (e.g. like the proposed one involving 'relative equals' at the start of the above quotation) designated as a 'rule of ordinary interaction', and then compared as such with some rule of court procedure. This contrastive device can be used to locate more and more instances, which not only appear to 'validate' the very contrast which was used to locate them in the first place, but also provide for court procedures to be continually and progressively discredited. For, as the rules on one side of the contrast are described as 'normal', variations or absences manifested by rules of court procedure can be displayed as not merely 'different', but as 'abnormal': or, as in the above extract from Emerson, as 'violations of appropriate rules of behaviour' governing 'normal interaction'.

To an extent, then, the object of such an approach seems to be to develop the commonsensically available contrast between 'legal' and 'ordinary' procedures into a description which ironicises and/or criticises the latter. But one problem this raises is that while it may provide versions of court-room interaction which are convincing and plausible for the practical purpose of mounting radical attacks on the way some hearings are currently conducted, the same method of reasoning used to produce them can be equally well employed to yield exactly opposite conclusions. That is, some rule which it is proposed operates in 'ordinary' settings could presumably also be claimed to be 'abnormal' or a 'violation' in comparison with some rule of court procedure. The radical critiques themselves, furthermore, would seem to involve practical implications which can be viewed as being more or less destructive and (at least in terms of some of the remarks made at the beginning of this section) as revealing something of a misunderstanding of some crucial properties of court procedures. For if the main thrust of an analysis is to complain about the 'special' legal procedures and to argue in favour of the greater appropriateness of more 'ordinary' procedures, then (taking the logic of the argument to its extreme) the most desirable situation would presumably be one in which there were no recognisably 'special' procedures at all, but only 'ordinary' ones: in which case, the situation itself would presumably no longer be recognisable as anything other than an 'ordinary' one. But, if it is the case, as was suggested earlier, that the existence of 'special' legal procedures may be related to the noticeable inadequacies of ordinary everyday procedures as effective methods for arriving at decisions which are (for practical purposes) unambiguous, definite and final, then it is not at all clear how such decisions could be reached in recognisably appropriate ways following the elimination of the 'special' legal procedures. ✕

In concluding this section it may be noted that no attempt has been made to present a detailed summary of the studies discussed, or anything approaching an all-encompassing review of the literature on court procedure more generally. Instead, the aim has been to outline some problems which arguably will inevitably arise so long as commonsensically available devices (like the ability of members to contrast the 'legal' with the 'ordinary') are used in an unexplicated way as a resource for analytic purposes, and so long as rules which seem to operate in one specific context are inspected with reference to those associated with other (purportedly more general) ones. That is, an attempt has been made to show how the recognisability and analysability (by members) of different procedures provides both the topic and the resource for analysis. This is not to suggest that researchers like Emerson and Carlen ought not to have used their everyday members' competences to recognise what is 'special' about court procedures, or that they or anyone else could not have done so even had they wanted to.[9] Nor is it to suggest that their detailed ethnographic observations are uninteresting or uninformative about the particular settings observed. Rather the general point is first that, having outlined 'noticeables', their analyses move too quickly towards imposing an order on them with reference to theories (both lay and professional) derived from outside the settings, thereby leaving open the question of what specific problems of the setting such 'special' procedures might resolve. Second, while many of these assertions about the nature of order in court (e.g. that hearings bewilder and confuse defendants) may be recognisable by members as plausible or 'possibly correct', the analyses are mainly directed towards establishing that they actually are 'correct', even though this is in principle not possible. For practical purposes in particular contexts, however, such a task is, of course, perfectly possible (in that members routinely recognise descriptions as correct for the particular purposes at hand and 'for now'), and it is presumably the availability of unexplicated interpretive procedures for doing recognitional work of this sort that enables observers (whether lawyers, professional researchers, or others) to construct such descriptions and have them regarded by others as 'possibly correct'.[10] The main implication of this to be elaborated in the next section is that, if recognisable orderliness is the product of the unexplicated and taken for granted procedures of practical reasoning used by members, then it is with the explication of such procedures that the analysis of social order in general, and order in court more particularly, should begin.

III   ETHNOMETHODOLOGY AND THE ANALYSIS OF SOCIAL ORDER

The sorts of problems touched on so far are obviously not confined to the sociology of law, let alone sociological studies of court proceedings. For the confusion which has persisted in the discipline more generally about the nature of the relationship between common sense and professional social scientific reasoning about social order has been central to most of the major theoretical debates in sociology. Conflict and consensus theorists, symbolic interactionists, phenomenologists and the rest all claim to have found the most appropriate model of social order and the most suitable methods for its study. And, in the absence of any recognised procedures for deciding between the competing versions, the various approaches continue to co-exist, and to provide the 'data' for yet further theoretical speculation aimed at producing some new synthesis or reconciliation between the alternatives. On at least three issues, however, there is general agreement between the majority of sociologists, irrespective of their particular theoretical persuasion. The first is that (in spite of all the evidence to the contrary) sociology, or the favoured approach to it, is capable of producing descriptions and explanations of social phenomena which correspond with the actual events in the world to which the descriptions and explanations refer. The second point of agreement is the widespread belief that professional sociological accounts of what is going on in the social world, and why it goes on, are of a different (and superior) order to the kinds of descriptions and explanations of social reality available to and routinely used by lay members in making sense of the events around them. And a third closely related theme common to most sociology is the view that the methods of practical reasoning which enable members to engage in descriptive and explanatory work are in some sense 'flawed', and hence must be avoided altogether, or at least repaired or modified, for the purposes of doing professional sociology.[11]

Now it might be thought that to reject any or all of these long-standing assumptions would be to deny the possibility of doing any kind of sociological analysis at all. For, if descriptions do not correspond with events in the world, if the distinctiveness of sociological accounts in comparison with common sense ones cannot be demonstrated, and if sociologists are unable to escape from or improve on the everyday methods of reasoning over which they had command long before they ever encountered professional sociology, then it is not clear what options remain other than the writing of journalistic reports, fiction, or political propaganda. During the last twenty years, however, ethnomethodology has developed an approach to social research which neither accepts any of these long-standing points of sociological consensus, nor recommends the abandonment of the systematic investigation of social phenomena. Not surprisingly, such an apparently paradoxical position involved a fundamental revision of sociology's traditional view of social order, of the sorts of question to be asked about it, and of the kind of empirical research to be done. To do justice to the range and complexity of the solutions proposed by Harold Garfinkel (especially 1967) and his associates who founded ethnomethodology is hardly possible here, but a brief summary of some of the main themes may help to locate and clarify the issues addressed in subsequent chapters.

Central to ethnomethodology's rejection of more traditional conceptions of social order is the idea that they presuppose a social world which simply could not work, or at least could only work in a very different world to the one in which most of us live. Thus, were it the case that descriptions and explanations of social order and particular social phenomena could indeed be arrived at, and empirically validated independently of the settings in which they are used, then there would presumably be not only a much greater degree of certainty in human affairs than appears to be the case, but also little scope for originality, diversity, innovation, conflict, or social change. The facts of any particular situation or event would never be in doubt, its causes would be identifiable with complete precision, and its consequences would be wholly predictable. In short, the dream of Auguste Comte, originator of the word 'sociology', of a society organised on an 'objective' or 'scientifically' warranted basis, and run by sociologist-priests, would long since have become more than a dream. Sociology would by now have succeeded in singling out *the* 'correct' version of social order from the multiplicity of versions which are to be heard in the real world, and the discipline would have achieved a greater degree of consistency and coherence than is suggested by the myriad of competing sociologies currently on offer.

The suggestion that traditional models of social order presuppose a world which could not work is not directed solely at those of the 'positivist' tradition in sociology, as might seem to be implied by some of the above remarks. In other words, it might be thought that the alternative views of social order associated with the 'interpretivist' tradition can be exempted from such a charge. And certainly it is the case that 'positivism' has been widely criticised by sociologists other than ethnomethodologists for having failed to give adequate attention to the 'meaningful' dimensions of social action, the understanding of actors' subjective orientations to action, the 'constructed' character of social reality, and related phenomena. But, in the very way that interpretivist sociologies replace the excessively determined, certain and objective models of positivism with variously indeterminate, uncertain and differentially experienced conceptions of social reality, they too appear to be proposing models of order which could not work. In the kind of world they provide for, the subjectively assessed meanings of actions and events would be so diverse and so utterly ambiguous, that it is difficult to see how members would be able to adhere to a single one for long enough to be able to accomplish anything at all, or how any semblance of order would be possible. Viewed in these terms, then, the two great sociological traditions of positivism and interpretivism can be viewed as having concentrated too exclusively on one *or* other of two dimensions exhibited by social reality, and have therefore failed to come up with a model of social order which would systematically accommodate *both*. For an adequate theory of social order would presumably have to provide for the way in which the social world is comprised of unique circumstances which are nevertheless recognisable as instances of generalised types, and is simultaneously flexible *and* patterned, subjectively experienced *and* externally objective, uncertain *and* certain, indescribable *and* describable. That is, the theory would have to be *neither* so inflexible or rigid that it lacks any sensitivity to the potentially infinite range of contextual variation in the world, *nor* so inflexible or loose that nothing at all is held to be general across different contexts. And the ethnomethodological interest in the methods of reasoning routinely used by members, both lay and professional, in finding *practical* resolutions to the basic theoretical dilemmas that divide positivist and interpretivist sociologies is informed by just such a model of social order.

As far as ethnomethodologists are concerned, then, the confusions of traditional sociology are inevitable so long as the search for descriptions and explanations of *the* realities underlying the commonsensically available appearances of social order is preferred to an examination of *how* such appearances are interactionally produced, managed, recognised and used *as if* they were *the* facts of the matter by societal members in living their everyday lives. In other words, the appearances of social order are viewed by ethnomethodology as the situated accomplishments

of hitherto unexplicated methods of practical reasoning which professional sociologists, by virtue of their societal membership, have used as a
taken for granted resource in pursuing their investigations. According to
Garfinkel, 1967, the major implication of this is that this resource should
become the *topic* for sociological analysis, and that empirical research
should thus be addressed to an explication of the methodic practices
employed by members in the production of social order. The basic
theoretical question was no longer to be the obstinately unanswerable
one of *why* 'in principle' social order is as it is (or claimed to be). Rather it
was to become that of *how* 'for practical purposes' are particular manifestations of social order achieved? In combining the terms 'ethno' and
'methodology', then, Garfinkel sought to encapsulate the revised topic
for research that was being proposed (on the origins of the word
'ethnomethodology', see Garfinkel, 1974).

Had ethnomethodology been no more than a critique of traditional
sociology and as a promise of better things to come, it would no doubt
have had little lasting impact on a discipline in which ambitious
programmatic claims are commonplace. But, in contrast with most
other purportedly new theoretical developments within sociology, ethnomethodology seems to have had an appeal for empirically inclined
sociologists, perhaps partly because Garfinkel's writings dealt with
problems which researchers will have inevitably encountered, and
partly because his solutions pointed to a hitherto largely unexplored
domain for investigation. Thus, even by the time Garfinkel published
Studies in Ethnomethodology, 1967, he was able to cite a dozen other
sociologists whose empiricial research, during the ten years prior to that,
had been directed by ethnomethodological rather than traditional
sociological questions (Garfinkel, 1967, p. vii). And the subsequent
decade has seen such work develop and diversify to a point where it is
now somewhat misleading to talk as if there were a single homogeneous
style of ethnomethodological research. One reason why a diversity of
approaches has developed from the earlier ethnomethodological writings may have been in response to the fact that they proposed so difficult
a way forward. Thus, while the new domain for investigation looked
interesting and exciting, it was not immediately obvious how it could be
subjected to systematic empirical study without falling back into some of
the old traps from which an escape was being sought. Garfinkel's stress
on the importance for social organisation of taken-for-granted methods
of practical reasoning, background expectancies, etc. seemed to suggest
that empirical research should be directed towards an examination of
the ways in which tacit rules and common sense theories were used by

members in accomplishing the orderliness of particular settings. In pursuing such studies, however, researchers were to operate under a number of analytic constraints or injunctions entailed by such a theoretical programme, most of which related to the analyst's own status as a 'competent member', and the implications of this for the way he was already able (as a 'member') to observe, describe and explain any of the activities he might encounter. Thus, general exhortation to view what seemed to be obvious, mundane and commonplace as 'anthropologically strange' was to be a constant reminder to analysts that obviousness was itself an orderly and methodic product of their *members'* interpretive competences. To ignore what appeared commonplace and mundane would therefore be to fail to regard the explication of the members' methods of reasoning which rendered them 'obvious' as the topic for analysis, and to rely on them as an unexplicated resource in much the same way as had been done for so long by traditional sociology. How work under such a constraint could actually be done, then, was a major challenge for ethnomethodological research.

A closely related and equally challenging constraint was entailed by the way in which Garfinkel's social actors were viewed as practical rule-using 'analysts', rather than as the pre-programmed rule-governed 'cultural dopes' portrayed by traditional sociological models of man. Thus, the professional analyst's major task was not to stipulate what rules members *really* were 'following' or 'governed by', but to locate rules to which they might be 'orienting to' and using in producing a recognisable orderliness in some setting. Thus, to find a way of making statements about rules and practices which could warrantably be said to be 'oriented to' by members then was another of the difficult challenges posed by ethnomethodology. For it demanded, among other things, that traditional sociological recommendations about the importance of looking at actors' orientations to actions, and of avoiding the imposition of observers' constructions were to be taken more seriously than in the past. That is, any solution which involved paying lip service to such matters as a prelude to stipulating observers' versions, would be regarded as unacceptable.

IV   ETHNOGRAPHY AND CONVERSATIONAL ANALYSIS

To find a way of doing empirical research which would meet the standards entailed by such constraints was, of course, a particularly ambitious and complex task, not least because there were no clear precedents as to how such work might proceed. One which did suggest itself, however, was the method that had been used by social anthropologists for several decades in their attempts to understand cultures other than their own, and which had more recently been rediscovered by sociologists who wished to find an alternative to the quantitative methods which had been predominant for so long in empirical research. Thus, most of the early ethnomethodologists made extensive use of ethnography and participant observation in their studies in practical reasoning. Many of the best of these were conducted in legal settings (e.g. Sudnow, 1965; Cicourel, 1968; Zimmerman, 1969a, 1969b; Wieder, 1974; Bittner, 1976a, 1976b), which may have had a special attraction because the kind of work being done there clearly involved members in finding practical and definite solutions to problems which could not be resolved in a principled, abstract or decontextualised way (e.g. deciding the 'facts of a case', 'what actually happened', who was 'really to blame', which general definition or rule held in 'this particular unique context', etc.). Indeed, it was during his association with the celebrated Chicago Jury Project that Garfinkel had coined the term 'ethnomethodology' (see Garfinkel, 1974) to refer to the phenomena of which the methodic procedures used by jurors to achieve and display their competences as 'legal' decision makers were an instance (Garfinkel, 1967, pp. 104–15).

But, as has been suggested elsewhere (Atkinson, 1978, p. 7), these studies often looked very similar to those of symbolic interactionists, who had also made extensive use of ethnographic field research, and it was relatively easy for a case to be made to the effect that there was little difference between ethnomethodology and symbolic interactionism (e.g. Denzin, 1971). Moreover, some of those who had become interested in ethnomethodology, and perhaps particularly those who encountered it later and from a distance (e.g. some British ethnomethodologists), came to doubt how far ethnographic ethnomethodology could come to terms with the sorts of analytic constraints outlined above in as adequate a way as that which appeared to be possible in the developing tradition of conversational analysis.[12] Thus, during the same period of the 1960s, when these ethnographic studies were being done, there had also emerged the approach to ethnomethodological research developed by Harvey Sacks, which took as its data tape recordings and transcripts of naturally occurring talk. Quite apart from the exciting possibilities which flow from a realisation that it is only very recently in man's history that it has been possible to record social interaction and subject it to repeated inspection, the mode of analysis developed by Sacks and his co-workers appeared to provide a way of conducting empirical investigations which was *both* addressed to the new topic *and* consistent with the analytic constraints proposed by Garfinkel.

The character of the solution provided by conversational analysis, and its advantages over ethnography can perhaps be most readily clarified with reference to a number of features of descriptive work, which had been at the heart of traditional sociology's methodological problems, and which also persist as obstacles to ethnographic observation and reportage. To discuss each in detail would be to write a separate book, so the following list, derived from a reading of studies by Garfinkel (especially 1967) and Sacks (especially 1963, 1966, 1972a, 1972b), will hopefully suffice as a brief summary of the main issues involved:

(a) A description of some object (which here and in the remainder of the list is taken to include persons, activities, events, situations, etc.) in the world can always be indefinitely extended and must at some stage be brought to a close, but

(b) a single descriptor can be used to do adequate reference to an object (e.g. one word).

(c) Any object can always be described in more than one way, thereby posing a continual problem of choice between alternatives.

(d) The 'recognisable appropriateness' or 'inappropriateness' of the selection of one description rather than another is context-dependent, in that one which does adequate reference in one setting may not do so in another.

(e) Descriptions are recognisable as 'appropriate' by members independently of their having to have observed the object in the world, and hence 'observational techniques' (or any other purportedly decontextualised methods) cannot provide an independent/objective way of warranting a 'certain', 'accurate', or 'correct' correspondence between a proposed description of an object and the 'actual object in the world' so described.

(f) Descriptions are a constituent feature of the settings and circumstances they describe, in that they are used by parties to a setting to monitor and produce its specific orderliness.

These characteristics of description have a continual relevance at every step in doing ethnographic research.[13] As is implied by the one last mentioned (f), descriptions of some field-work setting and its associated features will have been used by the ethnographer in organising his choice of that type of setting as one worthy of study, his decision as to where to find a particular one to which access might be sought, his activities in obtaining access and participating in it, his understandings of the actions and orientations of others in the setting, his selection of reportable items for inclusion in his field notes at the end of each day, his editing of these for research report, and his decisions about which particular items should be given analytic priority. The selection and design of the descriptions appearing in the final report can thus be seen to be only the latest practical solution to a long line of descriptive problems which will have been arising and being resolved continually during the course of the research. They are, in other words, merely the most recent orderly products of an extended process of descriptive work which could, in principle, have continued indefinitely, but which is drawn to a close in a manner appropriate to the latest practical contextual circumstances, namely those in which research reports are written up, presented, discussed, etc.

A general implication of all this is that there is a very considerable distance between the empirical data (the events observed in some setting) and those who read, hear and assess the reports on the data. That is, the audiences only have access to the researcher's necessarily selective and incomplete descriptions of what went on in a setting, and to his additional analytic interpretations of the described events which, in that they have to be described prior to any analytic comments, have already been organised by his own descriptive work. Readers and hearers of ethnographic reports are therefore totally dependent on the researcher's descriptive competences *both* for what they get to know (and not to know) about the data, *and* for their understanding of the analyses of the things they get to know about from the report (i.e. the 'data analysis'), just as the researcher had also depended on them in getting to the final writing-up stage of the research. For the ethnographer, then, the problem of coming to terms with the ethnomethodological constraint against the unexplicated reliance on members' competences in doing research is particularly acute. Thus, however reflexive he tries to be about the way his research was directed by taken for granted commonsense knowledge, and achieved through the use of everyday methods of practical reasoning, he will never be able to explicate them satisfactorily for his readers. For one thing, a pre-condition for being able to do such a thing would be that ethnomethodology's topic (members' competences) had already been extensively explored and documented to a point where a detailed explication of how members' methods worked to produce ethnographic reports could be provided. And another problem standing in the way of operating under such a constraint is that to attempt to describe *how* an ethnographic report was done would be to embark on yet another indefinitely extendible descriptive task concerned with data (i.e. the researcher's interpretive procedures) which, like the observed events themselves, would be irretrievably separated and distanced from the researcher's audience. Just as readers and hearers have no direct way of checking the ethnographer's selected descriptions of events in some setting against the events themselves, so too would they be deprived of any way of checking his descriptions of how he used his member's competences against his use of them.

In recognition of such difficulties, conversational analysis is based on a strategy of analysing data (i.e. recordings and transcripts) to which readers and hearers can have direct access. Indeed, it is probably the first and only form of social scientific research that insists on giving its audience equal access to *all* the data being analysed, and which thereby does not require readers either to make guesses about how some features came to be described rather than others, or to rely on the analyst's attempts to describe how such selections were made. Instead, they are provided with the opportunity to inspect the analyst's descriptions of what appears to be going on with reference to exactly the same material as that to which the analyst's descriptions refer. Any attempts by the analyst to explicate members' methods usable in the production of a particular description, furthermore, can be assessed by readers with reference to their own members' competences. It is not, then, that conversational analysts are claiming to be able to avoid a reliance on their members' competences as an analytic resource, but that they are attempting to explicate them in a way which is *open for inspection and scrutiny by others*. Readers and hearers of research reports which include the empirical data being analysed can, in contrast with what is possible in the case of ethnographic and other forms of social research, use similar methods to those used by the analyst (i.e. members' competences) in assessing both the contextual appropriateness of selected descriptions, and the attempts to explicate what methods might have operated to produce those selections rather than other possible ones. In the absence of anything other than analysts' *descriptions* of the data, attempts to explicate how members' competences might have operated as a resource in their production are likely to appear as personalised speculations and reflections on how they might have worked, which are insulated from any kind of rigorous public inspection. Given direct access to the data, however, readers can follow through the logic of any interpretations of it as well as proposals about how they were produced.

In this way, then, conversational analysis seeks to provide a workable way of doing empirical research which comes to terms with the constraint against using members' methods as an *unexplicated* resource for analysis. That such methods must inevitably be used is not in question, as is emphasised in the following summary remarks by Turner (1971, p. 177) about the way conversational analysis comes to terms with the problem:

> As a solution to the vexed problem of the relation between the shared cultural knowledge (members' knowledge) that the sociologist possesses and the analytical apparatus that it is his responsibility to produce, I propose the following:
> A. *The sociologist inevitably trades on his members' knowledge* in recognising the activities that participants to interaction are engaged in; for example, it is by virtue of my status as a competent member that I can recurrently locate in my transcripts instances of 'the same' activity. This is not to claim that members are infallible or that there is perfect agreement in recognising any and every instance; it is only to claim that no resolution of problematic cases can be effected by resorting to procedures that are supposedly uncontaminated by members' knowledge . . .
> B. The sociologist, having made his first-level decision on the basis of members' knowledge, must then *pose as problematic* how utterances come off as recognisable unit activities. This requires the sociologist to *explicate the resources* he shares with participants in making sense of utterances in a stretch of talk. At every step of the way, inevitably, the sociologist will continue to employ his socialised competence, while continuing to make explicit *what* these resources are and *how* he employs them. I see no alternative to these procedures, except to pay no explicit attention to one's socialised knowledge while continuing to use them as an indispensable aid. (Turner's italics)

Transcripts, then, enable readers or hearers of an analysis to check out *both* the proposed reading *and* the proposed analytic apparatus with reference to precisely the same data as those in which they were based, and with reference to their own members' competences. Criticisms or developments of a particular analysis may therefore *either* question a proposed reading and suggest another, in which case the onus would be on the critic to explicate an apparatus which would provide for whatever alternative reading is being proposed; *or* agree with the reading while disagreeing with the analysis, in which case the onus would be on the critic to provide a more convincing analytic apparatus.

In contrast with the momentary and fleeting observations which are the data base for ethnographic research, and which can be preserved only through the descriptive efforts of the researchers, the data of conversational analysis are thus preserved in such a way that they can be subjected to detailed and repeated examination, not just by the analyst, but also by anyone else who reads or hears his report. Attempts to explicate systematic features of the analyses displayed by participants in their utterances, then, will have a different character to the sorts of introspective and publicly inaccessible reflections which are all that can be offered when there is no opportunity to check them directly with the data. In other words, conversational analysis provides a way of doing research which is consistent with the first of the earlier mentioned constraints entailed by the ethnomethodological programme, namely that the normally unexplicated reliance on members' resources should not simply be avoided, but should become the central topic for analysis. In the way that it achieves this, furthermore, it also provides a way of coming to terms with the sorts of troublesome problems for social research associated with the features of description listed above. Thus, once the *situational* production, selection and recognition of a particular description by participants (c.f. item c in the list) becomes a focus for analysis, the relative 'completeness' of a description (c.f. items a and b) according to some purportedly decontextualised criteria ceases to be a matter of concern on which the analyst must take a stand. Similarly, the public availability of the data allows for any claims about the contextual appropriateness of a proposed description (c.f. item d) to be evaluated with reference to the context in which the described segment of data occurs, and its precise location within a particular sequence. And, given that an analysis starts from the assumption that there will always be alternative ways of describing the data (c.f. items a, b and c), the researcher does not have to claim, either explicitly or implicitly, that some particular reading is *the* correct or only one, and thereby again avoids having to assert that there exists a set of independently applicable decontextualised methods for warranting such a correspondence between a description and the data to which it refers (c.f. item e).

To this point in our summary of how conversational analysis seeks to come to terms with the first of the earlier cited constraints entailed by the ethnomethodological programme, the emphasis has been on how a researcher can go about explicating members' resources in such a way that the analysis is open to inspection by others. Much of what has been said, however, also has relevance for how such analyses also seek to work within the limits of the second mentioned constraint, namely that what is explicated should not be mere constructions of the analyst, but should be 'oriented to by members'. The traditional ethnographic response to this has been to the effect that, by immersing himself in some particular setting, the researcher can come to see the world and how it is ordered in the way that participants in the setting see it, and hence can describe these members' orientations when he returns from the field. As was noted earlier, however, the processes involved in the production of such descriptions are highly complex, and are largely irretrievable for inspection by others. But this is not the only set of problems facing the ethnographer, for there are also questions as to how his descriptions of members' orientations relate to the situated orientations of members in the observed settings. If, for example, it is proposed that members orient to this or that order of things in such and such a way, it may well be ambiguous as to how far the claim is intended to apply to a specific occasion encountered in the setting, to other occasions of a similar type within the setting, more generally across other organisational settings like the one studied, or more generally still across settings unlike the one studied. Similarly, there may also be ambiguity with respect to whether or not the orientations described are held to be specific to a particular individual, all individuals belonging to a particular category, all individuals involved in the setting, or others outside the setting, etc. And such descriptions of members' orientations may be held to apply to a particular person or class of persons in one setting, type of setting, or many, etc. But, as soon as the ethnographer attempts to eliminate any of these numerous sources of potential ambiguity by specifying limits to the generalisability of his descriptions of members' orientations, he will be faced with yet further methodological dilemmas, some of which may well have been important in his decision to focus on members' orientations in the first place. Thus, if he seeks to confine the relevance of his descriptions exclusively to the particular setting studied, or some specific occasion within it, he may well appear to have opted for a totally relativistic position which holds that nothing general whatsoever can safely be said about the social world. Yet if he proposes that they do have a relevance for other similar settings, or even more different ones, there is the question of how he could know enough to be able to warrant such a claim, if he has not also done field work in those other settings. This is particularly acute given how strongly the ethnographer's case for having his descriptions regarded as 'possibly correct' is based on his actually having been involved in the setting described, and the recognition by others (who have probably not been there) of such an experience as

giving him special rights to speak authoritatively about it.[14] In other
words, if extensive fieldwork is essential for producing 'adequate' descriptions of members' orientations in a particular setting, then presumably such descriptions could hardly be warranted as 'equally adequate'
in relation to settings which are outside the direct experience of a
researcher. Or, if such descriptions can be so readily held to be 'adequate' without having done the fieldwork, the force of direct involvement
as a warrant for the 'adequacy' of his descriptions of the fieldwork setting
would seem to be put in some doubt (c.f. item c on the list above).

A centrally important idea involved in the ethnographic approach to
research is that what participants say and do (and orient to each other as
saying and doing) in some setting may only be properly understood if a
great deal is known about the context in which such activities take place.
A considerable amount of effort is thus devoted by ethnographers to
providing detailed descriptions of specific contexts, so that readers will
be able to 'see the significance' of reported sayings and doings of
participants. In this way, the manner of presentation is held to be
consistent with how participants understand and orient to each others'
actions, in that they too need to know a great deal about the overall
context, the biographies and possible motives of other participants, the
previous course of the interaction, etc., in order to be able to design their
own next activities and to understand those of others (c.f. Garfinkel,
1967, pp. 4–5). But at least three related problems are entailed by the
view that the way participants organise their activities and orient to
them as organised can be reproduced by providing a detailed description
of the settings in which such things get done. The first is that the
researcher who follows such a course embarks on an indefinitely extendible task, namely the production of a complete description of all the
possibly relevant features in a setting which might in some way be 'taken
into account' by participants (or readers) in organising their activities
and those of others (c.f. item a on the list above). The second is that, in so
far as the first requires that the list of contextual features to be described
must be selected according to some criteria of relevance, such criteria are
likely to reflect what is 'noticeable', or 'special' about a setting, rather
than the more 'ordinary' features which, it is assumed, can be taken for
granted. Indeed, the sorts of settings studied by ethnographers are likely
to be selected precisely for their 'unusual' or 'exotic' character (e.g.
prisons, mental hospitals, police authorities, court-rooms, etc.) and,
with the notable exception of Erving Goffman, there are few researchers
who have made the mundane settings of everyday interaction their field
work locale. And a consequence of this is that it is the more noticeable

features of 'exotic' settings which are most likely to be included for description, which was a central theme in the earlier part of this chapter. Thus, court-room ethnographers notice and report on such things as the ecological environment of the court-room, the special attire worn by some participants, the unusual ways in which talk and bodily activities (e.g. standing up and sitting down) and co-ordinated, etc. But that many features of 'ordinary' conversational practice remain (e.g. that one speaker speaks at a time, that speaker change recurs, that speakers exhibit an understanding of what is going on, etc.) is not regarded as worthy of detailed report and analysis. By focusing on the more 'exotic' contextual features, therefore, ethnographers are likely to rely on their unexplicated knowledge (and that of their audience) of how activities in other more mundane settings are organised, and hence to refrain from reporting on anything other than the 'exotic'.[15]

The third problem with attempts to produce detailed descriptions of contextual features is that they are bound to fail in an important sense to do what they set out to do, namely to be faithful to the situated ways in which participants orient to the organised character of their activities. That is, participants seldom have to give running commentaries on what they are doing or on the settings in which their activities are taking place in order to achieve and display the orderliness of what they are doing. Rather such contextual features have, as Garfinkel (1967) so aptly puts it, a 'seen but un-noticed' quality and that they have been 'seen' by participants is more likely to be displayed precisely by *not* commenting explicitly on them than by constantly referring to them and to how they relate to what is being said and done. The analytic problems associated with the features of description listed earlier, it should be noted, are not merely ones which professional researchers face, but also have to be confronted and resolved (for all practical purposes) by participants.[16] Accordingly, the fact that any description can 'in principle' always be indefinitely extended means that members too can never 'say what they mean in so many words' (Garfinkel, 1967; Garfinkel and Sacks, 1970). A speaker therefore has no choice but to leave those with whom he is interacting to find a sense in his activities from what he says and does in specific *local* sequences. In other words, for an utterance to be oriented to and treated by others as a 'greeting', 'complaint', 'accusation', 'denial', 'excuse', 'justification', 'insult', 'expression of friendship', 'request', 'command', or whatever, it does not have to contain any direct reference to the fact that it is doing one of those things. Nor does an utterance have to be (or could ever be) 'definitely', 'unequivocally', 'exclusively' or 'certainly' any one of those things for members to be able to treat it and have it treated by others 'as if' it were certainly a particular one for the situated practical purposes at hand. Thus, just as members' 'actual' understandings in specific settings cannot be rendered 'certain' or 'correct' in any absolute sense by a detailed description of contextual features or any other method, so such procedures cannot assure such certainty or correctness to the interpretations of an ethnographic analyst.

But, while an analyst may not be able to arrive at *the* sense of what participants were *actually* orienting to in some particular context, his members' competences enable him, like them, to make *a* sense of what was going on by analysing what was displayed by the structure and location of speakers' utterances. The analytic importance of this has been concisely summarised by Schegloff and Sacks in the introduction to their analysis of the organisation of conversational closings:

> We have proceeded under the assumption (an assumption borne out by our research) that in so far as the materials we worked with exhibited orderliness, they did so not only to us, indeed not in the first place for us, but for the co-participants who had produced them. If the materials (records of natural conversations) were orderly, they were so because they had been methodically produced by members of the society for one another, and it was a feature of the conversations that we treated as data that they were produced so as to allow the display by the co-participants to each other of their orderliness, and to allow the participants to display to each other their analysis, appreciation and use of that orderliness. Accordingly, our analysis has sought to explicate the ways in which the materials are produced by members in orderly ways that exhibit their orderliness and have their orderliness appreciated and used, and have that appreciation displayed and treated as the basis for subsequent action. In the ensuing discussion, therefore, it should be clearly understood that the 'closing problem' we are discussing is proposed as a problem for conversationalists; we are not interested in it as a problem for analysts except in so far, and in the ways, it is a problem for participants. (Schegloff and Sacks 1973, p. 290)

In coming to terms with the second of the major constraints referred to earlier as being entailed by the ethnomethodological programme, namely that what is explicated should be 'oriented to' by members, conversational analysis thus avoids at least four of the problems which are likely to persist in ethnographic research. First, by concentrating on conversational materials, the analyst does not have to embark on the indefinitely extendible descriptive enterprise that necessarily follows from an ethnographic focus on contextual features. Second, by so doing, the analyst also avoids having to claim that the provision of detailed contextual descriptions somehow or other warrants a correspondence between what members in the setting might have been orienting to and his descriptions thereof. Third, the problem of what is to be selected as data is resolved, at least on one level, with reference to what is both observable and reproduceable.[17] And finally, the availability of the 'data' to anyone who reads an analysis ensures that the analyst's audience is not forced to take his descriptions 'on trust', but is in a position to assess any claims about the methodic ways in which a particular reading was produced with direct reference to the data in question.

V SUMMARY AND CONCLUSIONS

This chapter began with the observation that, while court proceedings have been a relatively neglected area for socio-legal enquiry, research in this area will be as sound or otherwise as the social scientific approach to it which is adopted. Previous sociological research into courts, it was suggested, have used taken for granted knowledge about the organisation of talk as an unexplicated resource for analysis, and such studies have accordingly tended to concentrate on the production of accounts which ironicise what goes on in courts by means of a commonsensically available contrast with what goes on in other settings of everyday life. The final sections sought to provide a summary of the ethnomethodological position taken in response to the problems of studying social order, and to locate some of the advantages conversational analysis has over ethnography in coming to terms with the major constraints imposed by such a programme. But the kinds of descriptive problems alluded to above, it should be noted, apply equally to our attempts in this chapter to provide a general summary of the central concerns of ethnomethodology and conversational analysis, particularly given that it has been presented for the most part in an abstract manner and without reference to data. Hopefully, however, what is involved in approaching the study of social order through an analysis of naturally occurring talk, the directions in which research has developed, and its implications for the study of court proceedings will become clearer in subsequent chapters.

2 Examination: a Comparison of the Turn-taking Organisations for Conversation and Examination

It was noted in the last chapter that a number of sociological investigations of interaction in courts have made considerable use of the readily apparent differences between the kind of talk which occurs in courts and that which characterises ordinary conversation. The contrast between the two has been used to support the argument that certain conventions can be identified as central to conversation, which constitute 'appropriate rules of behaviour' – rules which court-room procedures violate (Emerson, 1969, p. 202). In so far as court procedures facilitate such techniques as not allowing witnesses to tell their stories in their own words, denying witnesses their usual rights to avoid discussing sensitive and possibly discrediting matters, and generally controlling the information on which a court's decision is to be made, those procedures offend against the proprieties associated with normal interaction. On the other hand, the same contrast between talk in conversation and that in court-room interaction has been used by those who argue that the way in which talk is organised in courts is an important factor in ensuring the (reasonable) safety of the decisions of courts, by aiding the collection of relevant and impartial evidence and the assessment of its validity.[1] Thus through a variety of inferences and criticisms concerning the management of cases in courts, we find common reliance on the distinctiveness of the character of the talk which occurs in court settings. That distinctiveness is the topic of this chapter.

The phrase 'the talk which occurs in court settings' is perhaps misleading if it is taken to suggest that there is only one kind of talk in courts, for of course that is not the case. The stages of many hearings include the selection and swearing-in of jurors, the prosecutor's opening speech, the defence counsel's outline of his case, their respective closing speeches, the judge's instructions to the jury and his summing up, and so on – as well as the examination of witnesses, defendant, or plaintiff.[2] The talk in these phases of a hearing may differ to the extent that some consist of monologues whilst others involve at least two parties. Also the types of sequences in the talk differ at various stages of proceedings: for example, the selection of jurors consists of the nomination of a juror, followed by the state's or defence's acceptance or rejection of that nomination; whereas examination consists primarily of question and answer sequences. Despite these differences, the talk in each stage of court hearings shares the feature that although it occurs in a multi-party setting (in which a number of persons are present who might participate, or a number of conversations be held), the parties who may participate are limited and predetermined; so that, unlike conversation, not just anyone who is present may begin talking. Some aspects of the management of that feature of the talk in a multi-party setting are examined in the next chapter. In this chapter we are concerned primarily with the stages of a hearing which are often perhaps the major part of the business of most kinds of court, the *examination* of witnesses and defendants.

The rules of evidence which apply to the different types of examination (examination-in-chief, cross-examination, and re-examination) clearly have implications for the kinds of questions which may be asked, and for the distribution of certain sequences: for example, the rules applying to examination-in-chief not only affect the format in which questions may be put, but also result in the infrequency of sequences in which counsel challenge witnesses' evidence. For this reason it might be thought that any analysis of examination in court should start by addressing the various rules of evidence and their consequences. However our interest here is in the formal structural or sequential properties of the organisation of talk in examination, particularly its organisation into question-answer sequences – an organisation which is independent of the type of examination and hence of the rules of evidence, as well as of various content and other contextual matters. We do not intend by this to deprecate practitioners' knowledge of and respect for such practical procedural concerns as rules of evidence: the argument here is not about the relative 'importance' of such rules on the one hand, and the formal properties of the organisation of examination on the other. The point is rather that whatever is done in examination – the application of rules of evidence, as well as the co-ordination of other activities – is managed by participants within the constraints which the *turn-taking organisation* for examination imposes on the character of the turns in which they speak, constraints which are independent of the type of examination. Thus, for instance, the rules of evidence are fitted to that turn-taking organisation: they are expressed in terms of what may properly be done in questions or in answers. In order to consider some of the ways in which the organisation of talk in examination differs from that in conversation, and the constraints which may operate in the former, it is necessary to introduce some of the main features which characterise the organisation of conversation.

I THE TURN-TAKING ORGANISATION FOR CONVERSATION

A central property of conversation appears to be that it is organised into single-speaker turns, with regular transitions between speakers.[3] Participants take turns to talk, with one party at a time occupying a turn, then a next, then a next (though a 'next' can include a prior speaker) and so on until the end of the conversation. However many persons may be present and therefore available to speak, it is apparent that generally only one does so at a time, and on completion of his turn is followed by a next speaker.[4] Moreover the transitions from one speaker to another are achieved in an orderly fashion, without overlap between speakers (thereby preserving the property of 'one at a time') and without a gap between adjacent turns: co-participants may hold off from beginning their turns until the completion of the present speaker's, but then someone else may begin almost immediately. Thus conversation overwhelmingly consists of single-speaker turns which are co-ordinated so as to achieve minimal gap and overlap. As Sacks, Schegloff and Jefferson point out, this seems to be the case not only irrespective of such contextual variations as the identities of participants, what the conversation is about, the setting in which it takes place etc., but also despite the fact that the number of parties, the order in which they speak, the size of any particular turn (whether a turn is only a single word, or several sentences in length), what parties say, and the length of a conversation as a whole, can all vary, both within a conversation and between conversations. (Sacks *et al.* list these and other 'grossly apparent facts' about conversation, and propose that a formal model of the organisation of conversation should be compatible with, and able to account for, them: Sacks, Schegloff and Jefferson, 1974, pp. 700–1).

If the order in which parties speak, how long they speak for, and what they say in their turns, etc., all vary, then these cannot be specified in advance for conversations. Hence not only is the turn-taking organisation for conversation independent of various contextual features; it is also not subject to any external constraint on, or pre-specification of, turn order or turn size. If there *were* some such arrangement which pre-allocated turns to particular parties, that might be a way of achieving the central property of conversation outlined above: that is, a way of ensuring that a single speaker occupied a turn, and that the transfer to a next speaker occurred without gap or overlap, might be to have a rule specifying in advance of any actual conversation who should speak, how long a current speaker's turn should last, and who the next speaker is to be. These matters would be out of the hands of participants to manage, because they would be pre-specified – with the result that the order in which parties speak, and the length of their turns, would *not* vary from conversation to conversation, or within a single conversation. Clearly these *do* vary, and therefore for conversation there can be no rules pre-specifying turn order and turn size.

The fact that turn order and turn size vary for conversation, (together with some observations about the interactional difficulties which would arise were that not to be the case)[5] argues for there being some means whereby turn-taking is managed by co-participants on a local basis within given conversations. There must be techniques available to participants through which *they* can manage the co-ordination of transfers from one speaker to another, in such a way that we find these variations within and between actual conversations. At the same time, these techniques should be context-free insofar as they should be available across the range of local instances of actual conversations, and account for the variations in *any* conversation, whoever the participants, in whatever setting, whatever the topic, and so on. So the techniques for managing the turn-taking organisation for conversation should be formal (or not context-specific), and be interactionally managed by participants.

The techniques which Sacks *et al.* have identified, and which are compatible with the 'context-free but context-sensitive' requirement, concern the allocation of next turns. Their investigations of naturally occurring conversational materials reveal that next turns may be allocated either by a current speaker's selection of a next speaker, or by another party self-selecting. A current speaker's turn – which may consist of a word, phrase, clause, sentence, or number of sentences – may be designed to select who should speak next, and thereby to allocate the next turn. Alternatively, if the current speaker's utterance does not allocate the next turn, then other parties may allocate the next turn by selecting themselves to speak. Sacks *et al.* formulate a set of rules for the operation of these techniques, a simplified version of which is as follows: firstly, a current speaker may, if he chooses, construct his utterance so as to select the next speaker, by using certain speaker allocation techniques – only one of which, an empirically infrequently used one and which is really a special type of the more general class of techniques to be discussed later, is to select the next speaker by using a name. The person thus selected, and importantly *only* that person, then has rights and obligations to take the next turn to speak. However, if a current speaker has not allocated the next turn to some party, the second rule operates, which is that at a first point in the current speaker's turn at which the *completion* of that turn might be detected, another party may select themself as next speaker by starting to speak first. A speaker who self-selects may acquire rights for the next turn by being the first starter at a point at which it is understood the prior speaker has completed his turn, a point which can be treated as a 'turn transition-relevance place'. Finally, if a current speaker has not selected a next speaker, and if no one else self-selects at an initial transition-relevance point, then the third rule applies, which is that the current speaker may (but does not have to) continue until one of the first two rules operates, and transfer to a next speaker is effected.

These rules accomplish the close co-ordination of speaker turns, managing the transition from one turn to another with the minimum of gap and overlap, by operating on an utterance-by-utterance basis and being ordered relative to one another. A current speaker may exercise the option of allocating the next turn, for which the rule set applies anew. But to do so, a current speaker should select the next *before* the occurrence of an initial transition-relevance place, because if a next speaker has not been selected by then the second rule applies, allowing another party to self-select by beginning to talk at that point – the rule set now applying for that (new) speaker's utterance. Of course, if no-one selects themself at a first transition point then under the third rule the current speaker may continue, in which case the option of allocating the next turn re-applies: that is, the whole rule set, including the option under the first rule, re-applies to a current speaker's turn following each transition relevance place for which another has not been selected or does not self-select by beginning to talk. Thus to avoid the possibilities engendered by the third rule (which might result in missing the opportunity to say something in the conversation at the point at which it is relevant, and not being selected by current or subsequent speakers to say it), there is some constraint on anyone who intends to take the next turn to start at the earliest possible moment when an utterance completion can be detected. That motivation to self-select by starting as early as possible at a completion point also has to do with securing rights to the turn by starting before other intending speakers.

Hence, a current speaker may design his utterance so as to select the next, who should then begin his allotted turn immediately on the completion of the current speaker's turn. The notion of selecting a next speaker not only refers to situations in which more than two parties are present, say in the same room, where a speaker may select which of the co-present parties should have the next turn; it applies also for situations in which just two persons are available to talk, for example in telephone conversations. In the latter cases the selection issue may not have to do so much with who will take the turn following the current speaker's; but given that the length of the current speaker's turn, and what is done in that turn, are not pre-specified (the turn may be just one word long, or last several sentences; and he may ask a question, deliver some news, make an observation, etc., each of which can require certain responses by the other party), the non-speaking party in a two-party conversation still has the task of fitting his utterance with the last. Even though there may be no competitor for the next turn (other than by the current speaker continuing to talk), he has to monitor the current speaker's turn for whether he has been selected to do a particular response and when that should be done, or whether he is free to select himself at some point. Thus a current speaker's allocation of the next turn has to do with more than just indicating who should speak next; that will be discussed shortly.

Alternatively, if a current speaker's turn is *not* designed to allocate the next turn, other parties may be free to select themselves, and may do so at the first transition relevance place in the current speaker's turn. What is of crucial importance is that whether someone has been selected to speak next and what they have been selected to do in that turn, or whether others are free to select themselves, can only be detected in each and every current speaker's turn, because it is only in the course of that turn that the current speaker can accomplish the selection of a next. That is, the speaker selection techniques, ordered in terms of the rules, are operated on a turn-by-turn basis, and are therefore *locally managed*. Because the direction of turn transfer (i.e. to whom the next turn is allocated) is managed through the design of each fresh turn, hearers may monitor the progress of any current turn in order to find whether they have been selected to talk next, and if so what they have been selected to do, and when they should begin. These possibilities concerning the next turn are only accomplished in a present speaker's turn.[6]

A consequence of this is that co-participants will need to listen to a speaker's utterance, over the course of its production, to monitor the possibilities it may hold concerning the next turn. This achieves the 'one speaker at a time' feature of conversation, that is its organisation into single speaker turns. And the localisation of overlaps and pauses at transition relevance places is ensured through co-participants monitoring a current turn for its completion, which is the point at which they may begin speaking, thereby positioning the start of their turn correctly – not in, but at the end of, a current speaker's turn; and not some time after, but immediately after.

It is noticeable that co-participants themselves attend to the 'one at a time' condition in conversation, sometimes quite overtly. For example, if it happens that two speakers talk in overlap with each other, in certain circumstances that may be treated as some sort of trouble, as in the following extract from a telephone call:

```
(1)  (G:II:2:23)
     C:   .hhhh aa::of course under the circumstances Dee
          I would never:: again permit im tuh see im.
     D:   Yeah
          (0.7)
     C:   .tlk ⌐Be: c u z h e-
     D:        ⌊Wul did'e ever git-ma:rried'r anything?
  →  C:   Hu: ⌐:h?
     D:       ⌊Did yee ever git-ma:rried?
     C:   .hhhh I have no idea.
```

Both speakers in the above extract begin to talk simultaneously following a short pause, with the result that the whole of what C says, and part of D's turn, are done in overlap (it will help the reader to follow comments on data extracts, to look at the explanation of the transcription symbols in the Appendix). To some extent the overlap is minimised by C cutting off her utterance after 'Be:cuzhe-' and not going on to finish what she had to say. But the overlap still seems to result in some interactional difficulty. Instead of then carrying on as though that did not matter for the progression of the conversation, for what should be done next, one of the participants seeks a repeat of the other's utterance: C does that with her 'Hu::h?' in the arrowed utterance. Thus the sequence

```
C:    Hu:┌:h?
D:        └Did yee ever git-ma:rried?
```

repairs whatever difficulty is created by the overlapped talk in the prior sequence. The fact that C initiates the repair sequence rather than D can be accounted for by C being able to detect, from that part of D's utterance which is in the clear, that she is being asked a question, and thereby allocated the next turn, though too much of that utterance was obscured for C to give an answer. In this case then, the fact that one speaker (C) gives way to the other, and the repair sequence initiated by C following the overlapped talk, are evidence of co-conversationalists' orientation to the condition that turns should properly be occupied by a single speaker. Elsewhere this condition, and the difficulties which can arise if it is not met, are attended to in different ways, perhaps most dramatically when, as a result of overlapping talk, one speaker complains that *he* was talking ('I began first', or 'He interrupted me'), or when someone instructs others to 'talk one at a time'.

Thus extract (1) introduces two closely related points which are of some importance. Firstly, although the turn allocational rules minimise gaps and overlaps, they do not eliminate them; examining any conversation reveals the routine occurrence of generally very brief overlaps and gaps between speakers. Secondly, while the repair sequence initiated by C in extract (1) is a technique for managing 'breakdowns' in the 'one at a time' system, there are other more frequently used means of trying to prevent such difficulties as the obscuring or 'loss' of someone's utterance. It is worth giving some attention here to the occurrence of overlaps and gaps, because it may help illustrate how the formal apparatus of the turn-taking organisation can account for the variations in actual conversations, and also because the feature of single-speaker turns can be shown to be something to which co-conversationalists attend in their talk.

The rules provide for speaker transfers at the first point at which a current turn might be taken to be completed, points which can therefore be turn transition relevance places (this is unless a current speaker has provided hearers with certain instructions about the completion of what he has to say which can enable him to continue beyond a transition relevance place[7]). However, because a turn can consist of a variety of units (words, phrases, sentences etc), and any number of those units, whatever has been used to build a turn thus far may always be added to: a turn can be lengthened by adding more to what has been said, even though that might by itself be sufficient to constitute a turn. A consequ-

ence of this is that a next speaker can treat the completion of some unit as
also the completion of the turn, and therefore begin to speak, although it
may turn out that the first speaker had more to say, with the result that
the two speakers end up talking in overlap. This may happen in cases
where the current speaker has selected a next or where another party
self-selects. The following instances illustrate this basis for the occurrence of overlaps:

(2) (JS, I:22)
      E: D'you *li:ke* it?
      J: Uh, *Yeah,* ⌜(He looks)-
  →   E: ⌞I heard-=uh,
      E: I read two'r three columns en I heard it over TV
          thet it's become old- its becoming passe

(3) (RM, La 8)
      D: Is this e:r comment about one's own programmes o:r
      D: ⌜what exactly are (we talking) about.
  →   C: ⌞er (.) anything at all- anything at all up to now but *not*
      C: the new schedules which ⌜we're going to come to in a moment.
  →   D: ⌞No
      D: =No. (.) E::r no I don't think there's anything particular
      D: I want to raise at this point no.

(4) (AP, C: 5,21)
      D: Mm hm. Didju do any exercises in your trance?
      D: (0.2) Er ⌜didju jus-
  →   P: ⌞.hhh *Yes* yes
      P: the heaviness n' lightness with my a:rm.

(5) (PT:4)
      A: Be*c*uz uh:: u-may u-dz yer mom like t'*s*hop ov'r 'n look
      A: a*r*ou:n⌜(   )
  →   M: ⌞ng Ye:::s. Oh: yes. She luv-u-*S*he's

(6) (PT:1)
      M: .hhh O::::::::hh*he* didn:::need *it* e-*hm*-mmm.=
      M: =.hh⌜hh He *j*ist need'd it fer *t*hat one *thing* Agnes, =*hm*-mm.
  →   A: ⌞We:ll *D*ave gah-
      A: =.hh *Yah* b'djihknow we took about nine *b*ooks up there et
      A: the(p) (.) *u*h: the: e-*stamp* place'n he *got* a little pa:r tool

In each of these extracts the speakers whose utterances are arrowed begin speaking at, or very close to, a point in the current speakers' turns at which they project the *completion* of those turns, though as it happens those projections are wrong. For example, in extract (2) E begins speaking after J's 'Uh, *Yeah*,', which might of course be complete as an answer to E's question 'D'you *li:ke* it?'. Similarly, looking at the first of the overlaps in extract (3), C begins speaking when D has said enough ('Is this e:r comment about one's own programme (o:r what)') for that to be sufficient as an enquiry without the addition of '(o:r what) exactly are (we talking) about?'.[8] And in the second overlap in that extract, D begins speaking close to the point at which C's answer to her enquiry could be complete. In extract (4) the two-tenths of a second pause can be further grounds (i.e. other than the recognisable completeness of D's utterance as it stands, as a question) for P's projection of the completion of D's turn, though at the same time as P begins to answer, D begins to tag something more on to his utterance. Something like this also happens in extract (6), where M's inbreath just before 'He *jist* need'd it . . .' could be treated by A as some kind of pause. Again in each case, the result of those speakers *incorrectly* projecting the completion of the current speakers' turns is that both end up talking in overlap. Thus, although the turn allocational rules (specifying that whoever has been selected as next speaker by the current one – or, if no-one has been selected, whoever intends to self-select – should begin speaking at the first transition relevance place) can be designed to eliminate gaps between turns, in these instances the operation of those rules result in overlaps.

In extracts (2) and (6), E and A respectively appear to select themselves at those points (in extracts (3)-(5) the parties who begin in overlap have just been asked a question by the current speaker). Whereas in (2) and (6) just one speaker self-selected, it is to be expected that on occasions two or more speakers may self-select at the same point. This is because the recognisable completion of a turn through the production of some unit will be available to any of the co-participants, who may therefore independently project the same completion point. Furthermore if a current speaker has not selected the next, then the operation of the second allocational rule introduces a competitiveness into the system, given that the speaker starting first has rights for the next turn. A consequence can be that two (or more) speakers end up competing for the next turn by starting simultaneously at the point which they (independently) anticipate is the completion of the current speaker's turn. Two examples are these:

(7) (BR, PCM)

    NM: w(h) I kn*ow* tha' b but he said this mor:ning *I*
               cant do anything else b*u:* call a c*o*ntra:ct
               revie⌐w (because of what I said)
→ ( ):   ⌊(Well I don' see-)
→ NA: ⌊(Wel- in the pas') its a
    NA: contract review

(8) (BR, PCM)

    DA: . . . I mean he really came in en sai' he's got to *talk* to
    DA: someone = (very sor-) supp*o*rtive way ⌐towards you
    NK: ⌊(mmh)
          (.)
    NG: ⌐Think you sh-
    NA: ⌊Greg's (got wha-)
    NG: Think you should have *o*ne to: hold him

In extract (7), both NA and another (unidentified) speaker independently project the completion of NM's turn at the end of 'review'; because they happen to be wrong, the three speakers talk in overlap for a short while. In (8) however, NG and NA can detect the completion of DA's turn not only through its structural completeness, but also by the very slight pause which follows that utterance: they then begin together at an earliest opportunity, after only a sufficient pause to be able to tell that DA has finished speaking. Of course pauses may occur at the end of a turn which has not allocated the next, where for instance as in (8) it is used by participants to confirm that the speaker does not have more to say, if for a variety of reasons that might not otherwise be clear; and where no-one happens to start talking, given that others may, *but do not have to,* self-select. Thus if a current speaker has not selected the next, and if no-one self-selects, a pause may ensue until either someone self-selects, or the prior speaker exercises the option under the third rule.[9]

These extracts begin to show something of the systematic basis for the occurrence of overlaps and pauses in conversation,[10] and how their presence can be accounted for in terms of the turn allocational rules. Though the rules are for a system of single-speaker turns, with the close co-ordination of speaker changes, their operation can also result in gaps and overlaps. But it is noticeable that despite the occurrence of overlaps in these extracts, in no cases did those overlaps continue for any length of time: speakers do not both continue their separate turns without regard to the fact that they are talking together (except possibly in (7), where the overlap is very short because NM had little more to say). As in extract (1) the overlaps are minimised by speakers stopping in mid-turn,[11] by current speaker giving way as in (4):

```
     D:   Mm hm. Didju do any exercises in your trance?
→         (0.2) Er ⌈didju jus-
     P:            ⌊.hhh Yes yes
```

or by the next (i.e. interruptive) speaker giving way as for instance in (6):

```
     M:   =.hh⌈hh He jist need'd it fer that one thing Agnes, =hm-mm.=
→    A:       ⌊We:ll Dave gah-
```

or by both speakers stopping in their turns, as in (8):

```
→    NG:  ⌈Think you sh-
→    NA:  ⌊Greg's (got wha- )
```

In some of these cases speakers not only do not complete their turn, but actually cut-off in the middle of a word. It is further noticeable that, having temporarily given way or cut-off their turn, the manner in which speakers then re-start their utterances can attend to the kind of difficulty evidenced in extract (1), that recipients may not have heard some overlapped talk. They do so by restarting their turns in the clear with repeats or modified versions of their first starts, often having used various 'delaying' components to ensure that they will have the turn in the clear – components such as 'uh's', as in extract (2); inbreaths, as in (6); or the stretching of a sound, as in (5). Thus speakers do not merely begin again from the point at which they left off, but restart with repeats of what may have been lost in the overlaps, as in (8):

```
     NG:  ⌈Think you sh-
     NA:  ⌊Greg's (got wha- )
→    NG:  Think you should have one to: hold him
```

Other straight repeats occur in (3)-(5): a case of a modified repeat, in which the speaker re-starts with a slightly reorganised version of what she had begun to say, is (2):

```
     J:   Uh, Yeah ⌈(He looks)-
     E:            ⌊I heard-=uh,
→    E:   I read two'r three columns en I heard it over TV
          thet it's become old-its becoming passe
```

The features associated with overlapped talk – that one or both speakers may not take their turns to completion, and may even cut-off in mid-word; waiting to begin the turn in the clear, and possibly using 'delay' components which can be designed to secure that; and re-starts which are done with repeats, or modified versions, of what was started in overlap – are evidence for co-participants' attendance to the 'one at a time' property of the turn-taking system for conversation. Through these features, participants attempt to avoid the difficulties which might result from that property not being fulfilled – difficulties such as that in extract (1), for which more elaborate repair techniques may be required. Also, we have tried to outline in a simplified fashion how the very occurrence of overlaps and pauses can have its systematic basis in the operation of the turn-allocational rules. Those rules allow for speaker changes (i.e. next speaker beginning a turn) at a first possible transition relevance place; because of the different units which can constitute a turn, a next speaker's projection of the completion can happen to be wrong, with the result that he starts talking *in* the current speaker's turn. Overlaps can also result from the competitiveness introduced in the system by the operation of the second rule, allowing others to self-select if the current speaker has not selected the next (and for overlaps which can occur by virtue of the operation of the third rule, see note 9).

We have seen that a speaker may design his utterance to select a next speaker – for instance, E appears to do so in her first utterance in (2), as does D in (4) etc.; but so far little has been said about how that is achieved. The major technique for selecting a next speaker is the use of first parts of adjacency pairs.

A. ADJACENCY PAIRS.

It might be supposed that one way a current speaker might select a next is to *name* someone, or indicate that person by an address term such as 'Mummy', as in this exchange between a mother and child:

(9) (TW:C:76)
    Ch: Mummy
    M: Yes dear
          (2.1)
    Ch: I want a cloth to clean $\genfrac{}{}{0pt}{}{\text{(the)}}{\text{(ma)}}$ windows

The child's use of 'Mummy' here clearly achieves the selection of the next speaker: however, it is noticeable that the person thus selected, the mother, does not produce just any utterance, but *acknowledges* the child's *summons*. That is, we can anticipate that the class of things which the mother may do following the child's 'Mummy' is restricted in some way: she is not selected to speak next in the sense of then being able to say whatever she wants to. So the selection of a next speaker by naming him/her may not amount to an instruction, 'Right, now you go ahead and say whatever you like'; rather it seems to work by having that person do something in particular. To see that more clearly, one can consider a more frequent use of names; instead of constituting the whole of a turn as in extract (9), the name is merely one component in the turn.

(10)   (RM, La 8)
     C: Andrew do you want to raise any other =
     A: = Nothing special thank you no

C's utterance here is built with two distinguishable components: 'Andrew' [Address term] + 'do you want to raise any other =' [Question]; the person thus named then responds in a way which attends to C's utterance as a *question,* by his producing an answer. The component of C's utterance which appears to allocate the type of next turn is therefore the [Question], while the [Address term] component makes explicit to whom the question is addressed. Of course, the intended recipient of a question does not have to be named for a question to be understood to be directed to someone in particular (in which case other parties who are present may not answer): for instance, in extracts (2) and (4) the proterm 'you' achieves that; while in other cases, for example extracts (1) and (3), aspects of the content of the question may manage the speaker selection. So a turn may be designed to make it clear to whom a question is addressed through the use of a name or proterm, through aspects of its content, the direction of a speaker's gaze, or the fact of there being only two parties present, and so on. However, this presupposes the design of the turn as something which is addressed to that speaker – in extract (10) as a question. And it is that aspect of the design of a current speaker's turn which appears to allocate the next, by indicating what a selected speaker should do in that turn, which is the basis of the restriction applying to the mother's utterance following the child's 'mummy' in extract (9). Thus the child's utterance can allocate the next turn by being a 'summons', to which the selected speaker should produce an 'acknowledgement'. (Where they occur, Summons-Acknowledgement sequences are done as a preliminary to a subsequent action on the part of the initial speaker. For instance, in (9) the child then goes on to make a request.[12])

We can now begin to make out the more general properties of the way in which a current speaker may allocate the next turn through the production of such objects as questions and summons. Both are instances of *initial* actions to which a next speaker is selected to do some next *paired* action: on the completion of a speaker's question, the recipient should give an answer; and an acknowledgement should be given to a summons. But then it is quite familiar that an utterance is constructed syntactically as a question, but where that format is used to accomplish some other action:

(11)   (TW, Ga:E:73)
→   Ch: Will you read me this story
        M: Well, after I've washed the dishes I'll read
               you that story (.) yes

(12)   (SBL:10,-12)
→   B: Why don't you come and *see* me some ⌈times
        A: ⌊I would like to

In extract (11) the child's utterance may be heard to make a request, while B's utterance in (12) can be heard as an invitation. Both these utterances are formed as 'questions', but that is perhaps only incidental to their character as a request and an invitation – and it is to those characters to which recipients may be heard to attend in granting the request (though deferring it), and accepting the invitation. For instance, in (12) A does not begin to 'answer' the 'question' 'why don't you come and see me sometimes'.[13] The point that the 'question' format may not be critical to the way in which requests and invitations may select a next speaker is emphasised by the fact that both actions are commonly accomplished through a statement format, as in these cases:

(13)   (TW,Mu:E:35)
→   Ch: I want the radio o:n
        M: *No* darling

(14)   (SBL: 10,-14)
→   B: Uh if you'd care to come over and visit a little
               while this morning I'll give you a cup of *co*ffee.
        A: hehh Well that's awfully sweet of you, I don't think
               I can make it this morning .hh uhm I'm running an ad
               in the paper and-and uh I have to stay near the phone.

In these extracts the syntactic format of a statement is used to make a request in the child's utterance in (13), and an invitation in B's utterance in (14), thereby selecting the recipients to either grant or reject the request, or accept or reject the invitation. In both cases the recipients give a rejection. Therefore it is not necessary for an utterance to be formed as a question to allocate the next turn, for questions are only one of the utterance types which may be used: summons, requests and invitations are other types which can allocate the next turn independently of whether or not they are formed syntactically as questions. What these types have in common is that they are initial actions to which recipients are selected to do relevant next actions: they are *first parts* in sequences of paired actions (Questions-Answers; Summons-Acknowledgement; Request-Granting/Rejection; Invitation-Acceptance/Rejection), to which recipients should produce the *second part* (or one of the second parts) in the respective pair. This class of paired utterances was referred to by Sacks as *adjacency pairs*: extensive attention has been given, both in his work and elsewhere, to their central importance for the turn-taking organisation of conversation.

The analyses in the following chapters, which examine certain aspects of interaction and cross-examination in court-room settings, rely in various ways on the properties of adjacency pairs. The investigations into the action sequences which are initiated by the summons, 'Be upstanding in court . . .' at the commencement of a court's proceedings, into the interactional management of accusations, and into witnesses' production of justifications and excuses for their actions in the course of the hearings of a Tribunal of Inquiry, begin by noticing some of the sequential and interactional implications of the fact that such utterances as summons, accusations, and justifications/excuses are parts in adjacency pairs – summons and accusations being first parts, and justifications/excuses second parts. Because the adjacency pair format of the sequences in which summons, accusations, and justifications/excuses occur is so central to the development of the analyses in later chapters, it will be worth saying more about some of the general properties of adjacency pairs, before going on to compare the turn-taking organisation for conversation with that of cross-examination.

a. *Relative Ordering*

We have a short list of instances of adjacency pairs, questions-answers, requests (or invitations)-acceptances/rejections, and summons-acknowledgements; and we can easily add others, such as greeting-return greeting, accusation-denial/justification/counter-complaint/

apology, offer-acceptance/refusal and so on. The utterances in any given
pair have been described as either 'first parts' or 'second parts', which is
to say that they have a proper ordering within a sequence. Utterances
which are first parts of pairs should be produced in an initial position,
and should be followed, in second position, by an utterance which is the
second part in the relevant pair – or at least, one of the second parts; as
the list of possible second parts to accusations indicates, some adjacency
pairs admit alternative possible second parts in the pair. If a speaker
produces an utterance which by virtue of such features as its syntactic
form, or conventional properties, is heard as the first part of an adjacency
pair, the recipient of that may be expected to produce a second part in
the *same* pair. So not only are the parts in a pair ordered relative to one
another, but the next speaker's utterance which follows a first part
should not be any second part, but one from that pair to which the first
part belongs: hence, for example, return greetings may not be done to
requests.

The production of the first part of an adjacency pair selects the next
speaker to complete that pair, in the immediately adjacent (next) turn,
and not in some forthcoming turn. Hence participants may monitor a
current speaker's turn in order to check who is selected to speak next, at
what point that person should begin his/her turn, and what kind of
utterance (i.e. which second part) he/she should produce. Again, it
should be emphasised that the possibility of a current speaker selecting a
next through the production of a first part is present in any current
speaker's turn, so that this method of achieving transitions between
speakers is locally managed. It should not be imagined that an utterance
which is a response to a first part will not be monitored by listeners for
that same possibility; for a speaker who produces an answer or other
second part in a pair may also design that utterance so as to initiate an
adjacency pair himself – for instance, by designing that turn with two
components, as an [answer] + [question]. Thus *any* utterance in conversation may allocate the next turn through the production of the first part
of a pair, and may be monitored by participants for that possibility.

It follows from these points that a speaker may design an utterance
with regard to its *sequential placement*. Having monitored a prior speaker's
turn and found himself to be selected as next, a speaker produces an
utterance which displays his understanding of what the prior speaker
produced in that prior turn. For example, we saw that in extract (12) A,
who is the second speaker, produces an acceptance:

> B: Why don't you come and see me some⸢times
> → A: ⸤I would like to

That A gives an acceptance here, and not an answer (i.e. A does not answer B's 'question' by giving reasons why she has not been to visit B) displays her understanding that B is inviting her, and not, for instance, making a complaint about A's failure to visit. Although an alternative analysis of B's enquiry is conceivably that it is a question, and perhaps one which is part of a complaint, A doesn't treat it that way (neither, as it happens, does B go on to correct A's response, which she might have done had she recognised that A had misunderstood). The fact that A selects an utterance which is a second part in the invitation-acceptance pair, and *not* a second part in the complaint-excuse (defence etc.) pair, exhibits her understanding that B is inviting her, not making a complaint. The general point from this is that since a speaker may design an utterance so as to attend to its position in a sequence (i.e. what the utterance is placed after, though that will be revised somewhat in Chapter 5), then the type of utterance that the speaker selects displays to co-participants, and to the analyst, his understanding of the prior speaker's turn. For the most part, of course, the theoretical possibility of alternative understandings of utterances does not appear to create much actual confusion or misunderstanding between participants in conversations. However, it is an important strength of the analysis of the sequential organisation of conversation – into how speakers design their turns so as to attend to an utterance's sequential placement – that it can account for empirically occurring misunderstandings in the same terms as it accounts for the routine cases in which speakers 'correctly' interpret each other's utterances (i.e. agree on an analysis).[14]

b. *Conditional Relevance*

The link between utterance types in adjacency pairs has so far been described in the following way: on the completion of an utterance in which a speaker produces the first part of an adjacency pair, the speaker who is thereby selected should begin, and produce a second part in the relevant pair – thus, a second part is expectable following the completion of a first part. However, one can find, without too much difficulty, instances in conversation where questions do *not* appear to be answered, where a greeting does not get a return greeting, where a request gets no response, and so on – that is, cases in which a first part of a pair is not followed immediately by a second part. Such instances naturally raise the issue of what evidence there is for the kind of expectation, or constraint on a next speaker, which has been outlined. That constraint can be described as the *conditional relevance* of a second part following a first part. Following the production of the first part of a pair, a second part in that pair is a relevant next action on the part of the selected next speaker: and if the utterance in the next speaker's turn is *not* hearable as a second part in the pair, or if that slot is simply unfilled (i.e. if the selected next speaker does not begin his turn), then that is a *noticeable absence*. We can find (at least) the following kinds of evidence for the conditional relevance of a second part on the completion of a first part in a pair, and for the noticeable absence of the non-production of a second part in those circumstances.[15]

1. A first part (e.g. a question) which fails to get a second part is often *repeated*. Having produced the first part of a pair which is followed by a pause indicating that a response is not forthcoming, a speaker may repeat his original utterance, either in its entirety or in some truncated form: and such repeats may be continued until the relevant next action is done by the selected speaker. Two examples are these:

(15)　(BR:CM)
　　　A:　Is there something bothering you or not?
　　　　　(1.0)
→　　　A:　Yes or no
　　　　　(1.5)
→　　　A:　Eh?
　　　B:　No.

(16)　(TW:To,M,85)
　　　Ch:　Have to cut the:se Mummy
　　　　　(1.3)
→　　　Ch:　Won't we Mummy
　　　　　(1.5)
→　　　Ch:　Won't we
　　　M:　Yes

In these extracts, the first speakers (A, and the child respectively) do partial or modified repeats of their initial questions following pauses in which the recipients do not answer. They then do further reduced versions of their questions after another pause in which recipients still do not answer. These second repeats are successful in getting the looked-for responses. These repeats are therefore occasioned by the absence of the second part of a pair following the production of the first part, that absence being noticeable in a pause. Such pauses may not be very long (in (15) and (16) they are between 1.0 and 1.5 seconds), which again displays co-participants orientation to the close ordering of turns in conversation.

2. It is noticeable that in extract (15) none of the other persons who were present and who had been participating up to that point, and continued to do so afterwards, began speaking in those pauses. Generally, the pauses following the production of the first part of an adjacency pair, and before the recipient's response, may *not* be filled by other non-selected parties; this contrasts with pauses in other sequential positions, which may allow others to self-select, or the prior speaker to continue if no-one else self-selects – as happens in extracts (1), (4), and (8). Another case which is similar to (15) in this respect is the following:

(17)   (MH:GTS:B,053)
　　　P:　I think he should be at home doing it-
　　　D:　Well what was he *say*ing though
→　　　　(4.0)
　　　P:　I don't remember exactly =
　　　D:　= So you can't have been li*st*ening. What was he saying Mary?
　　　M:　He sais when he's in *com*pany he eats food that he
　　　　　doesn't really li*ke*.

This exchange occurred during a therapy session, at which several other persons were present who had been engaged in the talk. The four-second pause following D's question to P ('Well what was he *say*ing though') is clearly sufficient time for others to have self-selected – had they not monitored D's utterance as allocating the next turn to P. However, the fact that no-one began to speak in that pause is evidence for participants' orientation to the constraint that the second part of a pair should be done in the immediately adjacent position to the first part – that is, that the two parts should not be separated by other utterances, such that the second part would be done in turn-but-one, etc. The other parties' silence in (17) cannot be accounted for by their not being able to answer that question, because it turns out that another speaker *is* able to do so; it must be that other parties respect *P's* rights and obligations to the next turn. Thus the four-second pause is treated by those present as P's pause; a general feature of the pauses which occur after the first part of a pair is that they are not just anyone's pause, nor are they merely lapses in the conversation when no-one has anything to say, but are taken to belong to whoever has been selected as the recipient of that first part.

3. The noticeable absence of a second part of a pair is inferentially implicative. One obvious inference which might be drawn from a recipient's failure to produce a relevant next action to a first part of an adjacency pair is that that person has not heard the first part, perhaps

because they are not present, or because they were not attending or
listening; see, for example, D's second utterance in (17), and B's
utterance in (19) below. And that conclusion is certainly drawn on
occasions. However, the kinds of sequences which were found in extracts
(15) and (16) for example:

    (16)   (To:M:85)
            Ch: Have to cut the:se Mummy
                   (1.3)
    →   Ch: Won't we Mummy
                   (1.5)
    →   Ch: Won't we
            M: Yes

in which a speaker's repetition of a first part is only a *partial* or truncated
version of the original question (or whatever first part is involved),
displays the speaker's understanding that the intended recipient has
indeed heard the original utterance. The fact that certain information is
left out of the repeats indicates that the problem is *not* one of hearing. In
cases where the absence of a second part in a pair is not attributed to a
recipient's not having heard, that absence can be the topic of complaints
and the like, as in the following extracts:

    (18)   (BR:CM)
            A: What did *you* think (then) (.) Pete?
                   (5.7)
            A: Eh
                   (16.5)
    →   B: Don't shout all at once

    (19)   (BR:CM)
            (A's initial question in this extract is addressed to the 'Dave'
            named in C's utterance, and in B's enquiry)
    →   A: So you're just being awkward for the sake of it
                   (1.8)
            A: Why're you being awkward then?
                   (1.8)
            A: Eh
                   (8.4)
    →   C: You know summat Dave, the other day when I was (.)
                   saying and I was asking a question to everybody and

       , you butted in before I asked you and you sais Oh
       you never ask me anything. And when I do ask you
       you don't say nowt
       (2.5)

→   B: Are you listening Dave?
      D: Yeah

B's utterance in extract (18), 'Don't shout all at once', and A's initial utterance together with C's subsequent one and possibly also B's enquiry in extract (19), can all be heard as certain sorts of complaints concerning the failures by selected speakers to answer questions. But not only is the absence of an answer 'noticeable' in the sense that it can occasion complaints etc, but it can also be the basis of inferences, for instance that someone is being 'awkward'. The kinds of character and other inferences which may be based on someone's failure to produce second parts in adjacency pairs (e.g. failures to answer questions, to answer an accusation, return a greeting, obey a command, etc.) cannot be detailed here. But the fact that such absences may be complained about, and may support certain inferences about the person who has been selected by a first speaker, attests to conversationalists' orientation to the constraint that, on the completion of a first part of an adjacency pair, the second part of *that* pair is a relevant next action on the part of the selected speaker. That the selected next speaker should produce a second part in the *same* pair as was initiated by the first speaker is to be emphasised because, just as the complete absence of any utterance by the person thus selected is a complainable matter and may occasion inferences about that person, so too is his production of a second part from a pair *other than* that which was initiated by the first speaker. (Some of the interactional difficulties this can pose for witnesses in cross-examination are discussed below).

4. Finally, the following sort of instance might appear incongruous in terms of the constraint that a first part of a pair should properly be followed by the second part in that pair:

  (20) (BR, CM)
      A: What did y*ou:* think then Rod.   [Question 1]
           (1.5)
→   R: About Dave (.) ⌈(   )   [Question 2]
      A: ⌊No-
      A: N*o* I mean about the unit   [Answer 2]
      R: O::wa:(hh)
           (1.8)

R: ┌Er(   )
B: └We've (with Dave now)
R: Well I didn't erh (.) really think what the
      unit'd be like (   ).   [Answer 1]

Instead of immediately answering A's question, R himself asks a question ('About Dave'), which can be heard to be linked to A's (partly
through its truncated format) and directed back to A, its purpose being
to seek clarification of A's original question. Thus R initiates a question-
answer sequence which is inserted between A's initial question and R's
eventual answer to it, which gives rise to this (simplified version of the
above) sequence: Question 1 [Question 2, seeking clarification + Answer 2, giving clarification] Answer 1. However, the conditional relevance of an answer following a question has the effect that the recipient of
a question may not then produce just any question; for instance, it may
not change topic or otherwise direct talk away from the first speaker's
initial question, and following the completion of the insertion sequence
an answer to that initial question will remain to be given.[16] Insertion
sequences can be thought of as 'remedial', that is looking for a clarification or asking for a repeat (as in extract (1)) in order to be able to answer
the first question. They can occur in other sequence types besides
coming between questions and answers: notably they may come after
requests, to elicit further information on the basis of which the recipient
can decide whether to grant or reject the request. From this it can be seen
that the sense of 'remedial' should be widened to include 'delaying', so
that, for instance in the following extract, the mother can be heard to
delay her rejection (or deferment) of the child's request with her
'question' following the child's request:[17]

(21)   (TW:Ha,M,21)
        Ch: *Buy new tooth* .hh *paste for me*
→   M: Buy your new toothpaste for you?
        Ch: Uhuh
        M: Oh well but we can't get toothpaste (0.8)
               in the shops (0.3) we have to go down the town.

The general point here is that following a first speaker's production of
a first part of an adjacency pair (especially questions, but also requests
etc), where the next speaker produces a question (i.e. another first part
instead of the expected answer or whatever), that second question
should be heard as tied to the first, or directed back to it. So that not any

next question may go into that position. It should initiate an insertion sequence in which clarification is sought concerning the first speaker's utterance; and following the completion of the insertion sequence, which may last over more than one question-answer pair, the second speaker should then do the second part in the original pair (e.g. answer the original question).

The preceeding four points are evidence that participants in conversation attend to the constraint that given the production of the first part of an adjacency pair, the second part is expectable. That is, participants' attention to the *conditional relevance* of a second part following the first part of a pair is displayed through the *repetition* of the first part, on some occasions when the second part is not forthcoming; the occurrence of *pauses* following a first part in which, although the speaker who is selected to complete the pair does not immediately do so, other co-present parties may not begin talking as they might do following pauses which occur elsewhere; the possibility that the absence of the second part of a pair may be treated by co-participants as a *noticeable absence*, about which complaints may be made, or about which various inferences may be drawn; and lastly, through the occurrence of *insertion sequences*, on the completion of which the speaker who was selected by the initial first pair part should then complete that original pair.

c.   *The preference organisation for some adjacency pairs*

Some adjacency pairs have been described above for which there are *alternative* second parts. There are first parts such as questions, or greetings, for which generally only a single utterance type may be selected in order to complete the pair, answers and 'return greetings' respectively. By contrast with those, there are other first parts which can occasion more than one second part, either or any of which may properly be used by the next speaker to complete the pair. Obvious examples are that invitations may get either acceptances or rejections, as also may offers: and recipients of requests may either grant them or reject them. And for accusations there is a range of relevant next actions, such as denials, counter-accusations, justifications/excuses, admission (i.e. 'acceptances' of the charge), and apologies. The impression may have been gained that if there are alternative second parts to a given first part, the use of the alternatives is undifferentiated, or that they are equivalent actions. There is, however, evidence that this is not the case, but that one or some of the alternative available actions are *preferred*, while others are *dispreferred* actions.

A striking example is that following invitations, acceptances are preferred actions and rejections are dispreferred. The non-equivalent status of acceptances and rejections to invitations can perhaps be detected by comparing the acceptance of the invitation in extract (12) with the way in which A rejects B's invitation in (14):

(12) (SBL, 10-12)
      B: Why don't you come up and *see* me some ⌐times
→   A: ⌊I would like to

(14) (SBL: 10,-14)
      B: Uh if you'd care to come over and visit a little while
           this morning I'll give you a cup of *co*ffee.
→   A: hehh Well that's awfully sweet of you, I don't think
           I can make it this morning .hh uhm I'm running an ad
           in the paper and-and uh I have to stay near the phone.
      B: Well all right
      A: ⌐And- uh
      B: ⌊Well sometime when you are free give me a call
           because I'm not always home.

Whereas in extract (12) the recipient of the invitation straightaway (and in overlap) accepts it with no other components in her utterance than the Acceptance, the turn in which A *rejects* B's invitation in extract (14) is built with three distinctive components. They are, [Appreciation] ('Well that's awfully sweet of you') + [Rejection] ('I don't think I can make it this morning') + [Account] ('I'm running an ad in the paper and-and uh I have to stay near the phone'). A number of features of the design of that turn can serve to 'soften' the rejection and thereby attend to its dispreferred status. For example, the actual [Rejection] component is delayed in the turn, partly by A's slight hesitation, but primarily by the production of the [Appreciation] component prior to the [Rejection]. And the rejection itself is somewhat 'softened' by the inclusion of 'I don't think . . .', so that it is not done simply as 'I can't make it this morning'[18]; and perhaps most importantly, the rejection is done with an [Account] (by contrast the acceptance in extract (8) is not). That account is formed as a constraint ('I have to . . .') which for that particular occasion does not enable A to visit ('I have to stay near the phone'), and can thereby leave intact the possibility of an acceptance in the future – and in that respect it is noticeable that B treats the rejection as still allowing for that possibility, by going on to mention a visit sometime in the future 'sometime when you are free . . .': however it is noticeable that B leaves it to A to make a next proposal about a visit (with 'give me a call'), thereby avoiding getting further rejections. Thus the explanation which is given by A for rejecting the invitation can have the effect of deferring acceptance. By contrast with the acceptance in extract (12) ('I would like to'), which was uncushioned by any delay components such as an [Appreciation][19], and done without any [Account], the rejection in (14) is delayed in the turn, and is done with a reason contained in an Account.

Differences such as those between the designs of turns in which acceptances and rejections of invitations are given – and particularly the way in which the [Rejection] is delayed in A's turn, with the use of components which can 'soften' the rejection (and even give it its sense as a 'deferred acceptance') – is evidence for the non-equivalence of acceptances and rejections. Specifically they display the preferred character of acceptances and the dispreferred character of rejections. Hence the non-equivalence of the alternative second parts of a pair is observable in the different design and organisation of the turns in which such actions are taken. And in her work into these features of the design of turns in which dispreferred actions are done, Pomerantz (1975) notes that not only may dispreferred actions be delayed in a turn (for example, disagreements may be prefaced with [Agreement] type components), but they may also be withheld sequentially – that is, done not in the turn immediately adjacent to the first speaker's first part (the second speaker filling that turn with some relevant and possibly preferred action), but in a later turn.[20]

Of course, the fact that speakers may attend to the preferred character of some actions over others in the design of turns containing those actions should not be taken as exhibiting, or as proof of, participants' 'actual feelings' or intentions at the time. It is quite familiar that rejections to invitations are formed very like the one in extract (14), even though the speaker might have wished that the invitation had not been forthcoming, though the account was 'made up' for the purpose of rejecting it (accounts which are sometimes called excuses), and though the speaker has no intention of accepting any such invitation in the future, despite the account having been formed for *this* occasion. Thus the term 'preference' in this context does not refer to a speaker's psychological predisposition: instead it describes the systematic features of the design of turns in which certain alternative but non-equivalent actions are taken, as well as aspects of the sequential organisation of such actions.

An example which is of more immediate relevance here is that, for the *recipient* of an accusation (or complaint), some of the alternative conditionally relevant actions are preferred, whilst others are dispreferred.

Briefly, denials, justifications/excuses, counter-accusations and the like are preferred, whilst admissions and apologies are dispreferred: the former actions disavow or challenge the ascription of blame, while the latter accept the blame imputation. Evidence is beginning to show that, in sequential environments where a blame ascription has been made (e.g. through a complaint) or is anticipated, recipients design their turns so as to avoid self-blame. Speakers may exhibit the dispreferred character of actions which accept self-blame partly through their overwhelming use of the turn types which disavow blame ascriptions (i.e. denials, justifications, etc), but also through their design of turns in which the dispreferred types occur. For example, apologies — which appear to accept self-blame — are very often given with accounts or 'defence' components, so that turns containing apologies are generally organised as [Apologies] + [Defences], as S's apology is in this extract:

(22) (BR: CM)
      T: Steve er::m $\begin{matrix} \text{(alwes)} \\ \text{(always)} \end{matrix}$ seems to make sarcastic *c*omments
          en(s) things like (.) er:m its one of my:: yuhn the
          way I s*pea:k* (.) en things like *th*a:,
          (1.8)
      T: Sor'a goes round sorta speaking (.) very very *posh* °e(h)n
          (5.0)
→   S: Alrigh' I'm s*o*rry I do tha', (.) but some(s)times
          its jus *my* way uva jo:ke un I know no- hardly
          anybody likes my way (.) having jokes, =

The non-equivalence of action types which accept blame and those which disavow a blame ascription will be relevant at a number of points in later chapters. The general point to be borne in mind for the present is that where two or more actions are conditionally relevant second parts in an adjacency pair, one of the alternatives may be preferred over the other. That preference may be exhibited in the differential design of the turns, and the organisation of the sequences, in which the alternative actions are done.

We have seen that conversation is organised so as to ensure that only one speaker speaks at a time (i.e. occupies a turn at talking), and that transitions from one speaker to another are achieved with the minimum gap and overlap. Turn transitions are managed through two principle techniques for allocating a next turn: the first is that a current speaker may select the next, by the production of the first part of an adjacency

W: earlier in the day=
C: =Yes
W: Yes

Thus cases in which the (pre-allocated) positions of question and answer appear not to hold are accounted for by their being remedial insertion sequences, on the completion of which the examined party should then answer the original question; therefore they have the properties of insertion sequences discussed above.

Briefly, then, the argument is that the turn-taking system for examination allocates turns to just two speakers, and constrains what should be done in their turns, which should minimally be questions or answers. The pre-allocation of types and distribution of turns has the effect that the order in which parties speak is specified in advance: in this sense, turn transitions are not locally managed, but are provided for by court-room procedures. This lends to the talk of third parties its character as interruptive (where interruptions may or may not be violations), except for the provision that the examiner's slot in the question-answer sequences may be taken by the chairman (judge or whoever), thereby not affecting the turn organisation in the way that interruptions may temporarily do. And cases in which the examined party asks a question, which appear to contradict the distribution rule, are accounted for in just the same way as the production of the first part of a pair, followed by another first part, in conversation: that is, the latter may be heard as in some sense remedial, so that an answer to the first question will still be forthcoming.

A   ASPECTS OF THE TURN-TAKING SYSTEM FOR EXAMINATION WHICH ARE LOCALLY MANAGED

Earlier we saw that the turn-taking organisation for conversation is locally managed: the possibilities concerning any given next turn – when it shall begin, who (if anyone) is selected as next speaker, and what should be done in that turn – are accomplished in the course of each current speaker's turn. So the features of turn order and turn size, as well as what is done in a turn, are managed on a local turn-by-turn basis (for a fuller explanation of this, see Sacks *et al.*, 1974, pp. 724–47). By contrast, the turn-taking system for examination is organised such that the *order* in which the parties speak is fixed, as is what they should do in their turns. In these respects, turn transitions are not locally managed as they are in conversation, but are pre-specified. However, in two other very important respects the turn-taking system for examination does remain to be interactionally and locally managed by the participants. Firstly, turn-transitions need to be co-ordinated so as to accomplish the features of single speaker turns, with the minimisation of gap and overlap, which involves the local management of *turn size* and the *timing* of speaker transitions. Secondly, although respective turns should constitute either questions or answers, these are minimal characterisations of utterances in examination; other sequence types, such as accusation-justification, may be packaged in a question-answer format, and these are not pre-specified.

a. *Overlaps*

The turns in which questions and answers are done clearly vary in length: they can be constructed with just one word, with a phrase, or they may extend over several sentence units. There is no prespecification of how long a turn should last, although some control over the size of the next answer may be gained by designing a question which encourages an answer of a certain unit length, for example a 'yes' or a 'no'. Another technique for controlling turn size in examination (albeit one which operates *after* the turn) is evidenced in extract (29), and that is to object to components in the answer for which the question was not designed. Of course techniques for controlling the size of the next turn may be employed only in first parts of pairs, and hence by counsel in questions: this is then a topic in training manuals for lawyers, which contain explicit instructions about how to design questions in such a way as to restrict what a witness does in an answer, and thereby to control the production of information. Such techniques are also a basis for the kinds of sociological criticism of court procedures mentioned earlier.[24] However while turn size is not specified in advance, this is subject to the proviso that a turn might be recognised to have been completed at a point at which an utterance could count as either a question or answer; thus next speakers can, and sometimes do, begin their alloted turns at such points, though it may turn out that the current speaker had more to say. If that works as any kind of restriction on turn size by comparison with conversation, this is perhaps balanced by the bias towards larger turn size which can result from the lack of competition for a next turn. Whereas in conversation the competition among possible next speakers to self-select can inhibit long turns, in examination that pressure is relaxed, given that each speaker is assured of a next turn: hence speakers may more easily talk beyond turn transition-relevance places, and larger turns may result (these points are considered further in Chapter 6).

It follows from the fact that turn size varies that participants will monitor a current speaker's talk for the completion of that turn – that is, the completion of the question, or the answer – at which points they may begin their own (pre-allocated) turns. Thus the *timing* of turn transitions is locally managed. Arising from that, the overlaps which occur in court examinations are explicable in the same ways as they are in conversation: notably, they may occur at points at which either counsel, or witnesses/defendants, project the completion of a prior turn (i.e. anticipate the completion of an answer, or question, respectively) and thereby begin their own turns, but where it happens that the prior speaker had more to say.

(25) (Ou:43,5)
     C: An (.) about how long did you say you
     C: ta:lked before ⌈(this was   )
→   W: ⌊I don't remember
     C: (started ta kiss(h)a) =
     W: = I don't remember

(26) (Ou:45,3)
     W: A few feet away? =
     C: = Yeah ten feet fifty feet (.) ⌈something like that
→   W: ⌊I uh-   I
     W: still don' understand what you mean

In each of these extracts, the witness begins her turn at (or close to[25]) a possible transition point in the counsel's utterance: and because it happens that the counsel happens to have more to say, they end up talking in overlap, occasioning similar remedial devices – a repeat of the answer in (25), and a cut-off and re-start in (26) – as were discussed in relation to the conversational extracts (2)-(8).

b. Pauses

Another aspect of the local management of the timing of turn transitions involves the character of the pauses which occur between the completion of an answer and the start of counsel's next question. Earlier we saw that pauses in conversation may be inferentially implicative where they can be heard to belong to a selected next speaker. Where a next turn has been allocated to a speaker who does not then begin his turn, the absence of the second part of the pair is noticeable, and may be grounds for such inferences as that the intended next speaker has not heard, that he does not know the answer to a question, is stalling, or being 'evasive' or 'awkward', etc. Although similar pauses can occur between questions and answers in examination and can occasion such inferences, it is noticeable that often very long pauses may occur following the *completion* of a pair (an initial examination of some transcripts suggests that the noticeably longer pauses are often seven to twelve seconds, and longer pauses do occur). Whereas pauses in such positions (i.e. following the completion of a pair) in conversation may not be especially implicative, in examination, especially cross-examination, they can be recognised as interactional strategies employed by counsel, directed particularly at the jury, to display his disbelief or scepticism of the validity of an answer, to stress the particular significance of an answer and so on.[26] The pre-allocation of turns in examinations provides a technical basis for the inferentially implicative character of such pauses. Elsewhere, pauses following the completion of a pair may not necessarily be heard to 'belong to' anyone (given that a next speaker has not been selected, anyone present may if they wish self-select); but because the turn-taking system for examination allocates turns in one direction only, then following a witness' or defendant's answer the next turn automatically reverts to counsel, who should then self-select. Thus pauses which occur after a witness'/defendant's turn belong to counsel. It is by virtue of the pre-allocation of the turn-after-answers to counsel that the gaps which occur post-completion of answers are counsels' pauses, and so can be detected as employable by them as interactional resources, as an 'unspoken turn', to 'comment' on a prior answer.[27]

c. *The local management of action sequences*

The second aspect of the organisation of turn-taking in examination which is locally managed concerns the design of turns as questions and answers, but so as to accomplish other activities besides those. Whereas the characterisation of talk as 'conversation' is independent of the types of turns in that talk (including the activities done in those turns), by contrast we have seen that examination may be characterised as involving question and answer sequences only. However, that characterisation is only a *minimal* description of the turns in examination; other actions may be done in those turns, though they are done in the format of questions or answers.

One way in which that characterisation is only minimal – and a way which is most familiar to lawyers – is that not just any question may be appropriate, legitimate or allowable during the course of a hearing; nor may any answer to a question be allowable, even though it may *be* an answer to the question. There are various rules of evidence – for instance, concerning the relevance of the information sought in a question for the case at hand; whether evidence is hearsay; the use of leading questions; and the admissibility of questions as to issue (i.e. as to the facts of the matter) and to credit (i.e. as to whether the witness is the kind of person whose evidence is likely to be trustworthy) – the effect of which is possibly to exclude some questions from being put to a witness, and some answers from being considered as evidence in the case.[28] These exclusionary and other rules of evidence are local in that their application may be subject to the kind of court (e.g. Civil, Criminal, Coroner's; or a Tribunal of Inquiry), to the period or part of a hearing (e.g. whether the questions occur in examination-in-chief, or cross-examination), and to other circumstances.[29] As well as these technical considerations, there are also practical aspects of the application of these rules, by virtue of which their use will vary according to local circumstances. For instance, although the rules of evidence bar the use of leading questions during examination-in-chief, such questions may be permitted, and consented to by the opposing counsel, in a variety of situations: indeed Cross and Wilkins point out that almost any examination-in-chief begins with a series of leading questions (Cross and Wilkins, 1971, p. 61). Where such questions occur, then, opposing counsel may decide whether to consent to its being put, or to object to it. At any rate, the general point is that the format of a counsel's utterance as a question, or of a witness' as an answer to a prior question, does not assure the permissibility of either: thus questions, and answers, may not be equivalent, for some may be permissible (or legitimate) while others may be excluded. Clearly, although the rules of evidence can be specified in advance, their actual application is subject to decisions about whether a particular question or answer technically contravenes a given rule, and whether to allow or object to a question or answer which might appear not to be permitted under the rules.[30] Insofar as such decisions may depend on the various circumstances of a given occasion, the permissible/not permissible property of questions and answers is locally managed.

That is one sense in which the characterisation of turns in examination as questions and answers is only a minimal one, for now we have the condition that they should be permissible. But another sense in which that is so is that other actions may be done in question or answer turns. This point is developed further in later chapters (indeed it is the initial focus of chapters 4 and 5), and so it will only be briefly outlined here. In this context three main points are worth making: firstly, such actions as Accusations, Challenges, Justifications, Denials, Rebuttals and so on

may be packaged in the design of the questions and answers: secondly,
their recognition may be a noticeable matter, and the subject of complaints: and thirdly, the recognition and management of such action
sequences is interactionally co-ordinated (unlike the broad parameters
of the management of the turns as questions or answers).

1. We saw earlier in extract (12) that the 'question' and 'answer'
format of utterances may be used to accomplish a variety of activities.

(12)   (SBL: 10,-12)
        B: Why don't you come and see me some ⌈times
→   A: ⌊I would like to

A's return in this extract appears to treat B's 'question' as not really a
question, but an Invitation, through her (A's) production of an acceptance in the 'answer' slot. Hence one might begin to think of action
sequences (such as Invitation-Acceptance) being packaged in question-
answer sequences. Likewise it is easy to see that 'question' turns in
examination may be designed to achieve such actions as challenging a
witness as to the truth or adequacy of his evidence, to accuse someone, or
to allege they were implicated in something, and the like. Where
witness/defendants recognise that such actions (which are first parts of
adjacency pairs) are being performed in prior questions, they may
therefore design their answers as rebuttals, denials, justifications and so
on. Two such cases, in both of which Challenges and Rebuttals can be
heard to be involved, are these:

(27)   (ST: 91,21A)
        (('00.55' hours referred to in the second question
        is an entry in a police station log book))
        C: Was there firing in Sandy Row that night?
        W: Not to my knowledge
        C: Will you look at 00.55 hours: 'Automatic firing in
             Sandy Row'.
→   W: No, that is not correct.

(28)   (Ou: 43,5)
        C: And during that enti:re (.) *e*vening (.) Miss
             Lebrette (.) its your testimony (2.3) that there was:
             (0.9) *n*o indication as far as you could tell that the
             defendant had been drinking.
        W: No
             (3.1)

C: Now Miss Lebrette (1.2) when you were int*er*vie:wed by
the poli::ce sometimes later- sometime later that
evening (1.1) d*i*dn't *you* te:ll the pol*i*ce that the
defendant had been drinking (.) ⌐(did you tell them that)

→   W: └N*o* I told them that
there was a coo:ler in the ca:r and that I never opened it

In each of these extracts (the first of which is taken from a Tribunal of
Inquiry, the Scarman Tribunal, while the second is from an American
criminal trial), the counsel produces or elicits information in the first
question-answer pair, to which the information in the second question
can be heard to be discrepant. Thus the effect of the second questions can
be to *challenge* the witnesses' evidence in some way. What is most
important, however, is that that analysis appears to have been made by
the recipients of those questions, for in each case the witnesses' replies
display their understanding that the questions are designed to challenge
their evidence through their production of certain kinds of rebuttals. In
extract (27), the witness' response to the counsel's 'request' to look at an
entry in the police log is not merely to confirm that he has found the
entry, and then await a question about it (as happens very often in these
data); instead he denies the accuracy of the report, and thereby can be
heard to rebut the challenge to his evidence that there was no firing in
Sandy Row on a given night. In the latter extract (28), the witness'
answer, 'N*o* I told them there was a coo:ler in the ca:r and that I never
opened it', can be heard to attend to the way in which the cross-
examining counsel could have thought that she had told the police that
the defendant had been drinking, and in doing so, to attend to how the
counsel might (mistakenly) have thought that there was a discrepancy
between her present evidence and her earlier statement to the police.

These examples illustrate that such actions as challenges and rebuttals can be managed in the course of question-answer sequences, and in
later chapters we shall be considering the management of accusations
and justifications, denials etc in cross-examination. The important point
to notice is that what is of interest is not just that the occurrence of
sequence or action types other than questions-answers can be detected in
the data, but that *participants in the examination* may be seen to attend to the
occurrence of such sequences through the design of their turns. Just as in
extract (12) the second speaker's production of an *acceptance* displayed
her understanding of the prior utterance as an *invitation* – rather than a
question, or possibly a complaint, which might theoretically be alternative understandings – so the witnesses' (arrowed) replies in (27) and (28)

display their understanding of the prior questions as attempting to challenge their evidence. That understanding is exhibited in the design of their replies to variously rebut any such challenge. Hence we can expect to find that participants' recognition of the occurrence of certain action or sequences in 'questions' or 'answers' may be displayed in the design of their respective turns.

2. In conversation, the possible character of such utterances as B's in extract (12) as a question (by virtue of its syntactic structure) might well be incidental to the way in which they are treated by participants: in accepting the invitation, the recipient (A) does not attend to any constraint to actually answer the 'why don't you . . .' question. However, in examination the 'proper' characterisation of turns as questions or answers may be occasioned by participants as a constraint, in noticing that in his turn a speaker has done 'more than' answer a question, or that the question has not been answered (either not 'properly' or not at all). For instance, following the witness' second answer in (28), this occurs:

(29)   (Ou: 43,5)
        W: No I told them there was a coo:ler in the ca:r and
             I never opened it =
→   C: = The answer er: may the (balance) be here stricken
             your honour and the answer is *no*
        J: The answer is no
             (5.1)
        C: We- wz y*ou*:r testim*o*ny (.) as far as you can conclude
             (.) the defendant had not been drinking (.) ⌈(right)
        W: ⌊Right
        C: n you never told the pol*i*ce that the defendant had
             been drinking
             (0.6)
        W: I t*o*ld them about the coo:ler
→   C: You never told the police the defendant had been
             dri⌐nking (   )
        W: ⌊No

At two points here the counsel may be heard to treat the witness' prior answers as somehow inadequate; in the first place by requesting that part of the answer not be considered, and then by repeating a question. The first, the request to strike part of the answer, treats the witness' answer as more than was required by the question; it is noticeable that those 'additional' elements which he asks to be stricken are just those

with which the witness attempted to manage the possible challenge to
her evidence. Then later, in 'clarifying' exactly what her evidence was,
the counsel repeats the question, 'You never told the police that the
defendant had been drinking', thereby treating the first answer to the
question ('I told them about the coo:ler') as 'not answering'. In some
cases, as in the following, a counsel may quite explicitly reject an answer
by not only repeating it, but with some explicit rejection component:

(30) (ST: 90,10C)
    C: This is going back to the point which Mr Nicholson made
        a moment or two ago but it is an important point. Did
        you make any attempt to persuade the Catholic crowd to go
        back before you baton-charged them?
    W: I do not see how you could persuade them to go back.
→   C: Never mind that, just answer the question first and then
        give your reason. Did you make any effort to persuade
        the Catholic crowd to go back before you baton-charged
        them?
    W: No.
    C: Why not?
    W: I doubt if they could even hear me.

Of course, one of the things which the witness can be heard to do in his
reply that 'I do not see how you could persuade them to go back' is to
account for his not having tried to 'persuade the Catholic crowd to go
back' before baton-charging them. Thus his answer may be treated as
(at least part of) a justification for his action at the time. On occasions
participants explicitly refer to such alternative characterisations of a
prior speaker's turn – 'alternative' in the sense that an utterance
contained some such action, and was not (or was not primarily) a
question, or answer, as it should have been.

(31) (ST: 91,25A)
    C: Do you think or have you any views as to whether that
        suggests organisation to you?
    W: No, it does not suggest organisation to me. The fact
        was that there was heavy shooting coming from the
        Falls Road and people were highly incensed.
→   C: Are you seeking to justify that?
    W: They were out of control. My Lord, I am neither
        condoning nor trying to justify.

(32)   (ST: 91,31D)

    C: Let us examine that for a moment. Did you not know
           that there were arms in extreme Protestants' hands?

    W: I probably would have presumed that they may have a
→   few arms, but where they were I do not know. If you
           are suggesting that I was conspiring with the extreme
           Protestants about firearms

    C: Now, listen, Mr Bradley. Did you think my last
           question amounted to a suggestion that you were
           conspiring with extreme Protestants

→   W: A couple of questions before that, you made a very
           strong suggestion that there had been a Protestant
           crowd at the bottom of Percy Street and that I was
           asking them very nicely to go home. It seemed to me
           that you were under the impression that I was biased
           with regard to religion. I, my Lord, would resent that
           very much.

    C: We had better not carry on cross talk about this, but
           did you interpret my questions as suggesting that you
           had been conspiring with extreme Protestants?

    W: I did.

    C: To get back to the question which I asked you –

   Ch: Mr McSparran, you had no intention of making any such
           suggestion?

    C: Not the slightest, my Lord, and I do not think any
           reasonable person could possibly so interpret it.
           I hope, my Lord, that my phraseology is a little more
           accurate than that.

In both these extracts, speakers draw explicit attention to the possibility
that the other speakers have done something other than a 'question' or
'answer'. In the former instance, the counsel asks whether the witness'
prior answer was a *justification* for the 'retaliatory' actions of those
persons who were 'highly incensed' by the shooting from the Falls Road.
In the latter extract (32), the witness refers to the possibility that the
counsel has made a certain *suggestion* (allegation) concerning his (i.e. the
witness') sectarian bias. In each case, these alternative characterisations, of the 'answer' as a 'justification' and of the 'question' as an
'allegation' respectively, can be heard to be treated as *complainable*
matters. It is not just that the counsel in (31) and the witness in (32)
happen to notice the possibility of these alternative characterisations of

the answer and question: the point is that they can be heard to allege that the witness may have justified certain actions, or to complain that the counsel was accusing him of being biased in favour of Protestants. And it is noticeable that in each case the persons whose utterances have thus been described as a justification and 'suggestion' *deny* these possible characterisations.

Thus, while a variety of actions may be accomplished in 'questions' and 'answers', the question-answer character of examination may be attended to as a constraint on what should properly occur in speakers' turns, through the treatment of the interactional work or activity achieved in a 'question' or 'answer' as some sort of violation. This may be done, as in the above examples, by asking for a ruling that (part of) an answer be stricken and therefore not considered by the court; by rejecting a prior answer as possibly 'non-responsive', and repeating the question; or by 'naming' the action which the prior utterance is taken to be, possibly in the form of a complaint or allegation that the utterance was (the named action, which in extract (31) is a justification).

3. Finally, although the organisation of examination into question-answer sequences is not locally managed, but is provided for by the pre-allocation of the types and distribution of turns, the occurrence of other action sequences in examination is interactionally co-ordinated. It might, of course, be proposed that the production of such actions as allegations, complaints, challenges, denials, justifications, rebuttals and so on in court examination is accounted for by the close association which such actions have with blaming, which in turn has a special relevance in court settings. And in addition, some of those actions can be found to distribute differently for the different kinds of examination; as was mentioned earlier, challenges of witnesses' evidence may not distribute equally in examination-in-chief and in cross-examination, but will be very infrequent in the former. However, without denying that 'blame' may be an overwhelmingly relevant topic in court settings,[31] or that certain kinds of sequences may be more or less likely during different types of examination, neither of these points can account for their production and recognition by participants. Despite something like the general relevance of such actions in examination, especially in cross-examination, their occurrence in any particular speaker-turn is not assured or specified in advance: thus participants cannot guarantee that what is coming next is an accusation, or rebuttal, or answer. This is not to say that witnesses are not able to anticipate that a challenge or whatever is likely to come next, for clearly they are able to do so on occasions: but they have to monitor questions in order to recognise a

counsel's intentions, in a way which they do not have to do to know that a question is coming. So participants need to design their turns so as to accomplish certain actions, whilst at the same time producing 'questions' or 'answers' – here again lawyers will be instructed on, and having working knowledge about, how to accomplish such actions as challenges, etc., in the format of questions. Furthermore, co-participants may monitor each other's talk for what is being done in the prior turn, in order to find whether a relevant next action on their part is called for.

In later chapters (especially 4 and 5) we try to explicate some of the features of the design of questions in order to produce (the grounds for) an accusation: also, in the design of their 'answers', particularly through the production of justificatory components, witnesses can display their understanding that certain prior questions are part of, or leading up to, blame ascriptions which they thereby attempt to deflect – *where not just any question was treated by them as implicating a blame ascription*. We can observe, then, that the production of such actions as accusations, justification, denials, challenges, etc., is achieved through the specific *design* and the *sequential placement* of the turns in which they are done, and that participants may monitor each other's talk for the production of such actions, such that, for instance if a witness recognises that a question has the purpose of challenging his evidence, he may design his answer as a sequentially relevant next action, as a rebuttal. Although such actions may be thought to have a special relevance for court-room interaction, their occurrence in some questions/answers rather than others is *not* specified in advance: instead their occurrence is achieved on a local turn-by-turn basis, with the consequence that participants may have to monitor the talk for the possible production of such actions. Because that possibility is not pre-specified in the way in which the character of a turn as either a question or answer is, but is present in each current speaker's turn, this aspect of the turn-taking organisation for examination is *interactionally managed*, as it is in conversation.

III   THE DIFFERENCE THAT THE PRE-ALLOCATION SYSTEM FOR EXAMINATION MAKES

From this comparison of the turn-taking organisation for 'conversation' and that for 'examination', it can be seen that the major difference is that for 'examination' turns to speak are allocated between just two speakers (with provision for interruptive insertion sequences involving other speakers), to one of whom 'question' turns are allocated and to the other 'answer' turns, and thus turn order is fixed; there is no such pre-allocation of types of turns, or distribution of those types, to parties in conversation. It can easily be seen that the pre-allocation of turns in examination can have other consequences: for instance, that pauses of considerable length may occur within a speaker's utterance and in sequential positions where they might not ordinarily occur in conversation, as well as certain effects on the size of a turn, and so on. But although such technical consequences of the pre-allocation system may have certain inferential implications (see for example the points above on the possible 'use' of lengthy pauses by counsel, before asking a next question, to underline something about an answer for hearers), we want to conclude this chapter by drawing attention to a more general and pervasive consequence of the pre-allocation system – one which can confront participants as an interactional problem in examination – which is the constraint that whatever is done in examination has to be done in the sequential environment of questions and answers.

Before saying more about that, two points need to be made about the contrast between conversation and examination discussed above. Firstly it is *not* intended as a *definition* of examination. Other kinds of talk clearly share the pre-allocation of question and answer turns to just two parties, for instance interviews, quiz games, and tests; if one were interested in defining examination, a way would need to be found to differentiate it from these kinds of talk. One possibility might be to add certain conditions associated with court settings, but that ignores the fact that 'cross-examination' sequences can occur in other (non-legal) interactional situations. For instance, a sequence in which one speaker cross-examines another may occur in a seminar, a therapy session, or at the breakfast table; and the sequence may be preceeded and followed by 'ordinary conversation'. The system for examination which we have described might therefore be equally applicable to examination conducted in other settings besides courts, although whereas in courts the pre-allocation of turns is achieved through procedural rules, in other settings it will be interactionally managed: thus one speaker may manage the cross-examination of another by designing all his turns as questions to the other, and insisting on answers, whilst the recipient may try to avoid giving answers, or may try to change the topic or ask questions back, or even complain about being cross-examined. In order to take account of the non setting-specific character of examination, one needs perhaps to introduce the general relevance of issues to do with the commission of an offence and with the allocation of blame. But we suspect that even this feature, together with that of the pre-allocation system, might not be a uniquely defining condition for talk to be recognisable as examination.[32]

Secondly it should be clear that the purpose of describing the organisation of turn-taking for conversation at some length in the first half of this chapter was not simply to identify differences between conversation and examination: it was also to show properties of their organisation which they have in common. Fundamentally, of course, they are both organised into single-speaker turns, with turn allocational techniques used to effect transfers between speakers. The points made about the importance of adjacency pairs in the turn-taking system for conversation are particularly relevant here because of the central role of a particular pair type, Questions-Answers, in the organisation of turns in examination. So notions such as the relative ordering of parts in the pair and the conditional relevance of the second part following the first (the absence of a second part by the selected next speaker being a noticeable and inferentially implicative matter), all have a direct application for examination. It is important to see that this is so not just because examination is organised into question-answer pairs, but because other action sequences (i.e. other adjacency pair types) may be accomplished in them, and those points about adjacency pairs will be relevant to understanding how these other sequences are managed and co-ordinated in examination. This is to emphasise the main point of the last section, which was that while turns are pre-allocated to the extent that they should constitute either questions or answers, this is only a *minimal* characterisation of turns in examination. Other sequence types, such as challenge-rebuttal and accusation-denial, are *locally managed* in this system, as they are in conversation (as is the precise timing and co-ordination of speaker changes), which brings us to the concluding point mentioned above.

In conversation various syntactic structures may be used to package a number of activities: for example, requests and invitations may be made in either 'question' or 'statement' formats. So, for instance, whether an utterance is intended by the speaker to be a question or a request (or invitation, etc.) may be achieved through certain conventional features of the design of that utterance – so that, although the utterance is formed syntactically as a 'question' or however, it is designed to have recipients understand that it is a request. Also we saw that we have a way of detecting how participants analyse each other's utterances; for example, if the recipient of an utterance having a 'question' format responds with an acceptance, his production of *that* object (i.e. the acceptance) instead of an answer displays his understanding of the prior utterance as an invitation and not a question. This suggests at least two lines of investigation pursued in later chapters, firstly of how speakers design their turns so as to accomplish activities such as accusations, challenges, justifications, etc., and secondly speakers' analyses or understandings (which they display in the design of their turns) of prior speakers' turns.

However, in examination participants' design of their turns so as to achieve certain actions and display of their understandings of other speakers' turns, is constrained by the condition that they should attend to their placement as either questions or answers. Whereas in conversation the recipient of an utterance formed as a question may not have to attend to that character of the utterance, in examination a recipient will have to shape the alternative action (e.g. a justification) in an answer, that is, in a turn which can be taken to be an answer to the question. Moreover questioners, (usually) the examining counsel, will have to design whatever they intend to do (e.g. show that the defendant is at fault, challenge a witness' evidence, etc.) in a series of questions and answers, respecting the condition that the blame allocation, challenge, etc., should arise from the information which is asked for, or confirmed, in question-answer sequences. So that whatever an examining counsel may intend to do, it should be managed through the production of information in questions and answers.

That constraint can make a difference for a counsel who, for instance, intends to allocate blame to a witness or defendant.[33] First of all, in other sequential environments in conversation an accusation or blame imputation may be made straight out as a complaint in a statement format, as 'You did X'[34]; but in cross-examination such actions will have to be built out of the evidence which is collected in a stage-by-stage process in question-answer sequences. However, that can pose a problem for the counsel, were he not to get a certain expected piece of information in an answer, or were the witness/defendant to disconfirm some information proposed in his question. The difficulty that can thus be created is that the counsel does not have (or does not have agreement to) information which is a necessary step in building up the evidence for the blame allocation; and that piece of information may be necessary in order to move to the next stage in the questioning. Thus an (unanticipated) answer may obstruct or jeopardise a line of questioning. Faced with this sort of difficulty, a cross-examining counsel may design a next question so as to avoid the possible obstruction in the line of questioning, for instance by the use of a *conditional* question, as here:

(33)   (ST: 96,16C)
        1   C: You saw this newspaper shop being petrol bombed
        2   on the front of Divis Street?
        3   W: Yes

      4   C: How many petrol bombs were thrown into it?
      5   W: Only a couple, I felt that the window was already
      6   broken and that there was part of it burning and
      7   this was a re-kindling of the flames.
      8   C: What did you do at that point?
      9   W: I was not in a very good position to do anything.
     10   We were under gunfire at the time.
→   11   C: That shop of course could have been inhabited,
     12   could it not, it could have been the residents in it?
     13   W: Yes.

The witness, a policeman giving evidence to the Scarman Tribunal, produces a description of the petrol-bombing of a newspaper shop (in lines 5–7) and an account for his not taking action with regard to that (in lines 9–10). Those answers could thereby constitute good reasons for not taking action (or a justification) and thereby deflect a possible blame allocation by the counsel. However, the counsel's question in lines 11–12 can seek to avoid that implication of those answers by its design as a conditional, that despite whatever the witness has said, people *could have* been living in the shop (and though they are not reproduced here, the counsel goes on to ask two other similar conditional questions[35]).

This and other means by which counsel may seek to avoid the possible obstruction which a prior answer poses to an intended blame allocation are examined in more detail in later chapters (especially Chapter 5). The main point here is to draw attention to the special features of the design of questions so as to manage their *directedness* towards a blame allocation, and to handle witnesses'/defendants' strategies for trying to deflect blame allocations (for instance by disconfirming some information in the question, by qualified answers, or by 'don't knows' and 'don't understands' and the like). These features arise from the constraint that blame allocations have to be managed by counsel in the sequential environment of questions-answers. Similarly, the strategies which witnesses/defendants adopt to deflect blame are also designed for the sequential position of their utterances, as answers. So an analysis of how action sequences are managed in examination (and later we shall be concerned particularly with their production in cross-examination) should explicate how turns are designed to attend to their sequential position as questions or answers (i.e. exhibit their character as one of those utterance types), and to accomplish other actions in those turns: and, as was mentioned before, this also involves explicating the understandings which participants have of each other's prior utterances, understandings which are displayed in the design of their own turns. In short, a major difference which the turn-taking system for examination makes is that whatever actions are taken in examination will have to be fitted with the sequential environment of questions and answers: this can have important consequences for the interactional techniques employed by both parties, and for features of the design of turns in which actions are taken, and for the ways in which sequences develop.

The analyses in the following chapters have been developed from many of the issues introduced here, and illustrate some of the consequences of the turn-taking organisation of examination for what is done in examination. These chapters particularly examine the management of shared attentiveness to the restriction of rights to talk in court settings – that is, in a multi-party setting (Chapter 3); the design of questions to accomplish blame allocations, through an accusation (Chapter 4); the directedness of questions, the analyses which witnesses make of prior questions, and the design of their turns (answers) to deflect blame ascriptions (Chapter 5).

3 Opening a Hearing: Sequencing and the Accomplishment of Shared Attentiveness to Court Proceedings

I PRELIMINARY ANALYTIC ISSUES

A. INTRODUCTION

Two of the most noticeable features of interaction in courts which have recurrently attracted the attention of sociological observers, are *first* the way in which unspoken activities (such as standing up and sitting down) appear to be closely co-ordinated with spoken activities, and *second* the fact that speaking rights seem to be subjected to special restrictions which do not hold across all social settings. But, while such observations have provided important contrastive materials for the elaboration of complaints about court procedures and a variety of claims about the (mostly undesirable) effects they are supposed to have on some participants, little attention has been given to questions like whether and how their organisation might provide for the resolution or partial resolution of situated problems of the settings in which they are found. That unspoken activities, such as sitting down and standing up, seem to be somehow or other tied in with specific sequences in court hearings has presumably been regarded as too obvious to deserve serious consideration as a topic for analysis in its own right. Accordingly, as was elaborated in Chapter 1, both that 'somehow or other' and the obvious recognisability (to members) of similarities and differences between the way such activities are organised in courts, as compared with other settings, have been taken for granted and used as resources in the production of metaphorical and ironic accounts of court proceedings.

The approach adopted in this chapter, however, differs from those referred to above in that it seeks to remain indifferent to ironic and critical concerns, and to view the noticeability of continuities and disjunctions between court-room and other practices as a problematic and central topic for analysis. To this end it reports on some preliminary analyses derived from the early stages of a programme of research which conceives of court hearings first and foremost as one type of multi-party speech-exchange system.[1] Such a focus has not been prompted merely by a critical reaction to previous sociological work on court-room interaction, but it reflects also a more general interest in the possibility of adapting or extending conversational analysis to come to terms with two sorts of interactional problem evident in a variety of settings, of which courts are one example, but which have not been extensively dealt with in the existing literature on the organisation of conversations.[2] The first involves the question of how a mutual orientation or shared attentiveness to a single sequence of utterance turns can be accomplished and sustained by more than a few co-present parties to a setting. And the second general problem centres on the possible organisational significances of turns comprised of *unspoken* unit types, and the extent to which these might be incorporated into an analysis of sequencing. Some brief preliminary remarks about each of these may help to elucidate some of the analytic issues which may be involved.

B. SPEECH-EXCHANGE SYSTEMS AND GROUP SIZE

Most of the advances in conversational analysis have been derived from studies of data on talk between fairly small numbers of participants. But, as was suggested in Chapter 2, this by no means implies that such work is not or cannot be related to settings like courts where more than a few people are present. Thus, Sacks, Schegloff and Jefferson, 1974, were quite explicit in stating that, while they had sought to elaborate a model of the turn-taking system for *conversation*, their results had potential implications for the 'comparative investigation of the speech-exchange systems available to members of a single society, conceived of in terms of differential turn-taking systems' (Ibid., p. 729). More specifically, they noted the following:

The use of a turn-taking system to preserve one party talking at a time while speaker change recurs, for interactions in which talk is organisationally involved, is not at all unique to conversation. It is massively

present for ceremonies, debates, meetings, press conferences, seminars, therapy sessions, interviews, trials, etcetera. All of these differ
from conversation (and from each other) on a range of other turn-
taking parameters and in the organization by which they achieve the
set of parameter values whose presence they organise (Idem).

In developing this theme, they suggested that speech-exchange systems
might be ordered along a kind of linear array according to the extent to
which the ordering of turns is 'pre-allocated'. Whereas in conversations
next turn allocation is generally accomplished on a turn by turn basis
(c.f. Chapter 2 above), with one turn allocation being done at a time,
situations like those listed in the above quotation share the common
feature that turn allocation is, in various ways and to different extents,
done in advance. In court hearings, for example, many of the rules of
evidence and procedure are concerned with the pre-allocation of turns,
specifying (among other things) which categories of persons may do
what sorts of things at which points in the proceedings.[3] More generally,
it would seem to be the case that courts and other settings where turn
pre-allocation is an organisational feature are very often also ones where
quite large numbers of people may be present, and some of the earlier
findings of conversation analysis suggest that it may be no coincidence
that specialised turn-taking procedures tend to be found or initiated
when groups get above a certain size.

   Thus a crucially important property of the turn-taking system for
conversations is the way in which the requirement that parties must be
able to recognise possible turn endings, who may speak next, and what
may be appropriately done at any next turn, provides an inbuilt
constraint on conversationalists to monitor and pay close attention to the
ongoing talk if they are to be able to exhibit their continuing understanding of what is going on. This pressure towards attentiveness would
appear to be particularly strong in situations where only two parties are
present, in that there is no doubt under such circumstances as to whose
turn it will be next to deliver a sequentially relevant next utterance. But
where numbers increase a change takes place in the form of an increasing
strain on the capacity of the turn-taking system to preserve a shared
orientation of all those present to the same sequence of single utterance
turns. The larger the group, the less easy is it for a present speaker to
monitor closely the displays of attentiveness of all his listeners and, at the
same time, the less will be the likelihood that everyone present will be
able to take a turn to talk at all. Indeed, when some parties remain silent
for an extended period of time, it may become ambiguous as to whether

or not they are still parties to the same conversation. Under such circumstances, some of those present may, can, and often do, properly start up a concurrent conversation between themselves, the force of 'properly' here being to indicate that the second (or third, or . . . nth) conversation may receive recognition as a *separate conversation* by the failure of the active parties to the original one to invoke the 'one speaker at a time' constraint with reference to the recently started concurrent talk. In that this constraint no longer holds for all those present, but does so for members of different sub-groups within the setting, everyone may then be said to be orienting to there now being two or more conversations taking place where previously there was one.

Viewed in these terms, then, court hearings can be seen as one example of a situation where members face a rather general interactional problem of how a shared orientation to a single sequence of utterance turns can be sustained in the light of the probability that, if left unmodified, the turn-taking system for conversations provides for (and perhaps even exerts a pressure towards) the emergence of more than one concurrent conversation. And, more specifically, there is the problem of how transitions are accomplished from a situation in which several conversations are taking place to one where those involved in them have transferred their attention to the shared monitoring of a *single* sequence of utterances. An instance of such a transition at the start of a court hearing is examined below. Before proceeding to the analysis, however, a brief comment on the problem of analysing unspoken activities is necessary.

C. UNSPOKEN ACTIVITY TURNS[4]

As noted above, certain unspoken activities such as sitting down and standing up are particularly noticeable features of court proceedings, at least in the English legal system and others derived from it. And, as will be noted in one of the transcribed versions of the data to be considered below, descriptors of several such activities have been included along with the written representations of the utterance turns. That this has been done, however, is not intended to indicate that the selection and inclusion of activity descriptors for the purposes of analysis is a straightforward matter. For it raises a whole series of very complicated issues relating to, among other things, the inevitable availability of alternative descriptions of some activity in the world, the indefinite extendibility of any one description and, perhaps most important of all, the problem of how some unspoken activity may be warrantably said to

be 'oriented to be members'. In other words, the present study has
proceeded *as if* there were no such problems, rather than under the
auspices of some claim to the effect that they had been adequately
resolved *prior to* the empirical investigation.[5]

This raises the further question of why it might be deemed worthwhile
to include unspoken activities at all, given the unknown range of issues
associated with the organisation of spoken ones still awaiting exploration, and the sorts of analytic advantages associated with a more or less
exclusive concentration on talk. The preliminary references to the
noticeability of certain unspoken activities in courts would, however,
seem to suggest that they are oriented to somehow or other as organised
phenomena by participants and observers, whatever the details of some
particular description of them may be. More specifically, they would
appear to be *sequentially ordered* with the talk in a way which seems to
relate closely to what is already known about the sequencing of spoken
activities.[6] And this would seem to apply much more generally in a wide
variety of social settings, as can be exemplified by considering the way in
which an unspoken activity can constitute one or both parts of an
adjacency pair. Thus, a wave can be a perfectly proper first or second
part of a greeting pair, and a nod or shake of the head can similarly serve
as a second pair part of a question-answer sequence. Many sports and
games, furthermore, are characterised by sequences of unspoken activity
turns so that, for example, one stroke by a tennis player has clear and
limited sequential implications for his opponent's next turn, and so on,
until one player fails to deliver a proper turn. And, as will be discussed in
greater detail below, some utterances can be designed to elicit an
unspoken activity as a next turn, and may constitute a type of sequence
which is particularly suitable for doing certain sorts of interactional
work. More generally, given the extensively documented importance of
spoken-spoken adjacency pair sequences in the structural organisation
of talk, which was discussed in Chapter 2, a potentially promising line of
further research might be started by looking to as wide as possible a
range of naturally occurring social settings for instances of these other
adjacency pair types (i.e. where the first and second pair parts are
respectively unspoken-spoken, unspoken-unspoken, or spoken-
unspoken), as a prelude to considering their possible significance for the
sequential organisation of interaction.[7]

In summary, then, the suggestion so far has been that there are
reasonable grounds for supposing that the approach to the study of
sequential organisation developed by conversational analysts, as well as
some of their findings, might be applicable also to activities other than
spoken ones. This kind of proposed extension does, of course, raise a

number of interesting and difficult problems like the ones hinted at above, but it seems unlikely that either those or the question of how such work should be done will be resolved in the abstract and without reference to specific and relevant sources of data.

II OPENING THE HEARING: PRELIMINARY REMARKS

The data to be considered in the remainder of this chapter is taken from the first few moments of a coroner's inquest, which was one of a number originally observed during the course of an earlier study of how official categorisations of suicide are decided (Atkinson, 1978).[8] The main focus of that work was on the ways in which evidence about suicide and related phenomena was assembled and presented, and the data transcribed below were therefore collected with different questions in mind than the present ones. One consequence of this was that the transcription conventions used were fairly minimal and include, for example, no representations of intonation differences, breaks in words, etc. Consistent with these omissions, then, such events are not addressed in any detail in what follows.

A further general point about the data is that there are literally innumerable ways in which the proceedings could have been transcribed, and it is partly to illustrate this point, and partly to show how interesting issues can emerge during the very process of producing transcripts, that three versions of the same sequence are included. Thus, the first includes a record only of the audible utterances and their speakers, the second incorporates an inaudible utterance as well as the length and location of pauses, and the third introduces activity descriptors referring to unspoken activities which occurred during the pauses. A comparison of them quickly reveals that a good deal must have taken place during the time when the words from lines 1–3 of version 1 were spoken. Indeed, it is probably hardly necessary for any competent reader to go much beyond the first version in order to be able to fill in much of the detail included in Transcript 3, and to hazard reasonable guesses about a good deal more. It is obvious, for example, that something must have occurred *between* the first two sentences in that, if it had not, it is extremely difficult to envisage a situation where the three sentences could have followed on from each other in a continuous stream, and hence to make much sense of them as a 'single utterance' spoken by one party to the same recipient. 'Be upstanding in court . . .',[9] however, can readily be heard as projecting a next action which is to be an unspoken one and, in the absence of repeats by the speaker or repair initiations by another, readers of it who did not witness the original scene will presumably have little difficulty in locating a possible activity descriptor for what happened immediately after its completion.

Transcript 1

1	CO:	Be upstanding in Court for Her Majesty's Coroner.
2		Take the book in your right hand and read from the
3		card. That's it.
4	W:	I swear by Almighty God that the evidence I shall
5		give shall be the truth, the whole truth and nothing
6		but the truth.
7	CO:	Thank you. Could you just keep your voice up please.
8	C:	Now your name is Alfred James Smith?
9	W:	Yes.
10	CO:	Press Operator in a sheet metal works.
11	W:	Yes,
12	C:	And live at 33, Rose Hill Drive, Seatown.
13	W:	Yes.
14	C:	On (date) you came to Localtown General Hospital
15		and identified the body lying there as that of your
16		mother.
17	W:	Yes.
18	C:	Full name Amy Smith, formerly Amy Jones, and she was
19		a widow aged 48, born (date) at Docktown.
20	W:	Yes.
21	C:	And she formerly resided with you at 33 Rose Hill
22		Drive, Seatown.
23	W:	Yes.
24	C:	From which she became a patient at the (name of
25		mental hospital) here. She enjoyed good health
26		apart from minor ailments until 1968.
27	W:	Yes.
28	C:	Then what happened?
29	W:	She had an upset with my dad and she took some pills
		. . . . . .

Transcript 2

1	CO:	Be upstanding in Court for Her Majesty's Coroner.
2		(30 second pause) (inaudible utterance) (5 second
3		pause) Take the book in your right hand and read
4		from the card.
5	W:	I swear by Almighty God that the evidence I shall give

6   shall be the truth, the whole truth and nothing but
7   the truth.
8   CO: Thank you. Could you just keep your voice up please.
9   (12 second pause)
10   C: Now your name is Alfred James Smith.
11   W: Yes.
             . . . . . . (continues as from 10 in Transcript 1)

*Transcript 3**

1   (Some people standing, some walking about, some
2   sitting; several conversations going on)
3   CO: Be upstanding in Court for Her Majesty's Coroner

4   (The sitters stand, the walkers and some standers walk
5   a few paces before standing still. CO stands still;
6   everyone stops talking)
30 *secs*   7   (Coroner enters and sits down)
8   (Everyone else except CO sits down)
9   (CO walks to where W is sitting)

10   CO: (Inaudible utterance)

5 *secs*   11   (W stands up and walks with CO to witness box, which
12   he enters and stands still)

13   CO: Take the book in your right hand and read ⌈from the card
14   ⌊(W takes book
15   CO: That's it
16   W: I swear by Almighty God that the evidence I shall
17   give shall be the truth, the whole truth and nothing
18   but the truth
19   (W gives book to CO)
20   CO: Thank you. Could you just keep your voice up please

12 *secs*   21   (CO sits down; W remains standing)
22   (Coroner examines papers in front of him)

23   C: Now your name is Alfred James Smith
             . . . . . . (Continues as from 9 in Transcript 1)

(*Time elapsed between arrows is indicated on the left. Square brackets
indicate approximate points at which activities take place.)

The first proposed reading to be considered analytically below, then, is that 'Be upstanding in Court for Her Majesty's Coroner' can be heard as marking the beginning of the hearing as a whole and, more particularly, as marking the start of a transition from a situation where several concurrent conversations were taking place to one where everyone present starts to monitor the same sequence of activities. Hopefully, such a reading will be seen as utterly obvious and uncontroversial, and the almost unequivocal way in which the utterance can be heard to mark the start of the hearing is precisely what gave it an analytic attraction. Thus the problem becomes one of trying to provide for that recognisable *definiteness* by specifying some of the procedures usable by members (both participants in the setting and readers of the transcript) for recognising it more or less unambiguously as the first utterance of the inquest.

A general point which can be made immediately is that the utterance in question is hearable in this way *only with reference to its serial placement* in relation to what preceded it and what followed. Even the inferential work involved in identifying the first sentence as being separated from the second in Transcript 1 is prompted by the puzzle that would otherwise be posed by reading the second sentence as following on straight after the first. But, in addition to filling in some of that detail, the start of Transcript 3 refers also to what was taking place prior to the utterance 'Be upstanding in Court . . .', and what appears there would seem to be fairly typical of the kind of state of affairs found in many multi-party settings where nothing has yet been done to obtain the shared orientation of everyone present to a single sequence of utterance turns. We have, in short, *more than one* conversation going on at a time in a situation where those present presumably know that sooner or later they will all have to pay attention together to *only one* sequence involving one speaker speaking at a time and speaker change recurrence. In starting the transition to a situation where that is possible (i.e. where the previous conversations have been replaced by a silence which can be filled by a single speaker), the utterance 'Be upstanding in Court . . .' appears to be remarkably successful and economical. This is particularly so in comparison with other settings in which similar transitional sequences are found, such as before meetings, seminars or therapy sessions (c.f. Turner, 1972). For in those situations, several or many utterances may be required before a mutual orientation to their having started is achieved, and preliminary attempts to get them under way may, and frequently do, fail. And, while such transitional sequences may involve, like the present example, a first utterance (e.g. 'Is everyone ready?', 'Shall we start?', etc.) which can be heard as a *candidate* transition starter, such candidacy may fail for the moment, and the possibility of delaying further the start of the session is left open, an option which is not obviously present in the case of 'Be upstanding in Court . . .'. In parenthesis, then, it may be noted that the comparative study of different procedures for initiating such transitions would seem to be a potentially fruitful area for further investigation, though the present data do not of course allow for such an analysis. Bearing in mind that there are these other methods for accomplishing shared attentiveness, however, does serve to emphasise the effectiveness of the apparently simple utterance 'Be upstanding in Court . . .' in achieving the transition to a situation where all those present (a) stop talking and (b) end up sitting in silence monitoring the ongoing activities so closely that not only can the next audible utterance (lines 13–14 in Transcript 3) be heard, but the next inaudible one (at line 10 in Transcript 3) can be noticed. The analytic task addressed below, therefore, attempts to explicate three sorts of things: first, how it is that utterance gets to be heard as the first to which everyone present should orient; *second*, how it brings about a fairly immediate silence; and *third*, how what follows appears to bring about what is referred to below as the 'consolidation' of attentiveness.

III RECOGNISING AN UTTERANCE AS THE FIRST TO BE ORIENTED TO BY EVERYONE PRESENT

It was suggested above that a problem members may face can be that of identifying some single utterance more or less unambiguously as one to which attention is to be paid by all those present in a setting where several conversations are taking place at once. That is, there is no guarantee that everyone there will hear just any utterance as that, let alone respond to it in their next activities. Given that all those at this inquest did apparently respond to it, thereby displaying their shared understanding of it as such a first utterance, perhaps the most remarkable achievement of the utterance was the way in which the considerable potential for ambiguity and misunderstanding was avoided. In attempting to account for this lack of ambiguity, it will be proposed that it may have to do with the availability to members of not just one method for the recognition of 'Be upstanding in Court for Her Majesty's Coroner' as the first to which everyone should attend, but several. In other words, were there only one or two features of it which would allow for its possible recognition as the first, there would be a good chance that some of those present might fail to locate them and hence fail also to identify and respond to the utterance as the first. If, however, there are several features of its design and placement which would enable it to be so recognised, then it is presumably likely that each person present will manage to notice at least one, and hence to hear it accordingly. And, by implication, those of us (both participants and analysts) who can find a number of methods for identifying it as the first are likely to hear it more unambiguously as such. That is, it would sound like the first utterance of the hearing 'whichever way one looks at it'.

While various groups of people within the court-room may initially be engaged in separate conversations, there is, as was noted earlier, an expectation that something will have to happen to bring about the transition to a situation where everyone can orient to the same sequence of utterance turns, and there is also a predicted time when this might be expected to occur (i.e. the time set for the inquest). Thus, there is a prospective readiness to hear any utterance which could be interpreted as a first of the transition, as being indeed the first such utterance. Into this situation is delivered an utterance which is clearly hearable as having been recipiently designed *for everyone* (rather than just for the one or two others a person might be talking to at the time). The proposal that it can be heard as having been recipiently designed to be heard by everyone, is intended to draw attention to such features as the place in the court-room from which it was spoken, the type of person who uttered it, its content, syntax and, perhaps above all, its status as a simultaneous interruption of *all* the other utterances under way at the same time. To take the last of these first, its volume was much louder than any of the other concurrent utterances and, as such, it was readily noticeable not just as a violation of the 'one speaker speaks at a time' constraint being oriented to by parties to the various separate conversations, but as loud enough to have interrupted everyone else's conversation as well. An easy way to make sense of so flagrant and multiple a violation, then, is to hear it as having been designed to be heard by everyone, a conclusion which can be similarly arrived at by (and hence receive some confirmation from) other methods of reasoning too. Thus, at the same time as they hear it, those present in the court-room will presumably also see that it is delivered by someone standing on the raised platform and who is thereby set apart from everyone else. This can be taken as evidence that he is not a participant in one of the other conversations, which in turn makes it highly improbable that his remark could have been addressed *exclusively* to one or two particular people in the room.[10] That it was designed to be heard by all, therefore, is again a readily available method for making sense of it.

had the first turn constructional units been 'Stand up' rather than 'Be upstanding', it could well have been ambiguous for those present as to whether what had just been said was 'Stand up' or 'Shut up', or indeed almost anything else. To the extent that the form '*Be upstanding*' has an inbuilt delay of two syllables, then, it can be seen to have clear organisational advantages at this point over what is perhaps the most obvious possible alternative ('Stand up').

More generally, it can be noted in passing that such inbuilt delays of sequentially implicitive units at the start of turns may be a widely prevalent phenomenon in situations where preceding noise is a problem, and a possible line of further research might involve looking for further instances from similar settings. Other openings of court hearings would be one obvious source of such data and, while few of these have yet been examined in the course of the present research, it is perhaps worth mentioning how sessions of the United States Supreme Court began:

> Oyez, oyez, oyez. All persons having business before the Honorable, the Supreme Court of the United States, are admonished to draw near and give their attention, for the Court is now sitting. God save the United States of America.[12]

Thus, not only does it start with a *six* syllable silence initiating preface, but it also includes a much more explicit instruction for those present to be attentive than is the case with 'Be upstanding in Court . . .' Another interesting case of an unusual inversion (like 'Be upstanding'), which takes place in a setting where *both* noise *and* the sequential implicitiveness of an utterance for a collective unspoken next activity turn are involved, is to be found in the orders shouted at marching military squads. For while in most situations where directions to go left or right are being given, it is usual to say things like 'turn left', or 'go to the right', the inverted forms 'left turn', 'right turn', 'left wheel', 'right wheel', etc. are preferred for giving military orders, with the first word (containing the crucial piece of sequentially implicitive information) being typically long and drawn out compared with the short and snappily delivered second. And the sorts of organisational problems for military squads that might follow an utterance turn which delayed the directional word until the last second (as in the more usual 'turn left') can readily be imagined.

Following these suggestions as to how the first utterance is designed in such a way that the reference to the next projected action (i.e. standing up) can actually be heard, the problem of how it might be that it also projects an extended silence can now be considered. To begin with, then, it will be proposed that this may have to do with the fact that the utterance 'Be upstanding in Court . . .' can be heard as the first part of an adjacency pair which projects as a second part an unspoken activity turn rather than a spoken one. As a preliminary to this, two general points about its status as a command may be noted. The first is that commands can, of course, be the first part of spoken activity pairs (utterance-utterance), such as in examples like 'Answer the question', 'Speak to me', etc., as well as being possible first parts of spoken-unspoken activity pairs (utterance-activity). And the second point is that a range of syntactical formats other than commands (e.g. questions or statements) can serve as perfectly proper first parts of a U-A pair (e.g. 'Would you mind standing up?', 'I think we could do with a window opening', etc.).

The presence of one or other of these alternatives as a recognisable first part of a U-A pair may well have important consequences for the likelihood or otherwise of talk occurring after the completion of the first (spoken) turn. Thus, one feature of an utterance which can be heard as a command which has sequential implicitiveness for an unspoken next action is that one possible procedure for next speaker selection, namely 'present speaker selects next speaker' is *not* employed. But while this may substantially diminish the chances of the utterance being followed by talk (thereby increasing the probability of a silence), it nevertheless leaves open the possibility, at least in principle, that a next speaker will select himself. The likelihood of this occurring, however, would seem to be considerably less in cases where the first part of such a pair can be heard as a command rather than, for example, a question. Thus, there may be greater ambiguity as to whether a spoken or unspoken activity (or some combination of the two) should follow a first turn which is hearable as a question than is the case where it is heard as a command. For even questions designed to elicit some unspoken activity as a next turn will invariably have *simultaneous* sequential implicitiveness for a spoken activity (e.g. an answer to a question) as a possibly appropriate alternative or accompanying second part. Thus, a person who is expected to do an unspoken activity turn immediately after a question may reply with an answer to the question (e.g. A: 'Have you a cigarette?', B: 'Yes.', A: 'May I have one then?'), a request for further explication of the instruction, apologies for a delayed start of the activity, refusals to do it, etc. In short, then, utterances which can be heard as questions designed to elicit an unspoken activity at the next turn leave open a considerable range of spoken options which may be taken on their completion. By contrast, a first utterance hearable as a command to do an unspoken activity would seem to project a much narrower set of possible next actions, and to establish a clearer priority for an unspoken rather than a spoken activity turn to follow.[13] If this is so, then to speak immediately after such a first part could be seen as a failure (or refusal) to display an understanding of that priority, and would therefore be a particularly delicate and accountable matter.[14]

So far, then, the suggestion has been that the effectiveness of the utterance 'Be upstanding in Court . . .' in bringing about a silence may be at least partially provided for with reference to the way in which it involved *no* selection of a next speaker, and exerts a pressure against any next speaker selecting himself. But while no next speaker may be selected, the utterance does select a next actor to do the next turn, and this may further serve to diminish the chances of anyone selecting himself to speak immediately after its completion. As was noted in the previous section, this next actor can be heard to be *everyone together*, in that the utterance was apparently designed to be heard by all and permitted no exemptions from its auspices. Given that it also projected as a sequentially relevant next turn an unspoken activity (i.e. standing up), any other subsequent activity which might be recognisable as a next turn whether it be sitting down, waving at the speaker, walking out of the room, or, most significantly in the present context, talking, could be seen to be *misplaced*. Indeed, it would almost seem to be the case that a somewhat modified version of the 'one speaker speaks at a time' constraint for conversational turn-taking would be violated, in that one of these various sequentially inappropriate turns would be identifiable as an improper overlap or interruption of the sequentially relevant turn which should now be taking place. The kind of pressure against anyone selecting himself to talk involved here is arguably increased by the fact that the proper next action is projected to be done by a collective agent, namely *everyone together*. In that such collective action involves participants in the careful monitoring of each other's activities and in exhibiting to each other that they are all engaged in 'the same action', doing anything which could not be recognisably so described is likely to be highly noticeable and to invite a good deal of inferential work from everyone else. One way in which others could make sense of such an action would be to see the actor not merely as *an* incompetent member, but as *the only* incompetent member present in the court-room. Alternatively, such an action (or the total absence of the sequentially relevant action) may be seen as having been motivated by rebellious aims, which is of course an important resource for anyone who wishes to disrupt the orderly flow of proceedings or register a protest.[15]

The projection of an unspoken activity turn to be done next by everyone together may not only reduce the chances of any *one* person doing some activity which would clearly be recognisable as something else (whether that something else were unspoken or spoken), but the 'everyone together' requirement would also seem to exert a pressure specifically against the occurrence of verbal activity. Or rather this would seem to be so in situations like the present one, where participants have not been provided (either before the session or during the course of the first turn) with any pre-arranged script or instructions as to what it is that might be said together. Thus, were more than one, or all the parties present to speak at the same time, the result would be immediately recognisable as 'bedlam', 'chaos', 'Babel', etc. Conversely, situations where a group of participants (such as congregations at religious services, crowds at football matches, etc.) engage in spoken activities together are typically characterised by pre-arranged standardised responses, as well as a range of other organisational procedures designed to maximise the chances of simultaneous and co-ordinated delivery (e.g. music, drum beats, hand clapping, signals by cheer leaders, conductors, etc.). The suggestion here, then, is that a group of co-present parties are very unlikely to be able to speak, or chant, or sing, *in unison*, without some explicit or implicit prior instructions as to verbal content (whether these be known beforehand, contained in a script, or provided in an utterance which precedes the start of the collectively done turn).[16] To get such a group, as in the present case, to orient to doing a next turn together, without at the same time giving any details of spoken activities which could be done together, would therefore seem to be a potentially very powerful method for bringing about a collective silence.

To this point, the argument has been that the immediate silence which follows 'Be upstanding in Court for Her Majesty's Coroner' can be provided for in large measure with reference to the non-implementation of one procedure for next speaker selection ('Present speaker selects next speaker'), and the minimisation of the chances of the other ('Next speaker selects himself') coming into operation. It may be noted further that the third possible option under such circumstances, namely 'present speaker continues', is not taken up either. Thus, having successfully established his right to speak, the Coroner's Officer (CO) quickly reaches a possible turn completion point, after which he shows no sign whatsoever of continuing. In so far as everyone who heard the start of his utterance will presumably have been monitoring the turn during its course, they will also be likely to carry on monitoring for a possible continuation and, by doing so, they will be able to discover that what he actually does is to start to do what they have just started to do. That is, he too stands in silence, an activity which may provide visible confirmation for any doubters who may remain that this is indeed the sequentially relevant next turn that has just been projected. But it would also seem to be the case that, by joining with everyone else in doing this unspoken activity turn, the Coroner's Officer is also doing something which has prospective sequential implications for extending the silence and consolidating the shared attentiveness which has just begun. A brief consideration of how this might operate is presented in the following and final analytic section.

V CONSOLIDATING SHARED ATTENTIVENESS

The discussion so far has been concerned with the problem of how the various conversations taking place in the court-room prior to the hearing were closed down as part of the transition to a situation where everyone present can monitor the same sequence of utterance turns. But, while what has been said may go some way towards explicating how the initial silence was accomplished, it does not provide for how it was that the silence lasted for about half a minute. Nor does it say anything about how, by the time line 10 in Transcript 3 was reached, the attentiveness of at least one of those present (i.e. the author) had become sufficiently focused for an inaudible utterance to be noticed. In this section, then, the suggestion will be made that what occurs during the period leading up to the second utterance which can be heard by everyone (line 13 in Transcript 3) serves both to prevent any renewed talk from filling even such an extended silence, and to consolidate the shared attentiveness of those present to a single sequence of activities.

At the end of the previous section it was hinted that the Coroner's Officer's action in joining everyone else standing in silence might have some prospective sequential implications. What was meant by this was that his action could be seen as indicating a shift in the turn-taking system that had just been initiated. Up to that point the parties to it were the Coroner's Officer on the one hand and everyone together on the other, but by 'crossing sides' to join the other party he could be seen to resign from his erstwhile position as the person with whom everyone together should take turns, thereby creating a vacancy for someone else to fill. But, as was noted earlier, his first utterance had already projected the imminent arrival of the Coroner, an event which had to occur before the inquest could properly start. A candidate other party with whom

everyone together could now begin to take turns had, in other words, already
been established as someone who was about to arrive. Thus, once their
monitoring of the Coroner's Officer had yielded that he was, at least for
the moment 'one of them', the attention of *everyone together* could then be
directed to looking for the entry of someone who might be possibly
describable as the Coroner – under the auspices of some viewers' maxim
such as: 'see anyone who now enters as the Coroner if you can'. Such a
person does then enter and sit down behind the desk on the raised
platform (line 7 in Transcript 3), at which point there appears to emerge,
in the absence of any verbal or other signals to sit down, a greater degree
of potential ambiguity with respect to what should happen next than had
hitherto been the case. From the transcript, it will be noted that this slot
is filled with 'Everyone else sits down except CO' which, among other
things, can be seen as a report on the noticeability of CO's withdrawal
from continuing as a member of *everyone together* as some sort of potentially
significant marker. Thus, *everyone together* can now be seen to be, as it
were, 'on their own again' as far as doing a collective turn together is
concerned and, faced with the problem of what to do next, they all sit
down, while the person who had already established his identity as an
official and an initiator goes on to do something else which could well
turn out to ensure the orderly continuation of the proceedings.

Implicit in the above remarks is the idea that, by sitting down together
immediately after the Coroner has sat down (and by the Coroner's
Officer's failure to do so), those present exhibit their understanding that
the sequence of activities that was started by the first utterance has now
come to an end. That is, 'Be upstanding in Court for Her Majesty's
Coroner' may have indicated that there would be some sort of tie
between the activities 'Everyone stands' and 'Coroner enters', but it did
not provide any instructions as to *how long* everyone was to remain
standing and could thus be heard, at least initially, to carry with it an
'until further notice' clause. When no explicit 'further notice' is forthcoming, then, those present (except the Coroner's Officer) are left to find
for themselves when they may properly sit, and there would appear to be
at least three available methods for deciding this. The first is to see the
Coroner's seating himself as marking the completion of his entry and
hence also a possible termination of the obligation of everyone else to
co-ordinate their standing with his arrival. The second is, as was
suggested above, to see the Coroner's Officer's withdrawal from doing
the collective action together with everyone else as marking the possible
termination of that particular activity turn. And a third, perhaps most
obvious, thing to do is to monitor the activities of other officials (e.g.

policemen), who may be presumed to be familiar with court procedures, to see when they sit down.

In the previous section (IV), it was suggested that the active involvement of *everyone together* in an unspoken activity turn was important in bringing about an initial silence. From the above, it is possible to suggest further that both silence and shared attentiveness become increasingly assured by their involvement in a sequence of unspoken activities and with the interpretative problems they pose. Given that those present become active parties to a sequence of turn-taking with which few will have had direct experience, close monitoring of the unspoken activities of others (especially the Coroner's Officer, Coroner, and other officials) is essential to discovering what should be done next and when it should be done. Those present presumably know that there are certain standardised court procedures, but are unlikely to know precisely what they are. But, though there may be patterns there to be found, they have to be found *in the course of* the proceedings, and such a task must presumably require close attentiveness and shared monitoring.[17] This requirement is arguably particularly constraining at the start of a hearing, because it is at that point where those who are unfamiliar with the court have the least amount of data on the proceedings from which to start locating a pattern or, in other words, it is then that their uncertainty about the sequences that constitute the court procedures is likely to be at its greatest. Added to this, what does occur initially is largely unspoken, and the parties doing the turns keep on changing at frequent intervals before an extended stable pattern gets under way (i.e. turns are taken by CO and All; All and C; CO and W; C and W) after line 23 in Transcript 3. In such circumstances the pressure on those present to engage in close monitoring must be very great indeed, one result of which may be that the chances of finding what to do and when to do it are very good indeed. In this sense, then, the sequentially structured uncertainty can be seen to contribute in an interesting and important way towards both the consolidation of attentiveness and the orderliness of the proceedings more generally.

One final point which may be made in conclusion about the way in which attentiveness is accomplished relates back to what was said at the start of the chapter about the pressure for close monitoring being particularly strong in two-party conversations. Thus, the initiation of a series of two-party turn-taking sequences (between CO and everyone else together; everyone else and C; CO and W; C and W) may itself have powerful organisational implications for the consolidation of attentiveness in multi-party settings such as this.[18]

VI CONCLUSION

This chapter has sought to explicate how some of the 'formalities' found at the start of a court hearing serve to organise the transition from a situation where several conversations were taking place to one where sequences of single utterance turns (i.e. the examination of witnesses) can be monitored by all parties present. Obviously there will be differences in the details of how this is accomplished in different types of court, and the present analysis is at least suggestive of the idea that what members (and sociological analysts) gloss as greater and lesser degrees of 'formality' may have to do with the quantity and effectiveness of 'close ordering' devices employed to effect such transitions. There also seems little doubt that order in court (and indeed in any other multi-party speech exchange systems) could not be achieved without the use of some methodic procedures for the resolution of the sorts of organisational problems addressed in this chapter.

In the following analytical chapters, the focus shifts to phases of court proceedings where the main business of a hearing (examination and cross-examination) is well under way, and to a consideration of how some of the more explicitly moral work of courts gets done within the framework of extended 'pre-allocated' Question-Answer sequences.

4 The Management of an Accusation

Part of the purpose of questioning in cross-examination may be to try to challenge or in various ways undermine a witness's/defendant's evidence, or to show that the interpretation which should be put on the evidence is different from that which was put on it by the opposing side. Still more injuriously, persons being cross-examined may be subject to questions which attempt to attribute some fault or blame to their action. This is, of course, particularly so with respect to the cross-examination of defendants, but also often applies when a counsel directs his questions to show that a witness's action was such as to mitigate or perhaps even cancel the blame on the defendant's part. That happens, for instance, in some cases of alleged rape, in which the questioning of the 'victim' can be designed to impugn her action by attempting to show that it was partly or wholly responsible for the defendant's action.[1] Whether, therefore, the person being cross-examined is a defendant or witness, a counsel's questions in cross-examination may be designed among other things to dispute or challenge that person's evidence, or to attribute some fault or blame to his/her action.

We noted in Chapter 2 that the action sequences associated with such tasks as challenging or blaming are managed through questions and answers: whatever actions are undertaken by counsel in cross-examination (and this applies equally to examination-in-chief) have to be packaged in the organisation of the talk into question-answer sequences. The consequences of this are, firstly that challenges, etc., may be formed rather differently than they are in other sequential environments, that is where there is no constraint to produce them in question sequences. Secondly, the challenge, blame, or whatever, should arise from the information which is drawn out in the questioning. Thus a counsel has to design questions so as to elicit, or get the examined party's agreement to, certain facts or information, the effect of which will be to challenge or blame the witness/defendant.[2] Insofar as questions may be designed in these two respects to challenge or accuse a witness, these and all such actions are interactionally managed in the course of the question-answer sequences in examination. In this chapter we want to examine aspects of a counsel's design of questions so as to lead to an accusation against a witness.

The data through which this is examined is an extract from the cross-examination of a police witness giving evidence to the Scarman Tribunal (*Tribunal of Inquiry into Violence and Civil Disorder in Northern Ireland in 1969*, which published its findings in 1972). Tribunals of Inquiry do not have defendants, at least in a formal sense, though it is well known that questioning may often be intended not merely to find out 'what happened', but to blame a witness or show that he was at fault in some respect relating to the events which are being investigated. It is clear that dangers might arise from the inquisitorial element in tribunal hearings, given that witnesses do not have the same rights and legal safeguards which are usual in other kinds of proceedings. It was partly the recognition of such dangers which led to the recommendations of the Salmon Commission concerning the procedures which should be adopted to ensure that witnesses have adequate protection and opportunity to defend themselves from allegations made against them, recommendations which were later broadly accepted and put into practice.[3]

However, the analysis of the construction of an accusation here owes nothing to the special (and rather wider) powers of tribunals by comparison with other legal proceedings, because it is intended to explicate some features of the production of an accusation which are perhaps quite general. These features are that questions may be designed to build up the facts *progressively* – and get the witness's agreement to those facts – which form the basis for the accusation; and particularly that the counsel's *selection of descriptions* plays a crucial role in the design of questions to achieve that task. Clearly the descriptions involved in the data extract relate fairly specifically to incidents in Northern Ireland; indeed for much of the time the analysis concentrates on the use of the names of streets and areas in Belfast, places which may be quite unfamiliar to the reader. But again, the explication of how these description (place name) selections work to achieve the accusation makes use of an apparatus which is intended to be relevant to the interactional work achieved through any descriptions.

A major focus of this chapter, then, is the counsel's selection and use of descriptions with an eye to their interactional (i.e. accusatory) purpose, rather than to their descriptive adequacy. It is probable that we would rarely characterise a speaker's descriptive work as 'merely describing the scene', if that is an assertion that the descriptions were disinterested reflections or 'what is there' and were not motivated or purposed productions. Even the function that Toulmin and Baier (1963) attribute to descriptions, that of getting the hearer to recognise what the speaker is referring to, is a specialised task requiring considerable interactional skill. Routinely then, the descriptive work which speakers do is reported as 'telling a story (or a joke)', 'warning', 'blaming', 'justifying', 'sharing', 'dissenting', 'threatening' and so on – and may be reported as such even though no prefaratory or declaratory, 'here's a story...', 'well, I blame...', etc., was used. This is to emphasise that describing is not merely an appendage to other interactional work; rather it is often through constructing descriptions that certain interactional tasks may be accomplished.

I THE DATA

In the following extract a senior (RUC) police officer is cross-examined about events in which he was involved, events which occurred during the disturbances in Belfast in 1969.[4] In directing the cross-examination the counsel can be heard to draw attention to certain reports about these events, and to draw certain inferences from the descriptions contained in those reports. On the basis of those inferences the counsel can then be heard to accuse the witness that his action during these events was in some way defective. The descriptions which comprise the reports overwhelmingly employ place names, where these can be used to identify the religion of persons involved, and, in a variety of ways, thereby to document those persons' actions and the character of events.

(1)   (91:21F)

1   C: Then we have at 01.34 hours 'Crowd coming down Conway
2   Street from Shankill Road'.
3   W: Yes.
4   C: Then at 01.36 hours 'Crowd on Donegall Road from Sandy Row'.
5   W: Yes.
6   C: And again immediately below that 'Threat to burn Chapel at
7   Ardoyne' and 'Also man injured in Butler Street'.
8   W: Yes.
9   C: So there you have 'Fighting in Percy Street – crowd out of
10   control', 'Crowd coming down Conway Street from Shankill
11   Road' and 'Crowd on Donegall Road from Sandy Row'.

12	W:	Yes.
13	C:	All indicative of an invasion of Catholic areas by Protestants?
14	W:	I would say incensed at the shooting that was taking
15		place – scared.
16	C:	You say the crowd that were coming down there were incensed
17		and scared?
18	W:	Which crowd are you referring to?
19	C:	The Protestant crowd. Is that the crowd you are referring to?
20	W:	You mentioned shooting in Conway Street and I think the
21		Donegall Road.
22	C:	'Crowd in Donegall Road from Sandy Row', that would be a
23		Protestant crowd?
24	W:	That would be.
25	C:	Approaching the Catholic area?
26	W:	On Donegall Road, yes.
27	C:	And a crowd coming down Conway Street from Shankill Road?
28	W:	Yes.
29	C:	Then going down to 01.54 'Head Con. Rooney – about twelve
30		houses burning in Conway Street.
31	W:	Yes.
32	C:	So if we put the evidence we have heard aside for the moment,
33		viewed strictly from the context – and this is not
34		an absolutely reliable guide, I know – you have earlier an
35		intimation that a crowd are coming down Conway Street from
36		Shankill Road and then some minutes later houses are burning
37		in Conway Street.
38	W:	Yes.
39	C:	And those would be Catholic houses?
40	W:	Yes.
41	C:	Then at 02.00 hours 'Mothball – Cupar Street – fire
42		brigade needed at factory fire'.
43	W:	Yes.
44	C:	Then a message from you, Deputy Commissioner, 'Ask people i
45		Percy Street to go home as they can't stand there'.
46	W:	Yes.
47	C:	Did you send that message?
48	W:	Yes.
49	C:	Were those people you are referring to there Protestant people?
50	W:	Presumably they were.
51	C:	Were they in fact a Protestant mob that was attempting to
52		burst into Divis Street?

53 W: Prior to sending this message I must have known that there
54   was a crowd of people there.
55 C: You know in fact now that quite a lot of devastation and
56   damage was done in Divis Street at that immediate junction?
57 W: Yes.
58 C: And that there was a petrol bomb attack on St Comgall's
59   school?
60 W: Yes. Also fire was returned to St Comgall's school.
61 C: From it or to it?
62 W: To it.
63 C: Yes, we are coming to that shortly. I want to ask you about
64   the phraseology there, 'Ask people in Percy Street to go home
65   as they can't stand there'. Was that your message?
66 W: Yes, that is my message.
67 C: That was a rather polite way of addressing a mob who had
68   burned and pillaged a Catholic area, was it not?
69 W: I did not know that. The object of that message, if I may
70   answer it this way, looking back, was that there was such
71   heavy firing in particular areas that it was in the interests
72   of saving life that this message of mine was sent.
73 C: What I am suggesting to you is that you had information
74   or means of information that this mob had burned and
75   petrol bombed Catholic property and Catholic people.
76 W: No.
77 C: And that was rather a polite way to address them or
78   to address the command for orders as to how they were to
79   be dealt with.
80 W: No, that is not so.
81 C: What did you think those people were doing there?
82 W: From experience when you have trouble with rioting in one
83   area you get a crowd of people come out and stand there and
84   not do very much but stand there; you could not keep them
85   off the street. There is always a danger of confrontation
86   of different factions. That is the danger of shooting;
87   innocent people, women and children in the street will get
88   shot.
89 C: Do you know that about that time (and I use the word 'about'
90   advisedly) there is evidence that actual attacks were
91   being carried out from there on Catholic property?
92 W: There is.
93 C: Why did you not give an order or alternatively the senior

94		officer there, why did he not give an order to put that
95		crowd back up Percy Street?
96	W:	I had no evidence in my possession at that time that these
97		were the people, or I did not know yet that these were the
98		people that had committed any damage to Catholic property
99	C:	And you were the senior man in charge and at 2 o'clock you
100		did not have any evidence that these people had attacked
101		Catholic property?
102	W:	I did not know who they were.
103	C:	Did you make any effort to find out?
104	W:	I had a rather busy night; do not forget that.
105	C:	And of course the people who were living in those houses an
106		who owned that property were having a pretty busy night?
107	W:	They were, and if the IRA had permitted the fire brigade to
108		operate a lot of the property would not have been burned.
109	C:	We will be back to the IRA shortly. You did not give any
110		order to force those people or baton-charge them up
111		Percy Street,
112	W:	No.
113	C:	At that time, of course, you had had a message earlier at
114		01.33 hours from District Inspector 'B' – Mr Laggan – or he
115		had had a message, 'Fighting in Percy Street – crowd out of
116		control'.
117	W:	Yes.
118	C:	This was Mr Laggan's message and you were with Mr
119		Laggan at that time?
120	W:	I was.
121	C:	And you knew that when you sent this message that a crowd
122		had been out of control at Percy Street?
123	W:	I am sure I did; I just do not recollect it but I was in
124		the station, I was in the office.

In lines 67–8 of the data the counsel conducting the cross-examination can be heard to formulate the upshot of the 'facts' established in the preceding question-answer sequences, the upshot being that during the course of events under investigation the witness had politely addressed 'a mob who had burned and pillaged a Catholic area'. That is, in that utterance the counsel can be heard to extract from the prior talk the accusatory import of the descriptions (of scenes, persons, etc.) which are reported and constructed in that talk. An important feature of the questions which precede the accusation in lines 67–8 is that they use and/or elicit descriptions which include reference to *locations*, and particularly named locations, where these can be attributed some known identity in the normally organised religious geography of Belfast. There is certainly other descriptive work through which the counsel can design questions so as to lead to the accusation: for example, notice his use of 'mob' to refer to the persons to whom the witness sent his message, a term for which the witness substitutes the word 'crowd'.

> → 51   C: Were they in fact *a Protestant mob* that was attempting to
> 52   burst out into Divis Street?
> 53   W: Prior to sending this message I must have known that
> → 54   there was *a crowd of people* there.

However, the analysis in this chapter focuses on the way in which descriptions of locations are used to achieve the grounds for the accusation.

The analysis will attempt to explicate the ordered properties of these descriptions, through which they can be formulated as indicating that the people whom the witness ordered to 'go home' had 'burned and pillaged a Catholic area'. There are, of course, additional features of the question in lines 67–8 which give it its accusatory character: for instance it can be heard to propose a *shortcoming* in relation to the witness's action (through a device mentioned in the next chapter). But here the focus will be on how the descriptions managed in the questions can warrant an inference which appears to be central to the accusation: that is, it is the case not merely that the crowd in Percy Street had 'burned and pillaged a Catholic area' (as 'we can now see', or 'as evidence now available to us demonstrates'), but *that the witness knew, or should have known at the time he sent the message, what these persons were doing, knowledge in the light of which he should have taken appropriate action*. Notice that this is the analysis which the witness appears to make of the accusation.

> 67   C: That was a rather polite way of addressing a mob who had
> 68   burned and pillaged a Catholic area, was it not?
> → 69   W: I did not know that. The object of that message, if I may
> 70   answer it this way, looking back, was that there was such
> 71   heavy firing in particular areas that it was in the interests
> 72   of saving life that this message of mine was sent.
> 73   C: What I am suggesting to you is that you had information
> 74   or means of information that this mob had burned and
> 75   petrol bombed Catholic property and Catholic people.
> 76   W: No.

In the first part of his denial, 'I did not know that', the witness treats the counsel's prior utterance as implying that he *knew at the time* that the persons to whom he sent the message had 'burned and pillaged a Catholic area'. He does not deny the fact that that is what those persons are now known to have done, but he does deny that he knew at the time. Moreover, that denial is made *before* the counsel states, in lines 73–5, that he is suggesting that the witness 'had information or means of information that this mob had burned and petrol bombed Catholic property and Catholic people'. Thus the witness is able to recognise the implication of the accusation from whatever is done in the prior question-answer sequences, without having to wait for it to be explicitly formulated by the counsel. Hence the properties of the descriptions which are selected by the counsel for the purpose of managing the accusation are also the basis on which the witness can anticipate the main force of the accusation.

II   THE PROSPECTIVE MANAGEMENT OF AN ACCUSATION

We saw in Chapter 2 that accusations are one of the utterance types which are first parts in adjacency pairs, to which there are relevant next actions. So to an accusation the recipient should perform one of the second parts in that pair – make a denial, justification/excuse, counter-accusation, acceptance, admission, apology, etc. It was also mentioned that these second parts are not all equivalent, in the sense that some – those which *avoid* (deny or reduce) self-blame – are *preferred* on the part of the recipient, whilst others – those which accept self-blame – are *dispreferred*. The kind of evidence for that preference system is that, overwhelmingly, denials, justifications or other actions which avoid self-blame are made as seconds to accusations, whilst those which accept self-blame (such as admissions) are very infrequent (more evidence for this is mentioned in the next chapter). The adjacency pair format of accusations-denials/acceptances, etc., and the preferred character of denials, are a basis for anticipating that the recipient of an accusation will then make a denial, or perform one of the actions including justifications, excuses, etc., which seek to avoid or reduce self-blame (for the purposes of this chapter these are included under the rubric of 'denials').

It is worth emphasising the 'strength' of the expectation that the recipient of an accusation should produce a denial. Earlier, in Chapter 2 (see pages 51–57) we discussed how, on the completion of the first part of an adjacency pair, an utterance which is the second part in the same pair is conditionally relevant. That is to say, should a second part in the pair not be forthcoming from the recipient, that absence is a noticeable one, and one which may be the basis for drawing various inferences concerning its non-production. The inferential consequences of failing to deny an accusation are well illustrated in some difficulties surrounding the supposed 'right' which anyone who is questioned about, or charged with, an offence, has to remain silent. Formally at least, persons being questioned by the police in connection with a crime, and once they have been cautioned, have a protective right not to answer questions. However, according to McBarnet, 1978, cases in which such a right has been claimed by a defendant reveal how hazardous its exercise may be, given that on occasions an accused's silence (i.e. not answering questions or denying charges) may lead to inferences of guilt. McBarnet cites a number of rulings by trial and appeal judges which indicate the incriminatory force of not answering a charge.

> The law has long accepted that an accused person is not bound to incriminate himself; but it does not follow that a failure to answer an accusation or question when an answer could reasonably be expected may not provide some evidence in support of an accusation. Whether it does will depend on the circumstances. (Lord Justice Lawton, in R. v. Chandler, 1976, on appeal)

> ... it is reasonable to expect that (when a person is accused of something) he or she will immediately deny it and that the absence of such a denial is some evidence of an admission on the part of the person charged and of the truth of the charge. (Parkes v the Queen, 1976, 1, WLR: both quoted in McBarnet, 1978, pp. 1–2)

She finds that the implications of these rulings, which are particularly explicit in the latter one, are borne out in practice in actual cases in which the failure to answer a question/charge often lead to inferences being made by the judge or prosecution about a defendant's guilt. Very often this is because the accused's silence when charged may raise the issue of why the defence or explanation which was subsequently provided (e.g. in court) was not given earlier, at the first opportunity when being questioned about the offence.

> It is we think clear ... that it is wrong to say to a jury 'because the accused exercised what is undoubtedly his right, the privelege of

remaining silent, you may draw an inference of guilt'; it is quite a
different matter to say, 'this accused, as he is entitled to do, has not
advanced at an earlier stage the explanation which has been offered to
you today; you, the jury, may take that into account when you are
assessing the weight which you think it right to attach to that
explanation.' (Lord Justice Stevenson, in R. v Ryan, 1966, 50, Cr.
App. Rep.: quoted in McBarnet, 1978, p. 4)

Thus the constraints involved in the adjacency pair format of accusa-
tions-denials are emphasised by McBarnet's findings concerning the
inferences which may be drawn in practice from the failure to answer a
question/charge, even though formally the law provides for that as a
right.

However, to return to the implications of the expectation that a denial
will follow an accusation for the *management* of an accusation. That
expectation is then a resource which may be used by a counsel who
intendedly makes an accusation. Given that a denial is an anticipated
next utterance on the part of the recipient, the accusation may be
constructed so that a simple 'flat denial' can be seen to be unsuccessful;
for if a 'flat denial' were always to work there would be little point in ever
making an accusation (though of course we should not overlook that
simple rejections of a charge may not only be made but may also, on
occasions, be seen to work). Therefore a counsel may seek to forestall
such straightforward defeat of the accusation by doing some work to set
up the accusation (prior to its being declared or otherwise
acknowledged[5]), work which might be regarded as achieving the
grounds for the accusation and thereby orienting in advance to the
possible basis for a denial. Such work can include the production of
'facts', and of descriptions of events, etc., from which the inference that the
witness did X (or did X in some special way) can be made – and
designing questions to get the witness's (or defendant's) confirmation of
or agreement to those facts. This can involve the witness in a closely
ordered task to defeat the accusation, because he may now have to show
either that the facts/descriptions, etc., from which the inference that 'he
did it', etc., are wrong, or that other inferences may be made from the
same facts. A consequence of this is that participants may occasion a
rather closer constraint with regard to the adjacency pairing; that is, it
may be expected that the utterance in the next slot after an accusation
may not be just any denial, but a denial which is addressed to the 'facts',
etc., from which an accusation is formulable, in the same way that the

utterance following a question should not be any answer but one which is specifically an answer to *that* question. Thus if the denial cannot be heard to address these facts, *that* is a noticeable absence and accountable grounds for holding that the witness has 'failed to answer the accusation', or for inferring that he has not understood the accusation properly.

The fact that a counsel can be expected to do some work to set up an accusation suggests that accusations may be *prospectively managed*. That is to say, a counsel may be expected to manage question-answer sequences so as to establish progressively the facts, etc., out of which the accusation is built, before actually declaring that he is accusing the other person of doing X. In the data one of the counsel's strategies for managing the interaction appears to be to report information which is already known to him through the police records, and to have the witness confirm that information and/or add other relevant information, in such a way that were agreement not to be given by the witness at some stage, then that might perhaps jeopardise or forestall making the accusation. Thus a speaker who intentionally makes an accusation may, given the conventionally paired occurrence of accusation-denials, orient to the likelihood of the recipient's denial in managing the talk so as to build the materials (facts, descriptions, etc.) which are the grounds for accusation. And this is in turn a resource available to participants (especially witnesses) for locating accusations in talk, for if a counsel can be expected to do some work to set an accusation up, then a witness may look to see whether *that* kind of work is presently being done.

Support for this are those occasions prior to the accusation in lines 67–68, when the witness gives *qualified* answers in an attempt to avoid what he recognises as the implicativeness of the information which is sought or asked about in the prior questions. We have already seen that in lines 53–54 he qualifies his confirmation of what is proposed in the question by substituting 'crowd of people' for 'mob'. But it is noticeable that his answer is qualified in another sense. The question in lines 51–52 proposes that a mob was 'attempting to burst out into Divis Street', while the witness confirms that he knew 'there was a crowd of people there': that is, he omits the reference to what they were doing. Other places where the witness can similarly be heard to give qualified answers (prior to lines 67–8) are these:

13   C: All indicative of an invasion of Catholic areas by Protestants?
→   14   W: I would say incensed at the shooting that was taking place
→   15   – scared.

49 C: Were those people you are referring to there Protestant people?
→ 50 W: Presumably they were.

In lines 14–15 the witness does not directly confirm the counsel's assessment that the log reports are 'all indicative of an invasion of Catholic areas by Protestants'. Although he does not actually deny that assessment, which would have involved him in disconfirming that that could be inferred from the reports, the witness nevertheless holds off from a direct confirmation by adding information which may account for the Protestants' action. In doing so, he omits reference to (and thereby avoids confirming) the descriptor 'invasion', which is of course similar to his avoidance of any reference to the actions of Protestants in his qualified answer in lines 53–54. The qualification in line 50, that 'presumably' the persons to whom he sent his message were Protestants, is noticeable in the light of the earlier outline of what the participants appear to treat as the main force of the accusation. The qualification that 'Presumably they were' (Protestant) can be heard to treat that identification as one which can be inferred from what is *now* known to be the case, thus allowing for the possibility that he may not have known that at the time. So this is an earlier occasion than that noted above (i.e. in line 69) on which the witness appears to detect the particular force of the anticipated accusation.

Hence in giving these qualified answers the witness can be heard to anticipate the 'point of' the questioning, or what the questioning is leading to. He can monitor the question-answer sequences for their non-discrete overall organisation – in this case, the progressive production and accumulation of facts out of which an accusation will be made (see for example the counsel's utterance in lines 9–11, where information is brought together). Thus in his qualified responses to counsel's questions, the witness can be heard to attend to the whole sequence (comprising prior, and anticipated future, question-answer sequences) to which the production of certain pieces of information is seen to be integral. This suggests that the utterance in lines 150–51 may be formulated as an 'accusation' not because it is exclusively there that the counsel can be heard to make the accusation, but because it can be treated by co-participants as an occasion for displaying what has been the self-explicating character of the prior talk. That utterance is not, therefore, the point at which the sense of prior talk is suddenly revealed or discovered. Rather it is a point at which co-participants may attend to what has been – during the course of its production – their sense of the talk's underlying character, the recognition of which enabled them to achieve the ordered coherence and sense of the particular question-answer pairs, and which has brought them to *this* point.[6]

III   THE SELECTION OF 'LOCATION' DESCRIPTIONS

Prior to lines 67–8 the cross-examination can be heard to consist of eliciting the witness' first-hand accounts of certain episodes, scenes, etc., and producing reports contained in police station logs (whose entries are announced as 'Then at 01.36 hours we have . . .'). Looking initially at lines 9–11, we can notice that the log entries selected for the witness' (and tribunal's) attention contain descriptions of *locations*.

```
 9   C:   So there you have 'Fighting in Percy Street – crowd out of
10        control', 'Crowd coming down Conway Street from Shankill
11        Road' and 'Crowd on Donegall Road from Sandy Row'.
12   W:   Yes.
```

As well as describing where persons are (e.g. '. . . down Conway Street'; '. . . on Donegall Road'), 'place name' categories are used here as *identifications of the persons involved*, as '. . . from Shankill Road' and '. . . from Sandy Row'. These identifications are a *selection* from other ways in which the same persons might have been referred to. Because the description which can be given of a person, a group, an action, etc., is indefinitely extendible (that is, there is always more that might be added to the description), any empirical description is in principle a selection from alternative ways of describing the 'same' person, etc. And it happens that description selections in talk display a remarkable economy, for in referring to persons etc., speakers overwhelmingly employ just a single category or descriptor, which is commonly (and wherever possible) a proper name.[7] Among the considerations which enter into the selection of an identification or other descriptor is the interactional task or purpose for which the selection is being made: concomitantly, the selection which a speaker makes can be an important means through which co-participants are able to recognise that speaker's task. An initial issue this raises, which is discussed later, is how a certain category or identification selection may be used and heard to accomplish a given interactional task, here an accusation. At any rate, among the various ways in which groups of persons are referred to elsewhere in the Tribunal hearing are the composition of the crowd (in terms of the age and/or sex of its members – 'they were all male and aged, I would say, probably between 16 and 24 . . .'); the mood of the crowd ('this aggressive crowd . . .'); locations, other than place names ('the crowd at the barricade . . .', and 'the people in the flats . . .'); the numbers of persons involved ('the larger group . . .', and 'Occasionally one or two managed . . .'); and persons' activities ('those who were throwing petrol bombs . . .', 'those who broke through the police line . . .', and 'the people who were defending their homes . . .'). However, instead of these and other possible alternative descriptions which might have been used to identify persons in the setting, in lines 9–12 the counsel occasions the relevance of *place names* to achieve identifications by drawing attention to entries in the police log which contains such identifications.

The way in which place names achieve person identification here is that they can indicate the *locations of origin* of the crowds: that relies on hearing the preposition 'from' in 'crowd . . . from Shankill Road' and 'crowd . . . from Sandy Row' as stating something about where the crowds are originally 'from', rather than where they happen to have appeared from or came by way of. The identification ascription 'from Shankill Road' may not, of course, need to be supported by evidence about the residence of individuals in the crowd. Instead its adequacy in referring to the crowd relies on the attribution of a common property to members of the crowd, in terms of which they are treated as a collectivity and for which 'from Shankill Road' can stand perhaps as a sort of shorthand.[8] For this reason, identifying a collectivity by a 'named location of origin' may be finely discriminative in a way which other categories (such as size, activity, mood, positional location, etc.) may not: for a 'place name' category may be used to provide for the *religious identity* of persons so categorised.

	9	C:	So there you have 'Fighting in Percy Street – crowd out of
	10		control', 'Crowd coming down Conway Street from Shankill
	11		Road' and 'Crowd on Donegall Road from Sandy Row'.
	12	W:	Yes.
→	13	C:	All indicative of an invasion of Catholic areas by Protestants?

And

| → | 22 | C: | 'Crowd in Donegall Road from Sandy Row', that would |

→ 23   be a Protestant crowd?
   24   W: That would be.

In each of these cases (and this occurs elsewhere in the data, for instance in lines 32–9) the counsel uses the identifications of the crowds as 'from Shankill Road' and 'from Sandy Row' as the basis for categorising them as Protestant crowds: that is, he maps an alternative category, Protestant, on to certain place names.[9] The warrant for this mapping procedure lies in participants' knowledge about the 'religious identity' of certain streets, areas, ends of streets, etc., in the city, knowledge which they may invoke in order to identify persons as members of that religious group to which the street, etc., 'belongs' – given the condition that the normal ecology (i.e. organised religious geography) has not been disturbed. Thus, one of the means whereby that category selection may be relevant for the task at hand is that the category (place name) should expectedly be recognisable as having some 'known religious identity'. And therefore an 'inappropriate' selection may be one that does *not* enable hearers to recognise the 'religious' identity of persons so categorised. Hence the examining counsel's selection of certain log entries for consideration by the witness and by the Tribunal can be heard to orient to the expectedly recognisable religious identity of the place names used to describe persons, where those log entries *not* selected may not contain place names or other categories which could serve as 'religious identity' descriptions. Routinely, the matter of the recognisability of some location's religious identity may not be left to chance; participants may at the outset or during the course of an enquiry into an event, etc., collaboratively produce, remind themselves about, or check the details of, that religious identity, so that it is not merely *expectedly* recognisable but there before them. English army officers giving evidence to the Tribunal are commonly asked about their knowledge of the religious identity of streets or areas, given that their ability to interpret incidents properly and therefore act appropriately may be seen to depend on knowledge which for them does not result from native competence but is learned knowledge.

However, it is important to emphasise two aspects of the way in which the counsel progressively builds up descriptions of these events, initially through the use of 'neutral' place name identifications of the crowds, on to which he can then map a 'religious identity' category. The first is that he can thereby get a witness's agreement to the religious identity of the crowds as a consequence of their place of origin, before coming to consider the witness's action in relation to these crowds – which can avoid the kind of difficulty (for the counsel) which occurs in this extract:

(2)   (ST: 84,33,G)
       C: No-one went very far past you, you say?
       W: No-one got more than a few yards past me.
       C: So some people did go past you?
       W: I was hit in the leg by a stone and went down and that is
            when they went past me.
       C: These were Protestant civilians?
   →   W: They were civilians.
       C: Did you think that they were Catholic civilians?
   →   W: I did not give consideration to it. They were in the crowd in
            Shankill Road.
       C: So you did not think of the question of religion?
   →   W: It did not even enter my mind. This was a conflict between
            two sides and I did not even think of religion.

In this extract, the counsel first of all obtains the witness's confirmation
that certain persons had got past him, though notice again the qualified
character of that confirmation. The counsel subsequently goes on to
introduce the religious identity of those persons ('They were Protestant
civilians?'). Instead of getting the witness's agreement to that identification *before* raising issues about these persons' actions and what action the
witness took regarding them, the effect of the questioning in extract (2) is
that the witness disconfirms or denies the relevance of the religious
category (i.e. that they were Protestant). In lines 9–13, and 22–4 of
extract (1), however, the counsel attempts to manage the witness's
agreement to the origin of the crowds, and subsequently their religious
identity, in a step-by-step fashion before any mention of the witness's
own action, which is not introduced until lines 44–5.

   The second aspect of the counsel's initially drawing attention to
descriptions of various crowds which employ 'place name' identifications is that naming the 'place of origin' of a crowd can be used to
accomplish the *separate identity* of each crowd, where other categories
which might be used to refer to one or more of the crowds (e.g.
'Protestant') would *not* do this separate identification. The 'named place
of origin' is an important resource in describing scenes, not only because
it may be used to monitor the movement of groups (for narrative, as well
as more immediate, purposes) in a way which other categories or
location formulations may not, but also because it can enable the counsel
to distinguish between what each of the separate crowds (which have a

tant' crowds. But the ascription of certain areas as 'belonging to' either Catholic or Protestant can be used to do more than establish the identity of persons from such locales. Here the conventionally 'owned' character of an area may be the basis for inferring the hostile intentions of 'non-locals' in the area, where an identification for those can be 'Protestant'. A number of the reports to which the counsel draws attention in lines 1–40 can be heard to establish either the presence of Protestants in, or their movements towards, a Catholic area. An instance of the former is in lines 32–40:

```
32   C:   So if we put the evidence we have heard aside for the
33        moment, viewed strictly from the context – and this is not
34        an absolutely reliable guide, I know – you have earlier an
35        intimation that a crowd are coming down Conway Street from
36        Shankill Road and then some minutes later houses are burning
37        in Conway Street.
38   W:   Yes.
→  39   C:   And those would be Catholic houses?
40   W:   Yes.
```

From the report that houses burning in Conway Street 'would be' Catholic homes, the counsel infers (and gets the witness's agreement) that any house in the street must be Catholic; hence Protestants 'coming down Conway Street' are located *in* a Catholic area. (Other reports which can similarly provide for the presence of Protestants *in* Catholic areas are in lines 6–7 and 9). Secondly, there are reports which are formulated by the counsel as indicating that some Protestants were '*approaching* a Catholic area'.

```
22   C:   'Crowd in Donegall Road from Sandy Row', that would be a
23        Protestant crowd?
24   W:   That would be.
→  25   C:   Approaching a Catholic area?
26   W:   On Donegall Road, yes.
```

In lines 22–26 Donegall Road is taken as being a location 'on the way towards' a Catholic area for people who started from Sandy Row. It should be emphasised that places do not have any automatic status as 'places on the way towards' somewhere else: their identity as such is contingent upon members' reasoning about the circumstances, including the setting in which the crowd was observed and features of the

crowd itself. So determining the direction of a crowd's movement, and
identifying its intended destination, can often be problematical and a
matter for dispute etc. However, the inference that the 'crowd from
Sandy Row' is approaching a Catholic area is not challenged here.
Hence a contrast has been set up between the religious composition of
members of the crowds (established by named location of origin), and
the religious community to which areas in which the crowds are located,
or towards which they are moving, belongs. It is the ascription of
'ownership' of and rights in an area to a particular religious group which
enables such contrasts to be made so as to warrant inferences about the
hostile intention of 'outsiders', and here that Protestants are 'invading'
Catholic areas.

An important feature of the way in which the location of members of
one religious group in, or moving towards, the territory of the other may
be used to occasion inferences about 'hostile intention' and the like, is
that such inferences require the categories 'Protestant' and 'Catholic' to
be treated as categories from the constrastive device 'sectarian groups'.
Thus members may occasion their already-constituted knowledge of
typical patterns and of social structures in order to document or decide
what is happening in a particular setting. But events whose character is
thus documented may then be taken as evidence that such social
structures exist and that the event is a product of those structures, that is,
a normal routinely occurring event in the course of religious conflict in
Northern Ireland. Thus location descriptions are employed in the data
as a way of documenting 'what was happening'; but the efficacy of these
descriptions as grounds for ascribing the activity 'invading' to certain
persons depends on members' knowledge that the ecology is organised so
as to segregate *hostile religious groups*, a fact for which this event, whose
character has thus been occasioned, can be instanced as evidence. It is
this which was referred to earlier as the reflexive property of members'
use of their knowledge about the organised religious ecology of the city as
an interpretive device with which to document the character of an event
or scene. That is so pervasive a property of members' (including
sociologists') reasoning about events that it deserves to be a topic in its
own right.

The descriptions constructed during the cross-examination can thereby warrant inferences about the identity of the 'aggressors' and 'victims'.
It is, of course, in relation to these identities that we can begin to see
judgements about the action of the police, and particularly the witness,
being set up. Taking the identification of the aggressors as 'Protestant', it
is noticeable that in formulating the upshot of the police records as 'all

indicative of an invasion of Catholic areas by Protestants' (line 13) the counsel can be heard to attribute that activity to *each* of the groups of Protestants. Though this does not occur, it could have been disputed whether this was a correct description of *all* the particular incidents mentioned in the log (lines 9–11), while allowing that it is correct for *some* of them. The way in which a number of distinguishable incidents are reported, and agreement sought that they do all indicate an invasion by Protestants, is an important feature of the construction of the accusation (that the witness knew, or should have known, what the people in Percy Street were doing, and that he should have acted in the light of that knowledge), so as to orient to a possible denial. Until now the analysis has given attention to how participants can treat 'Protestant' as a category from the device 'sectarian group'. But at the same time as 'Protestant' may be a category in some device's collection, it may also itself be treated as a device, whose collection includes among others, 'the residents of Sandy Row', 'the residents of Shankill Road', etc. Given that, as we have seen, activities and other characteristics are ascribed to members of a population on a *category* basis, then for some purposes it may be necessary to construct these as separately identifiable categories within the device 'Protestant'. This gives members a conventional basis for contrasting the action of (Protestant) residents of one area with those of another – for example when making claims about 'infighting' among Protestants, where at least one of the parties to a dispute can be identified by an area, street, etc., from which it draws its members and/or support; about the 'independent line' being followed by residents or a certain area; about the 'disloyalty' of residents of a given area to the Protestant cause; or about the 'militancy' of persons living in a certain area compared with residents of other areas.[15] These kinds of claims seem to trade on an expectation or presupposition about the relationship between the categories, 'residents of named locations', and about their organisation within the device 'Protestant'. It is perhaps an expectation that 'Protestants' have a common cause and should 'work together' in their common interest which gives force to the contrasts in such claims; they are groups who are not merely fighting, but 'fighting among themselves', not merely taking a stand, but an 'independent stand' on some issue (compare this with, for instance, the possible difficulty a speaker might have in getting acceptance for similar contrasts made about Conservative, Labour, and Liberals taken as categories within the device 'political parties').

This expectation that (groups of) Protestants should and/or routinely do 'work together' can be occasioned through the *duplicatively organised* property of the device 'Protestant'.[16] Sacks noted that a central property of some devices is that they may be used to denote a team-like unit, and its categories organised as co-members of the unit. He gives the example of the device 'family', whose categories are 'father', 'mother', etc.; if the device 'family' is applied to some population, what is done is that its categories are taken to define the unit, and members of the population treated as co-incumbents (e.g. a father) of the unit. Sacks further points out that some duplicatively organised devices have a proper number of incumbents for certain categories in the unit; for example, a family may have only one father, a baseball team only one shortstop on the field, etc. It can therefore be a noticeable matter if a particular population to which the device has been applied is found to have more, or less, than the proper number of incumbents of such categories (which is a conventional basis for counting 'fatherless families' and so on). Taking the device 'Protestant', it commonly happens that appeals are made to the integral relationship of certain groups to the Protestant cause: so that to be an 'adequate' or proper member of the Orange Order, the Unionist party, the Ulster Workers' Council, or a resident of a given area, one has also to display consistency with or loyalty to the Protestant cause. We can add to Sacks's explication that if a population has been defined with a device so as to have the property of 'duplicative organisation', certain activities can be ascribed to members of the population with respect to that organisation. The team-like quality of the categories as comprising a unit may be used to occasion the *interdependence* of the categories as members of the unit, which in turn may warrant claims that persons belonging to the constituent categories should work together, co-operate, display loyalty to one another etc. Observe that the attribution of activities in this way can work not only as *prescriptions* (to contrast what some group is observed to be doing with what it should be doing, for instance when imputing 'disloyalty'), but also as a *prediction*: the interdependence of categories in a unit may be invoked to predict that an action which is asserted to have been done by incumbents of one or some categories defining a unit (or device) will also be, or have been, done by persons identified by other categories from that unit.

An expectation or prediction that identifiable groups within a 'religion' device might 'work together' is frequently oriented to by speakers when, for instance, explaining why an incident occurred:

(3) (ST: 74,87E)

C: One has to try and understand what was in the mind of people that night: Catholics who saw the houses of their co-religionists

going up in flames and they were being driven down to the Falls
Road where they could not protect them might well react extremely
angrily against the police who were so driving them, might they
not?

W: That is quite possible.

Here the counsel invokes the expectation that a group of Catholics would
want to help or protect their co-religionists in accounting for that group's
angry reaction towards the police, whose action prevented them from
giving such protection. And later in the cross-examination from which
extract (1) is taken, the participants may be heard to attend to the issue
of whether these attacks, though spatially separable and involving
different groups of Protestants, were linked in some way. They investigate whether the separate attacks were the result of 'organisation', a
common response to firing from a single position (St Comgall's school)
directed at some Protestants, or whether some were 'unprovoked'
attacks on Catholic areas – enquiries bound up with apportioning blame
for the incidents, and negotiating whether there was any justification or
excuse for some or all the attacks.[17]

(4)   (ST: 91,25,C)

C: You say that there was heavy shooting coming from the Falls Road,

W: Yes.

C: And you have these different and diverse attacks almost simultaneously on Catholic property?

W: Yes.

C: Do you say that those were precipitated or caused about the same
time by the heavy shooting that was coming from the Falls Road.

W: Yes, this is my view, that had it not been for the shooting the
police, although limited numbers, would have been in control of
the situation.

However, returning to extract (1), in his question in lines 9–11 the
counsel refers to three incidents, including 'Fighting in Percy Street –
crowd out of control', and then in line 13 proposes that these incidents
are 'All indicative of an invasion of Catholic areas by Protestants'.
Without engaging in a separate inquiry into the parties involved in each
of these separate incidents, he subsumes each incident in the assessment
that Protestants were invading – despite the fact that no explicit
identification of who is involved in the 'fighting in Percy Street'; or which
crowd is 'out of control', or the aggressor in two of the incidents – and this
is treated as grounds for inferring that should trouble be reported

elsewhere, but without positive identification of who was involved, it is nevertheless reasonable to suppose that the other incident is also part of an invasion by Protestants. In lines 14–15 the witness mentions a single 'threat' (i.e. shooting, which turns out to be from one location, St Comgall's School) to which each group responds. Thus he proposes that each group is acting for the same reason (reacting to a common threat) and they are therefore engaged in concerted action. Hence by line 16 the counsel comes to include all the groups of Protestants in the singular form 'crowd' (in 'the crowd that were coming down there'). The witness, however, again avoids direct confirmation of that singular form, and thereby avoids confirming that his explanation applies to the crowd who were out of control in Percy Street, which would be to presuppose that they were Protestants.

> 14   W: I would say incensed at the shooting that was taking place
> 15   – scared.
> 16   C: You say the crowd that were coming down there were
> 17   incensed and scared?
→ 18   W: Which crowd are you referring to?
> 19   C: The Protestant crowd. Is that the crowd you are referring to?
> 20   W: You mentioned shooting in Conway Street and I think
> 21   the Donegall Road.

By asking 'Which crowd are you referring to?' in line 18, the witness can be heard to attempt to re-introduce the separateness of these incidents: this is emphasised by his also avoiding agreeing that he is referring to 'the Protestant crowd' when, in lines 20–21, he does not answer 'yes', but cites two incidents in response. It is that avoidance strategy on the part of the witness which occasions the further check in lines 22–40 that these groups were Protestants, that they were in Catholic areas, and the result was 'houses burning' and other evidence of hostility; however, the identification of the crowd in Percy Street is not included in this check, but left until a later point in the questioning.

VI   THE WITNESS'S ACTION

Having thus managed the prior question-answer sequences to show that various distinguishable groups of Protestants were engaged in hostile actions towards Catholics, and to have the witness concur with that inference (though already with the qualification in lines 14–15), the counsel introduces the action which the witness took with respect to one of the groups, the 'people in Percy Street'.

44 C: Then a message from you, Deputy Commissioner, 'Ask people
45   in Percy Street to go home as they can't stand there'.
46 W: Yes.
47 C: Did you send that message?
48 W: Yes.

In the log entry which the counsel reads out in lines 64–5, the witness is reported as having sent a message to persons who have already been included (in line 13) in the depiction of Protestants invading Catholic areas. The counsel then checks that those persons were Protestants – and of course it is particularly at this point that the witness gives qualified confirmations.

49 C: Were those people you are referring to there Protestant people?
→ 50 W: Presumably they were.
51 C: Were they in fact a Protestant mob that was attempting to
52   burst out into Divis Street?
→ 53 W: Prior to sending this message I must have known that there
→ 54   was a crowd of people there.
55 C: You know in fact now that quite a lot of devastation and
56   damage was done in Divis Street at that immediate junction?
57 W: Yes.

The counsel goes on to document the damage and other evidence of hostility at the junction of Percy Street and Divis Street (lines 55–62), and then again cites the witness's message to those people.

At this point the accusation in lines 67–68 may be glossed as follows: the action which the witness ordered to be taken, sending a message to 'ask people in Percy Street to go home as they can't stand there' was insufficient to control a crowd which was likely either to have already, or would go on to, attack Catholic property. A little later the counsel underlines the assessment that the witness's action was insufficient, when (in lines 93–5) he asks why he did 'not give any order to put that crowd back up Percy Street', or (in lines 109–11) 'did not give any order to force those people or to baton-charge them up Percy Street'. Thus, in citing 'stronger' action which might properly have been taken, the counsel proposes that the action which the witness took was disjunctive (and specifically, not strong or 'forceful' enough) compared with the actions of the crowd in Percy Street.

We can now see how the counsel may be heard to occasion the

duplicatively organised property of 'Protestants' in constructing this accusation. Given the known character of other events occurring in the vicinity (that each involves an invasion of Catholic areas by Protestants) the duplicatively organised property of the device 'Protestant' can occasion the probability that *this* event is one of the same kind. Though in some respects certain features of the event might make its character ambiguous (see, for example, the witness's remarks in lines 82–8), the work done prior to lines 67–8 in documenting the character of other events can be designed to show that the witness could have assessed the messages that he was receiving (that there was 'Fighting in Percy Street – crowd out of control') and have decided that that, too, was part of an invasion by Protestants.

A possible denial to the accusation as glossed above (and the one which we have seen the witness gives in line 69) is that despite what *other* Protestant groups had been doing, there was no evidence of *this* crowd's intention available to the witness at the time he took his action (i.e. sent the message). Although it transpires that 'in fact' the crowd in question either had already, or subsequently, succeeded in attacking and damaging Catholic property, information was not available to him *at that time* that that was the case. But occasioning an expectation concerning the crowd's activity through the duplicative organisation of 'Protestants' can prospectively orient to such a denial. In that the property is proposed as an 'objective' feature of the world, it can be claimed that the witness, from the information which it is ascertained he already had at the time he sent the message, *should have predicted* what the (Protestant) crowd in Percy Street were doing there, *despite* his having no other information (reports, etc.) about what they were doing. Thus the counsel's reformulation of the accusation in lines 73–5 that the witness had '. . . information or *means of information*' about the activities of the crowd can be heard to propose that although the witness may not necessarily have had 'direct' observational information (the counsel can be heard to leave it open that the witness may not have had direct information at the time, for instance when he said in lines 55–6, 'You know in fact *now* that . . .', etc.), the information which he *did* have could, in the light of shared and 'objective' knowledge of the structured or organised basis of social activities, have enabled him to deduce what the crowd were doing there. And notice in this respect that the counsel's questions in lines 99–101, and 113–24 can be heard to check that the witness *was* in a position to have information from which that deduction was possible, by getting the witness's agreement that he was the person in charge at the time, that he was in the police station and with the person receiving messages, and that the relevant messages had been passed on to him.

Thus the descriptive work done over the course of several utterances provides for the inference that what was happening in Percy Street could have been predicted or decided in advance of confirmatory (e.g. forensic) evidence, by consulting the character of events elsewhere. The availability of that prediction is thus accountable grounds for inferring that the action which the witness ordered the police to take was in some way *defective*. That is, in addition to the inappropriateness or unsuitability of that action, the availability to anyone in the witness's position (i.e. who had the information which has been collaboratively documented) of the expectation, supposition, prediction, or whatever, that the crowd in Percy Street were invading a Catholic area, can be grounds for inferring the *culpability* of the (inappropriate) action. It is in the sense that the inappropriateness of the action can be taken to have been more than a 'chance' misreading of the situation, or a mistake 'anyone might have made', that the word 'defective' is meant. The ascription that the witness was in a position from which he 'should have known' what the crowd were doing can perhaps be used to set up the defective nature of his action in (at least) two analytically distinguishable ways. Either it can provide for the likelihood that he *did* actually know at the time he took the action that the crowd in Percy Street were invading, but for some reason failed to act appropriately. This raises questions about his *reasons* for not taking the appropriate action, and therefore proposes the intentioned or motivated character of his failure to order suitable action to be taken. Alternatively it may be used to contrast his apparently not drawing the 'obvious conclusions' about the intentions of that crowd from the information available to him, with some requirement that to fulfil adequately certain organisational duties he *ought* to have assessed the situation correctly; thus his failure to do so is at least a culpable neglect of his duty. Bearing in mind these alternatives, it is of interest that the witness makes this remark later in the cross-examination.

(5) (ST: 91,31,E)

W: A couple of questions before that you made a very strong suggestion that there had been a Protestant crowd at the bottom of Percy Street and that I was asking them very nicely to go home. It seemed to me that you were under the impression that I was biased with regard to religion. I, my Lord, would resent that very much.

It appears, then, that what the accusation was 'about' is formulated by the witness in terms of the imputed motivations, interests, etc. (e.g. 'religious bias') which might account for the proposed defectiveness of the witness's action – and this may be achieved irrespective of whether or not hearers agree with the substance of t'.e accusation.

VII CONCLUSION

The preceding explication of this data suggests the descriptive work done over the course of this extract is finely *discriminative*, in the sense that it can be used to manage certain tasks such as identifying the parties concerned, and so as to preserve and display features of the setting as resources for constructing an accusation. For instance the descriptions reported enable certain groups to be identified as Protestants, while preserving the distinguishable identity of separate groups of Protestants. This in turn can be heard to occasion the inference that *each* group of Protestants was invading Catholic areas (lines 9–13), and thus that groups of Protestants were acting in concert. Thus the work which can be done with location descriptions includes not only occasioning the activities of persons in the setting, but also the grounds on which the message that there was 'Fighting in Percy Street – crowd out of control' might, or should, have been interpreted. The analysis suggests how the counsel can be heard to manage the production of descriptions in the question-answer sequences so as to be able, in lines 67–68, to formulate the upshot of those descriptions in such a way as to propose a judgement about the witness's action, where other descriptive work which could have been done might not have served that purpose.

It is important to emphasise that not only can the descriptive work managed in the course of the question-answer sequences be designed for the counsel's purpose in setting up the grounds for the accusation; it can also be the basis on which the witness may detect that purpose in the questioning. In the early part of this chapter we saw that, given the constraint that a subsequent action should be topically linked with an initial action, we have a means for seeing what the witness took the substance of the accusation to be. That is, given that for instance an answer should be connected topically or in terms of its content with the specific question to which it is addressed (so not just any answer will do), similarly a denial should be addressed to the specific charge which it is intended to rebut. The nature of the witness's denial in line 69 exhibits his understanding that the accusation was designed to implicate that he knew at the time he sent his mesage that the people in Percy Street had 'burned and pillaged a Catholic area'. It is the fact that he knew that at the time which he denies, not the fact that as it turns out from later information that is the case. Again, it is noticeable that the witness produced that denial before the counsel made that implication explicit, though afterwards the witness goes on to repeat and elaborate that denial, and his explanation for sending that message, in lines 82–88, 96–98 and 102. It is this intersubjectivity of the (blame relevant) inferences which can be drawn from the description selections – that is, the objective availability of such inferences to participants, hearers, etc. – that the formal apparatus of membership categorisation devices attempts to account for.

5 The Production of Justifications and Excuses by Witnesses in Cross-Examination

In the data extract discussed in the previous chapter, we saw that the witness sometimes gave qualified confirmations in response to the counsel's questions (see for example, the answers in lines 14–15, 50 and 53–4 of extract 1, Chapter 4). It was noted that these qualified answers can indicate the witness's anticipation that the questions are leading to a blame allocation. That is, he may recognise that the implication of the facts which he is being asked to confirm is to attribute blame to him for his action: his qualified answers can therefore attempt to avoid or mitigate that implication by at least withholding agreement to the items in the questions which appear to be relevant for the anticipated blame allocation. This chapter focuses specifically on witnesses' recognition that questions are leading to blame allocations, though in the data to be discussed here that recognition is displayed not just in withholding agreement to some items in prior questions, but also in the production of justification/excuse components in answers.

The materials for this chapter are some instances in the (Tribunal) data in which, during cross-examination, police witnesses give answers which contain, or are primarily, justifications/excuses – or, more generically, defences – for their actions. A noticeable feature of such answers is that they generally, indeed overwhelmingly, occur in response to questions which do not appear to directly or formally accuse the witness. Given the relative ordering of parts in adjacency pairs, and the fact that justifications and excuses are second parts in the accusation-denial (justification etc.) adjacency pair, one might expect defences to occur in the sequential position *following* an accusation or other form of blame allocation (see Chapter 2, pp. 49–51, on the relative ordering of adjacency pair parts). However, on the face of it that expectation is not borne out by the data. An example in point is the following.

(1)   (ST: 96, 16C)
      1   C: You saw this newspaper shop being bombed on
      2   the front of Divis Street?
      3   W: Yes.
      4   C: How many petrol bombs were thrown into it?
  →   5   W: Only a couple. I felt that the window was
      6   already broken and that there was part of it
      7   burning and this was a re-kindling of the flames.
      8   C: What did you do at that point?
  →   9   W: I was not in a very good position to do
      10   anything. We were under gunfire at the time.

In two of his answers in this fragment, the witness produces defence components in response to what might appear as 'straightforward' questions – in the first case 'How many petrol bombs were thrown into it?', and in the second 'What did you do at that point?'. There are components in the answer in lines 5–7 which may be designed not so much for the descriptive adequacy of the answer (for which 'a couple', 'two', or some other numerical assessment may have been sufficient), as to exhibit the relative non-seriousness of the incident. A more detailed explication of the 'defensive' character of that answer will be given later, but we can note here that the witness's attempt to minimise the seriousness of the petrol bombing seems to be related to his not having taken certain action, possibly to investigate whether anyone was still inside the premises or injured. And in lines 9–10 he gives an explanation for not taking such action, though that is done in answer to a question which does not, explicitly anyway, ask for the reasons for his action; it only asks what he did at some point in a sequence of events, and an answer could have been given to that 'narrative' sense of the question.[1] Instead, the witness treats the question 'What did you do at that point?' as asking whether he took any action with respect to the incident referred to in the prior sequence, to put a stop to that petrol bombing or to protect life or property, etc. His explanation that 'I was not in a very good position to do anything. We were under gunfire at the time' can be designed to defend his not having taken such action, by mentioning a constraint which did not enable him to do so.

   Questions such as those in lines 4 and 8 of extract (1) might, then, be characterised as straightforward, or factual, or even innocent,[2] in the

sense that they do not actually contain any blame-relevant assessments
of witnesses' actions. Nevertheless, in their replies, witnesses often
display an alternative analysis of such questions: their production of
defences (or components which are part of defences) displays their
understanding that the business of prior questions is to lead towards the
ascription of blame to themselves – ascriptions which, of course, the
defences are designed to avoid or undercut. Having said a little more
about how witnesses may be seen to treat some questions as *prefacing*
anticipated blamings, our main interest in this chapter is to identify
some systematic features of the ways in which replies are designed so as
to manage – to attempt to avoid or mitigate – projected blame allocations. As in the previous chapter, the data to be discussed here are taken
mainly from the Scarman Tribunal; but the emphasis throughout will be
on properties of defences which we do not think are dependent on the
specific setting of the incidents being investigated in the cross-
examination (i.e. in Northern Ireland).

However, as a preliminary, we should just mention what decided our
use of the term 'defences' to refer to the justificatory/excusatory components in answers, when perhaps a more familiar one to sociologists might
be 'accounts'. The term 'account' is widely used in the literature on
deviance, and elsewhere, to refer to the motivational or explanatory
objects with which accused persons try to undercut or at least reduce the
allocation of blame to themselves: and justifications and excuses are
sometimes written about as though they were synonymous or coterminous with 'accounts'.[3] But accounts are routinely produced with such
actions as *rejections* of invitations, and of requests etc., as in this extract.

   (2) (SBL: 10,-14)
       B: Uh if you'd care to come over and visit a
           little while this morning I'll give you a cup
           of *co*ffee.
       A: hehh Well that's awfully sweet of you, I don't
   →   think I can make it this morning .hh uhm I'm
   →   running an ad in the paper and–and uh I have to
   →   stay near the phone.

As was mentioned in Chapter 2 (pp. 48–9), A rejects B's invitation
with an [Account] component, 'I'm running an ad in the paper and–and
uh I have to stay near the phone': this is in marked contrast with
acceptances of invitations, which are usually done without accounts. We
saw that the inclusion of [Accounts] with rejections of invitations etc.

was part of the evidence for the dispreferred status of rejections. The [Account] may be included by someone who rejects an invitation in order to avoid having the other person make certain inferences about why their invitation is being rejected, and thereby avoid giving offence to that person – given that issues to do with friendship, personal estimations, and lines of solidarity can be bound up with accepting or rejecting invitations. But while accounts produced in the sequential environment of post-invitations may attend to the interactional sensitivity of rejecting an invitation, defences are given in response to allegations and the like, and are designed specifically to avoid or reduce blame allocations. And, given that they are designed specifically for their placement in blame sequences, the probability is that defences are formed differently from accounts produced in other sequential environments[4] (though we shall look later at the details of how accounts in defences are formed, we do not provide comparative evidence for the different format of these by comparison with accounts done, for example, with rejections of requests). So a point in favour of using the term 'defences' rather than 'accounts', is to draw attention to the fact that the former occur in a different kind of sequence from other kinds of accounts (i.e. in blame sequences), and do work which is specific to that type of sequence.

Another point is that 'account' rather easily connotes a *reason* for action, which is perhaps why that term is widely used in the sociological literature on offenders' motivations. But looking again at extract (1) – and this will become increasingly plain as more data is considered – only one of the witness's answers was formed as a reason for his (in)action (in lines 9–10; 'We were under gunfire at the time'). His other answer in lines 5–7 consists primarily of *descriptions* of the scene, which although they might be associated with his reasons for not taking action, are not formulated at that point as 'reasons' in the sense of being an answer to a 'why' question (at that point neither the counsel nor the witness have yet introduced any mention of the witness's action). From this it is clear that the witness can attempt to defend his action partly through aspects of his descriptions of scenes, as well as by providing reasons for his action. And as this extract illustrates, not only may defences consist of descriptions as well as accounts or reasons, but both types of components may be used in relation to the same action. Very often when a sociologist cites the account which someone gives for an action, that is taken as having located the justification or excuse which the speaker offered.[5] Hence the term 'account' is misleading, partly because it might prompt the analyst to look for *the* account which a possible offender gives for his action, as though there was just one such object – where the close examination of

most court cases (and certainly of the data here) reveals that there is no
single component which carries all the work which a witness or defendant does to defend his action. Instead a variety of work is done vis-à-vis
the ascription of blame for a particular action, and that work is done in a
number of sequential positions. But the main point is that 'account' is
misleading because many of the defence components in witnesses'
answers are primarily descriptive, rather than overtly providing reasons
for actions.

   Finally, in this analysis we have not attempted to classify the defences
which occur in the data into either justifications or excuses. There is a
now familiar distinction often made between 'justifications' and 'excuses', one most clearly articulated by Austin (1970), which is that in
justifying an action, a speaker proposes the correctness of his action in
the circumstances, that it was the right thing to do. Excuses, on the other
hand, admit the faultiness of the action, but deny full (or any) responsibility for it. 'In the one defence, briefly, we accept responsibility but deny
it was bad: in the other, we admit that it was bad but don't accept full, or
even any, responsibility' (Austin 1970, p. 176). One difficulty with this
distinction is that it does not seem to capture the claims which people
may make about their action through excuse-type accounts. Interestingly, Emerson noticed this inadequacy of the Austinian distinction, with
respect to the 'accounts' offered in juvenile courts.

   While this distinction may be adequate on an abstract level, it fails to
   describe accurately the actual use of justifications and excuses observed in the juvenile court. Within the concrete situation of defending
   conduct, to deny responsibility represents a partial claim that the act
   was not 'really' wrong. That is, in reference to an actual situation, an
   act's wrongfulness derives from the actor's responsibility (in terms of
   intent and foreknowledge) for it. To claim that an 'offence' resulted
   from *accident*, for example, is not only to deny responsibility but also to
   depict the act as something other than wrong. The act becomes
   wrongful in some sense because the actor knowingly intended it to be
   wrong. (Emerson, 1969, p. 143).

Similarly, while police witnesses' accounts may, as we discuss later,
accept that some action should have been taken if that had been at all
possible, they deny that it was possible, and hence may also be heard to
deny that their inaction was in any way faulty. And, again as is discussed
later, both (justificatory) descriptive strategies designed to exhibit the
correctness of their actions (or inactions), and excuse-type accounts,

invitation could not be accepted, while ostensibly at least still only having answered A's question, and therefore without doing a rejection. And the consequence of her 'discouragement' of the projected invitation is to forestall it:[10] A acknowledges the import of her reply for an invitation he had intended to give, with 'but if you're going out you can't very well do that', and marks that invitation as not now being made through the preface 'Oh, I was just gonna say . . .': thus A withholds the invitation, though informing her – in response to her 'Why' – that that is what he had in mind.

So there are components of B's answer to A's pre-request, including her description of what she is doing, which can be heard to be selected with a view to the anticipated invitation, while still in this case answering the question. Similarly, in lines 5–7 of (1) the witness can be seen to treat the prior question as prefacing some sort of blaming, through components in his answer which can attempt to mitigate his not having taken certain action.

(1) (ST:96,16C)
    4   C: How many petrol bombs were thrown into it?
    5   W: Only a couple. I felt that the window was
    6   already broken and that there was part of it
    7   burning and this was a re-kindling of the flames.

Through the use of 'only' to modify the numerical answer to the question in line 4 (and notice that that modifier is compatible with the selection of 'a couple' rather than, say, 'two'), and then the inclusion of descriptions of the scene which were not required for a literal answer to the question, the witness can be heard to show that no action was necessary (that will be explicated in more detail later). Thus terms are selected in the answer which are designed to mitigate a failure to take action, and these terms therefore count as defence components: but it should be emphasised that these terms are nevertheless managed in an answer to the prior question. That is quite easy to see in relation to the addition of the modifyer 'only' to something which answers the 'how many . . . ?'. But notice that the rest of that utterance contains descriptions which can be heard to relate to the newspaper shop (that a window in it was already broken, that it was burning) and to the petrol bombs being thrown (that they re-kindled the flames). These are matched to terms used in the question: the pro-term 'it' which is used in the question to refer to the shop is preserved in the description, and the throwing of petrol bombs, which is the topic of the 'how many' in the question, is pro-termed by 'this' in the answer. So that although some components in the witness's reply may be recognisable as in some sense additional to an answer to the question, having as their main task something to do with the anticipated sequence, they nevertheless display close attention to certain properties of the question in line 4.

That is one way in which witnesses may display their understanding that some questions preface blame allocations – by including components and descriptive terms in their replies, which seem to be there, not so much for the descriptive adequacy of the answers, as with a view to the projected sequences. But an alternative method by which recipients of pre-sequence questions may design their responses is illustrated by V's response to M's enquiry about the fishtank in extract (4). Here, V's understanding that that enquiry prefaces a request for the tank is displayed in his reply (which follows some hesitation) that 'I'm not intuh selling it or giving it. That's it.' Instead of answering the question in the way that we have seen B answers A's question in (5), for instance by saying whether or not he's using the tank, what he is using it for etc., V's reply is formed as a response to what he expects M to be going on to do, to make a request for the tank: and that reply straightaway *rejects* the projected request. In many other cases, recipients of pre-request or pre-invitation questions directly grant the request – or, make an offer – and so on, without waiting for the first speaker to formally make the request. But the general point is, recipients may design their turns following pre-sequence items specifically as *moves in* the projected sequences, where 'moves' are relevant next actions, or second parts, in the pairs initiated by the anticipated but as yet unannounced actions. For example, a recipient may directly grant or reject the request which it is anticipated the speaker was going to make, without first answering the question in such a way as to enable that speaker to decide whether to go ahead and make the request, or to withhold it. Such responses obviate the need for the request (or whatever action), and hence by omitting the request result in a collapsed form of the sequence.[11]

Something like this second method – the design of replies as relevant next actions in the projected sequences – is employed by the witness in (1), in part of his reply to the question in line 8.

(1)   (ST:96,16C)
    8   C: What did you do at that point?
    9   W: I was not in a very good position to do anything.
→ 10   We were under gunfire at the time.

Both parts of the witness's reply here can be heard as reasons for not taking action. However, it is noticeable that the first part ('I was not in a very good position to do anything') is formed directly as an answer to the prior question, though in such a way as to defend his not taking action. By contrast, the latter part of his reply ('We were under gunfire at the time') is more clearly an answer to a projected 'next' question: in that explanation, he treats his failure to take action as an accountable matter, which can therefore be expected to lead to a subsequent question, for instance, 'Why didn't you do anything?'. Thus he anticipates that a consequence of it turning out, from the first part of his answer, that he did nothing, will be further questioning directed at showing he was at fault for failing to take necessary action. He does so through the design of the second part of his reply, in line 10, as an answer to an as yet unasked, but anticipated, question. So, as with V's response to M's pre-request in (4), the second part of the reply here is designed as a move in the projected blame sequence – as an answer to an expected 'why' question. That occurs also in this fragment.

(6)   (ST: 84,15A)
   C: While this was going on and you were carrying out these activities was the Protestant crowd staying back at that stage?
   W: Yes, they were quite good at keeping behind us. They did not try to go beyond us. Occasionally one or two would dart forward and throw something towards the Divis Street crowd and then would retreat back into the street again,
→   but taking any action against them would have been taking
→   our strength off our general purpose of keeping the whole
→   crowd back.

In answer to the question '. . . was the Protestant crowd staying back at that stage?', it emerges that 'one or two' did not stay back, but 'darted forward' and threw missiles at an opposing crowd. The fact that the witness did not take action against those who had broken through is displayed in his explanation that 'taking any action against them would have been taking our strength off our general purpose of keeping the whole crowd back'. Again the witness can be heard to anticipate a blaming by including what are, in effect, answers to two possible future questions, which might be 'Did you take any action against those who broke through?', and then 'Why didn't you take action against them?'. As in the witness's reply in line 10 of extract (1), the witness here does not await the unfolding of that projected sequence. Instead, recognising the implication of his 'admission' that he did nothing, he addresses that by adding his reasons for not taking action, reasons which will be analysed below as defence components.

So in both these cases, in line 10 of (1) and in the latter part of the reply in (6), witnesses produce answers not really to prior questions, but to anticipated questions in projected blame sequences – which as in many other instances in the data are answers to 'why' questions. But whereas it will be recalled that in the conversational extract (4), V's response was designed *solely* as a next action in the projected sequence, as a rejection to the anticipated request, without his actually answering M's question (i.e. V did not answer what he was doing with the tank), it is noticeable that in these cases from cross-examination in the Tribunal data, the explanations which the witnesses give – formed as answers to anticipated future questions – are nevertheless prefaced by answers to the prior questions. In this way, witnesses orient to the constraint resulting from the pre-allocation of turns to participants in examination, discussed in Chapter 2: there we saw that sometimes when a witness does not attend to that constraint, and without first answering the prior question anticipates a 'next' question, the counsel may reject that answer by repeating the question.[12] At any rate, a major basis for witnesses attaching additional components to answers to prior questions, for instance by implicit or explicit 'Yes(no), but (because) . . .' constructions, is their recognition that from the information given so far (e.g. in the earlier part of the answer) a further line of questioning is likely, directed at blaming them. The 'additional' components are, therefore, addressed to anticipated questions in that projected line of questioning. However, it should be remembered that witnesses also display their recognition that questions preface future blame sequences through the very selection of terms with which they *do* answer the prior questions. Both these methods are employed by recipients to manage pre-sequence questions, both therefore resulting in aspects of their answers which, because they address the projected blamings, can be counted as defence components.

FAILURES TO TAKE ACTION

In comparing these few conversational extracts with others from the Tribunal cross-examination, we have been identifying some of the general ways in which recipients of questions display their understanding that those questions preface projected action sequences. And of course the argument has been that in these cases from the Tribunal data, witnesses treat some questions as prefacing blame allocations, and specifically blamings for failures to take action. In part, the evidence that they are anticipating such blamings is contained in the later detailed descriptions of the defence components in their replies. However, at this stage it is worth drawing attention to aspects of the replies in the extracts already considered and in others, which clearly display their anticipation that they are to be blamed for *failures* to take some necessary or expected action. We saw that in (3) the witness replies to the question 'How far did you drive the Catholic crowd at that time?' with the report that nobody from a Protestant crowd went very far past him (i.e. past the police), or got as far as the Catholic area ('on Divis Street'). So that part of his answer attends to the fact of some Protestants getting beyond the police, and is designed (in ways to be explicated in the next section) to mitigate his not having done anything to stop them, or whatever – when another possibility might have been for him to have addressed the issue of his action against the Catholic crowd. That is, it is at least conceivable that the witness might have treated that question as directed towards blaming him for the measures he took vis-à-vis the Catholics (e.g. for baton-charging them unnecessarily): instead, he treats the line of questioning as one concerning what he did – or as it turns out, did not do – about the Protestants.

In some of their replies, witnesses quite explicitly attend to the possibility that they might have been expected to have taken certain action, and to the fact that they did not do so. For example in (1),

(1) (ST:96,16C)
   8 C: What did you do at that point?
→   9 W: I was not in a very good position to do anything.
   10   We were under gunfire at the time.

instead of replying to the question in line 8 in terms of what he did then, as a next move in a sequence of events (see note 1 for such an example), the witness reports (and defends) his not having done anything – again attending to, and anticipating a blaming for, a failure to take action. Similarly in (6), having mentioned that some Protestants darted forward and threw things at the opposing crowd, the witness proceeds to explain why it was not possible for him to take any action against them. And in his last reply in the next fragment, the witness very clearly anticipates the issue of his failure to take action against people who had thrown petrol bombs.

(7) (ST:95,73F)

    C: How many climbed onto the railings thereby?

    W: Very few, two or three.

    C: And threw in petrol bombs?

    W: Yes.

    C: And then returned?

    W: Yes.

    C: You were in a position to observe that?

→   W: Yes, but not in a position to carry out the action I would

→   have liked.

Extracts (1), (6) and (7) are some of the frequent instances of witnesses' explicit references to their not having taken some action, references which are often contained in explanations as to why they could not: and it will be noticed that in these cases the witnesses themselves are the first to draw attention to any expectation that they should have taken action, and to their failure to do so. These self-initiated references to their failures to take action are perhaps the strongest evidence for witnesses anticipating that questions preface blamings for such failures, especially as these references are often managed by *transforming* the subject of the prior question into the witnesses' own actions – or inactions.

(8) (ST:95,72C)

    C: Between 10 and 20. What did they do after they discharged
        their petrol bombs?

    W: They disappeared in amongst the crowd again.

    C: They came back then into Percy Street?

    W: Yes.

→   C: Did they come through a police line again?

→   W: Again the few police that were there: I had not deployed
        all the men, because, as I said, I was prepared to face
        more risks than I was prepared to allow my men to do.
        They were not all deployed.

For instance, the subject of the last question in (8) is 'they' (i.e. a group who had 'discharged petrol bombs'): but in the answer that is transformed into a new subject, which becomes the witness and his party, in a reply which can count as an explanation for not taking measures against persons who are the subject of the prior question.[13] In other cases, the *action referent* which is the topic of a prior question is changed in the answer to a new action referent, to become specifically the action which was not taken (see, for example, the last question-answer pair in (7)).[14] In thus initiating reference to possible failures on their part to take action, witnesses appear to anticipate – and take an earliest opportunity to defend themselves against – blamings for such failures.

In other cases, though, counsel make the first reference in a sequence to some actions which witnesses might have been expected to take, as happens in the following instances.

(9) (ST:74,69H)
    C: Are you telling the Tribunal that at no time did any petrol bombs make their way down from Beverley Street?
    W: No, I am not telling the Tribunal that.
    C: You did not see any?
    W: I saw one crate.
→ C: Did you take any steps to stop it?
    W: I could not have done so.

(10) (ST:84,34B)
    C: In any event, when you mounted that second baton charge
→   you took no steps to prevent the Protestant people following you?
    W: I was not in a position to take any steps. If I had taken any steps to prevent them I would have left more than half my party and the other three or four of us would have had no effect on chasing them from this fire that had been started at the Sarsfield Hall.

In each extract, the counsel asks a question concerning an action which the witness might have taken – that is, to stop petrol bombs being transported in (9), and to prevent Protestants following a police charge in (10). Only in (10) is such a reference made in the form of proposing a failure to act, for in (9) the question is only whether certain action was taken: however, both are instances where it is the counsel, rather than the witness, who first draws attention to a possible or expected action on the part of the witness, action which it turns out in (9), or it is proposed in (10), he did not take. The collection of defence-type objects which are analysed in this chapter were all produced in anticipation of, or in response to, assessments of failures to take action. Naturally this does not exhaust the range of things for which witnesses may find themselves being blamed during the Tribunal cross-examination: other particularly common matters which seem to have to do with the allocation of blame are, whether some action which the police took was overreactive, or in some sense too forceful in the circumstances; or, as was the issue in the data analysed in the previous chapter, whether their action was insufficient or inadequate. There may, of course, be no strict conceptual division between, say, the possible insufficiency of an action, and a failure to do something: for example, it may be claimed that a consequence of not doing enough to control a given crowd was that a witness thereby failed to protect property belonging to the other faction. But in the sequences analysed here, participants – both counsel and witnesses – treat the issue as being one of a possible failure to do something: so that at some point in all these sequences, either counsel or witnesses or both make explicit reference to an action which was not taken.

In the collection of these sequences, one finds that in a large majority of instances witnesses themselves initiate reference to a possible failure to take some action, without waiting for counsel to do so. However, whether such references are initiated by witnesses or by counsel, all the sequences have a discernible structural similarity: they consist of a *reporting of another party's action/incident* in an initial position in the sequence, followed by a *noticing of a failure* by the witness to take some action. A clear instance illustrating that is extract (7).

(7)   (ST:95,73F)
      C: How many climbed onto the railings thereby?
      W: Very few, two or three.
      C: And threw in petrol bombs?
      W: Yes.
      C: And then returned?
      W: Yes.
      C: You were in a position to observe that?
      W: Yes, but not in a position to carry out the action I would
           have liked.

In the first part of the sequence, the questions elicit information, or seek confirmation, about the actions of 'two or three' infiltrators (as they are described just before the first question in this fragment): thus the questions consist of reports that these persons climbed on to railings, threw petrol bombs, and returned (these are 'reports' in the sense of drawing attention to these incidents, as the topics of questioning, and clearly not in the sense that the counsel is informing the witness of news). These reports of the actions of another party (a party other than the witness, or those under his command) are followed sequentially by a reference to an expected action on the part of the witness ('. . . the action I would have liked'): as we have seen, this reference is initiated by the witness, in a reply formed as an acknowledgement or noticing of a failure to take that action ('. . . not in a position to carry out' . . .). Similarly in (1), lines 1–7 consist of the report of an incident, the petrol bombing of a newspaper shop, and as in (7) that report is elaborated over several turns: that is followed, in lines 9–10, by the noticing of a failure to take action ('I was not in a very good position to do anything'). A similar sequential organisation will be found in (6),[15] (8) and (9), but it also characterises all the sequences from which other fragments have been taken. This sequential organisation – the report of an incident or other party's action in an initial position in the sequence (though often occupying more than one question-answer pair), followed by a noticing of the fact that a witness failed to take some expected or relevant action – seems to reflect the way in which an incident is taken to occasion the relevance of a subsequent, paired action on the part of the witness. Thus participants treat the incidents/actions reported in the prior questions as implicating paired actions on the witnesses' part, that is actions which they might have been expected to take in view of (and subsequent to) what other persons were doing in that setting.[16] Thus witnesses can anticipate that, as those expected actions were not taken, the questions are leading towards the attribution of blame for failing to take appropriate or necessary action.

DEFENCES

A consequence of that organisation is that it locates two sequential environments in which turns containing defence components occur: these are *prior to*, and *post*, noticings of failures to take action. We will be describing the two major defence types whose occurrence corresponds with those positions. That is, the data exhibits a sequential move from the use of one type of defence object in turns prior to noticings of failures, to a quite different type of object post such noticings. These types can be identified despite considerable variations between instances in the actual content of defences, in the facts and reasons which are appealed to. What seems to be a systematic feature of both these defence objects is that they represent solutions to coincidental interactional tasks; but because the solutions are fitted to the sequential environment in which the answers are done, they emerge as different types.

These coincidental tasks are witnesses' avoidance of the allocation of blame to themselves, which will be referred to as the avoidance of self-blame; and the avoidance of disagreement with the position or information in a prior question. Avoiding self-blame can involve witnesses in not letting some information be put, in either questions or answers, without somehow disavowing or mitigating the blame which they anticipate is implicated by that information. Hence they may withhold agreement with the forms in which information or proposals are put in questions, where those forms appear to be blame implicative. At the same time, outright disagreements – for instance through explicit disconfirmations – are comparatively rare in these extracts, which suggests that witnesses also avoid disagreements with positions in the prior questions. It should not be supposed that this is simply a consequence of the more general preference for the avoidance of disagreement which has been identified for conversation:[17] the 'avoidance' of disagreement here may instead be a product of questions being built in such a way as to elicit certain preferred answers, and hence to create difficulties for witnesses to disagree (looked at this way, witnesses may be 'condemned' to agree). However that is, we can observe that witnesses design replies so as to avoid self-blame, hence often withholding agreement with something in the prior questions, while at the same time avoiding outright disagreement with some proposal or position held in these questions. We shall be interested here in how turns are designed so as to manage those coincidental tasks, and thus with how different types of defences emerge from their management in response to questions which occur before any reference has been made to a witness's failure to take action, and those which occur post the noticing of such a failure.

A general point about the sequential move from one defence type to another, a point which will perhaps become clearer as the types are described in more detail, is that it involves a shift to successively 'weaker' defence strategies. 'Weaker' here should not be taken to imply anything about the potential efficacy of a given defence type in mitigating blame, compared with another: instead it describes a property which results from the sequential positions in which these defences are done. Because replies are designed to avoid disagreement with the proposal or presuppositions in prior questions, a defence which occurs *post* the noticing of a failure to act is produced in a turn managed to avoid disagreeing with the proposal that an action should have been taken, but was not: in that sense, defence components in the latter sequential position do not 'deny' a possible failure. By contrast, defences in the former sequential position, pre-noticings of failures, occur in an environment in which the projected fault (a witness's failure) is as yet unstated, or unacknowledged explicitly: so here, in avoiding disagreeing with the prior questions, replies do not thereby implicate any concurrence that some expected or appropriate action was not taken. But despite that apparent 'weakness' of the later defence type, we shall see that they nevertheless manage to avoid accepting the proposed failures, by withholding agreement to the presupposition in questions that witnesses ought to have taken particular actions.

DESCRIPTIONS OF OTHER PARTY'S ACTIONS

The first major defence type occurs, sequentially, *prior to* noticings of failures to take action, and thus in the environment of questions and answers concerning other party's actions/incidents. Replies in this environment are designed to defend 'possible' or projected failures, by describing the other party's actions/incidents in such a way as to *minimise* or diminish their seriousness – thereby exhibiting the fact that no actions on the witness's part were necessary in the circumstances. So where it is anticipated that questions are leading to the proposal that a witness ought to have taken some action, given what other persons were doing, the descriptive terms selected in replies to those questions are designed to undercut the relevance of a paired action on the part of the witness. An instance is the witness's reply in lines 5–7 of (1)

(1) (ST:96,16C)

1	C:	You saw this newspaper shop being petrol bombed
2		on the front of Divis Street?
3	W:	Yes.
4	C:	How many petrol bombs were thrown into it?
5	W:	Only a couple. I felt that the window was already
6		broken and that there was part of it burning and
7		this was a re-kindling of the flames.

Up to this point, of course, no reference has yet been made to any action which the witness might have been expected to have taken, nor to his failure to take such action (that reference is not made until his reply to the next question). But in lines 5–7 he anticipates that issue, by managing a description of the petrol bombing of the newspaper shop, designed to warrant his inaction. The seriousness of that incident is minimised partly through the use of 'only' to qualify the number of petrol bombs thrown into the shop (and 'a couple', instead of 'two', also lends ιo that effect): and then the descriptions in the second part of that reply indicate that the shop had already been damaged ('a window was already broken') and set on fire ('there was part of it burning and this was a re-kindling of the flames'). These descriptions minimise the seriousness of the incident, by conveying that there was no further danger to life or property as a result of the 'renewal' of the burning, and therefore that the witness did not need to do anything about the burning of the shop. Two other fragments from extracts already cited, which are rather clear cases of the other party's action being described so as to minimise its seriousness, are these.

   (7) (ST:95,73F)
        C: Did you see them climbing onto the railings in front of
             St. Comgall's?
        W: Yes.
        C: How many climbed onto the railings thereby?
→   W: Very few, two or three.
        C: And threw in petrol bombs?
        W: Yes.

   (9) (ST:74,69H)
        C: Are you telling the Tribunal that at no time did any
             petrol bombs make their way down from Beverley Street?
        W: No, I am not telling the Tribunal that.
        C: You did not see any?
→   W: I saw one crate.

In (7), 'very few' qualifies the numbers who had thrown petrol bombs; and instead of just reporting that he did see petrol bombs, in (9) the witness reports he 'saw one crate': in both cases, the effect is to minimise those incidents. However, looking back to lines 5–7 of extract (1),

  5   W: Only a couple. I felt that the window was already
  6   broken and that there was part of it burning and
  7   this was a re-kindling of the flames.

we saw that the reply can be heard to be designed to forestall a projected blaming for failing to help anyone who might have still been inside or to prevent damage to the shop. Thus the major part of that reply is concerned with the possible *consequences* of the other party's action, that is of the petrol bombing: the descriptions attend to whether or not the witness needed to have done anything with regard to these consequences. But something of interest about that is, that the witness manages the reply so as to avoid addressing another matter about which blame for a failure might be attributed – that is, the matter of whether he should have taken action against those who threw the petrol bombs, perhaps to have prevented them doing so, or to have arrested them. There is a sense, then, in which the witness chooses which out of a possible set of projected failures to mitigate, thus selecting the ground for his defence (to that extent that form of the reply is successful; for later questions focus particularly on whether anyone might have been left inside the shop). Something like that also happens in (3).

(3) (ST:84,33F)
   C: So when you baton charged the Catholic crowd for the second time you knew, because of your previous experience, that the Protestant crowd were liable to follow you?
   W: I did.
   C: How far did you drive the Catholic crowd at that time?
→ W: I stopped in Dover Street and nobody went very far past me
→   and no-one went on Divis Street from the Protestant crowd.
   C: No-one went very far past you, you say?
→ W: No-one got more than a few yards past me.
   C: So some people did go past you?

The witness's descriptions of how far past him some Protestants went – 'nobody went very far past me', 'no-one went on Divis Street', and 'No-one got more than a few yards past me' – all minimise the seriousness of, or the possible danger posed by, their having gone beyond the police. While that might mitigate his not having taken action against them at that point, for instance to force them back away from Catholic territory, it avoids the issue of his failure to prevent Protestants following the police and getting past them in the first place. And there is good sequential evidence that the counsel is treating *that* as the blameable failure, when he asks later, 'In any event, when you mounted that second baton charge you took no steps to prevent the Protestant people following you?' (extract (10)). The avoidance of that issue in the reply, however, is achieved by putting the report of the other party's action in the form of 'nobody went very far past me' etc., rather than in a more 'positive' form of admitting that 'some of them went past me' – which is of course just the form that the counsel uses in a subsequent question, in 'So some people did go past you?'. So replies not only contain descriptions minimising the seriousness of, or the threat (or danger) posed by, the other party's action, and thereby seek to avoid self-blame by displaying the fact that no action by the witness was necessary. They may also be designed to formulate a particular version of the 'failure' (though that formulation is implicit, given that the failure is as yet unstated), a version to which the minimising, descriptive components are fitted. Hence witnesses may avoid certain blame-implicative forms in which the report of the other party's action might have been put – the very forms in which, in some cases, as in (3), they *are* subsequently put by the counsel. (See also extracts (6) and (8), where witnesses describe persons as having gone forward to throw things at the opposing crowds, in a form which avoids reference to their getting past the police to do so: in (8) the counsel subsequently draws attention to that aspect of the other party's action, in his question 'Did they come through a police line again?'.)

The replies in which we have seen descriptions are designed to minimise the seriousness of the other party's action are produced in response to questions which ask for certain information (e.g. 'How many petrol bombs were thrown into it?'); so the questions do not themselves propose a version of that information, which might for instance be a proposed upshot of a witness's previous evidence, for the witness's confirmation. In these cases, then, defence components are managed in an environment in which witnesses avoid disagreements with proposals or positions in prior questions, because those questions do not contain any such proposals. But a similar descriptive defence strategy is sometimes used in replies which qualify a proposed version in the prior questions, as in these fragments.

(11) (ST:84,36C)
      C: If some of those, if, as Mr Allen has said (if he did say it) threw petrol bombs, that would indicate that they were in an extremely hostile mood?
→   W: They were obviously hostile.

(12) (ST:95,72B)
      C: When the ten or twenty people had unloaded or discharged their petrol bombs –
→   W: Ten–twenty is putting it high. Between ten and twenty; it might not have been more than ten.
      C: Very well; we are going to get to numbers later on.

Both fragments are from extracts which arrive at explicit references to the witness's failure to take action with respect to those persons described in the initial questions. In each case the witness qualifies the counsel's description of the other party, with terms which tend to *diminish* the seriousness of their action (i.e. by comparison with that proposed in the questions). In (11), 'they were in an extremely hostile mood' is diminished to 'they were obviously hostile'; and in (12) the witness qualifies the assessment of the size of the crowd, from 'ten or twenty' to 'Ten—twenty is putting it high . . . it might not have been more than ten'. Though qualifications of this sort may on occasions be treated by recipients as implicating disagreement (and in (12) the counsel can be heard to withhold full concurrence with the witness's qualification about the size of the crowd), the turns in which these 'diminishers' occur avoid overt disagreement, or disconfirmation, forms.[18]

So the first type of defence components occur pre-noticings of failures to take action, in the environment of reports of other parties' actions. They are fitted to that environment, by being formed as descriptions designed to minimise (or, in cases where they qualify descriptions in prior questions, diminish) the seriousness of (or threat or danger posed by) the other parties' actions – and thereby mitigate anticipated failures by displaying the fact that it was not necessary to take action. The turns in which these defence components occur are also designed to avoid self-blame, through the selection of particular formulations of those aspects of the other parties' actions with respect to which failures on the witness's part may be located – where the selected formulations allow for, and are matched to, terms which minimise those aspects. Thus the turns are built to avoid other possible formulations of the failures (which in many cases are subsequently explicitly addressed by counsel), which may not admit such a strategy. Finally, they can attempt to avoid self-blame by being done in an environment in which the projected relevant next actions on the part of witnesses have not yet been referred to, and the 'offences' which they are defending themselves against are *unstated*. Thus these defence components – terms which minimise the seriousness of the other parties' actions – can seek to forestall noticings of failures for which they may be blamed. And there is good evidence that witnesses look for the opportunity of doing such defences. Not only do they overwhelmingly occur in sequences where some sort of defence is given for a failure, always in an initial position in such sequences, as a first strategy:[19] they also employ the kinds of 'transformations' mentioned in the previous section, which create the chance to use this strategy in response to questions which might not otherwise afford them that opportunity. This is well illustrated in (3), for instance,

> C: How far did you drive the Catholic crowd at that time?
> W: I stopped in Dover Street and nobody went very far
>   past me and no-one went on Divis Street from the
>   Protestant crowd.

in which the defence components in the second part of the reply are
managed by transforming the subject from 'How far did *you* drive' in the
question, into the actions of the other party – the Protestants, who are
not even cited in the prior question. That part of the reply is, of course, in
a sense added to an answer to the question, again indicating that the
witness is creating the opportunity for such a defence (which is supported by instances like lines 5–7 of (1), in which again defence
components are managed in an 'additional' part of the reply). It is also
noticeable that in (12), the witness interrupts the counsel (one of the very
few cases of interruptions transcribed in this data) in looking for the
opportunity to diminish the seriousness of that incident.

ACCOUNTS

Although the defence components just discussed may attempt to forestall future references to witnesses' failures to take certain appropriate
actions, it happens that they are rarely, if ever, successful: for as was
mentioned earlier, all the sequences in the corpus on which this analysis
is based arrive at noticings of failures to take action, whether initiated by
counsel or by witnesses (a later section discusses ways in which questioning may be directed towards such noticings, by getting round attempts to
forestall them). So those first strategies never terminate these blame
sequences: witnesses always go on in subsequent replies, in the environment of the actual noticings, to produce defences of a second major type.
This type of defence occurs, then, in turns post noticings of failures,
where these are initiated by counsel; or, where they are initiated by
witnesses, in conjunction with and in the same turn as the noticings.
Such defences broadly consist of two components, the primary one being
an [Account], though that is often prefaced by a [Rebuttal]. The two
components may be done in separate terms, the [Rebuttal] in an earlier
turn and the [Account] in next position: or more usually, they may be
combined in the same turn, retaining that order. Again, we shall try to
explicate how the components are built to avoid self-blame, but at the

same time avoid disagreeing with prior questions leading up to blame allocations.

The witness's reply in lines 9–10 of (1) consists of these two defence components.

(1) (ST:96,16C)
    8   C: What did you do at that point?
    9   W: I was not in a very good position to do anything.
    10   We were under gunfire at the time.

That reply is organised into a [Rebuttal], 'I was not in a very good position to do anything', which prefaces an [Account], 'We were under gunfire at the time'. We have called such objects as that first component 'rebuttals', because they seem to counter what is taken to be a presupposition in the prior questions, that not only *should* a witness have taken certain action (that is, that that action would have been preferable, or appropriate in the circumstances), but that he *could* have done so. But as we shall see later, although they rebut the presupposition that they could (were in a position to) have taken certain action, they are designed nicely to avoid disagreeing with the presupposition that such action might have been relevant. The latter [Account] components are perhaps more familiar: they provide reasons for not having taken a given course of action, and are often done in overt 'because' clauses.

To begin with, both these kinds of components are designed to avoid self-blame, by *avoiding outright acknowledgements or announcements of failures to take action*. For instance, in cases where counsel are the first to draw explicit attention to witnesses' failures, in questions which propose that the witness did not do X, witnesses may – instead of giving straight confirmations of those failures – often produce a [Rebuttal] in first position in the reply.

(10) (ST:84,34B)
      C: In any event, when you mounted that second baton charge
           you took no steps to prevent the Protestant people
           following you?
→   W: I was not in a position to take any steps. If I had
           taken any steps to prevent them I would have left more
           than half my party and the other three or four of us would
           have had no effect on chasing them from this fire that
           had been started at the Sarsfield Hall.

Generally, in replies post *other-initiated* noticings of failures to take action, witnesses use [Rebuttal] components in place of direct confirmations of failures – as happens here in (10). The witness is asked to confirm that 'you took no steps to prevent the Protestant people following you'. But in his reply he withholds direct confirmation of that proposed failure, though the [Rebuttal] 'I was not in a position to take any steps': which, by not simply confirming that he did not take such steps, avoids a form which could be taken to acknowledge a failure[20] (where an acknowledgement might be acceptance-implicative, and hence an acceptance of blame).

[Rebuttals] and [Accounts] are also used to avoid direct *announcements* of failures to take action, in *self-initiated* noticings of failures. It will be recalled that in most of these sequences, witnesses themselves are the first to draw explicit attention to the fact that they did not take some action. Often, they do so in response to questions which ask whether a particular relevant or expected action was taken: although such questions do not propose a failure on the witnesses' part, they may put witnesses in the position of then having to admit to not having taken the named action – as in these fragments.

(13)   (ST:74,69H) (This occurs immediately after extract (10))
         C: Did you take any steps to stop it?
➔   W: I could not have done so.

(14)   (ST:95,72E)
         C: At any stage did you take action by baton or otherwise
              against the ten or twenty that had broken through?
         W: I was quite certain those who had broken through – I was
              surprised they were not shot, because the shooting was
➔   going on at that time. A baton-charge to clear that
➔   street would certainly have been desirable if I had been
➔   in a position to mount it from a proper position of
➔   strength whereby I was not being shot in the back.
              Certainly the impression which is now being forced to me
              to give that we were not taking any action against any
              Protestant crowd, I want to get it over is not the
              impression that we were out to portray or to carry out
              when we were doing our manoeuvres.

In other cases, witnesses initiate noticings of failures, in response to questions which (unlike the questions in (13) and (14), for instance) make no mention of that action which might have been expected of them. As we have seen, that happens in lines 9–10 of (1), and in (6) and (7).

(6) (ST:84,15A)

C: While this was going on and you were carrying out these activities was the Protestant crowd staying back at that stage?

W: Yes, they were quite good at keeping behind us. They did not try to go beyond us. Occasionally one or two would dart forward and throw something towards the Divis Street crowd and then would retreat back into the street

→ again, but taking any action against them would have been
→ taking our strength off our general purpose of keeping
→ the whole crowd back.

(7) (ST:95,73F)

C: You were in a position to observe that?

→ W: Yes, but not in a position to carry out the action I
→ would have liked.

As so frequently occurs in the data, where witnesses are faced with possibly admitting that the action asked about in the prior question was not taken, as for instance in (13) and (14), or where they anticipate that issue, as in (1), (6) and (7), they avoid direct admissions or announcements that they did not take some action by using [Rebuttals], particularly in the former kind of case, and [Accounts] in the latter. For example, the effect of the reply in (6) is to convey that some Protestants got past the police to throw objects at a Catholic crowd, but the police did not take action either to prevent them doing so, or to arrest them (or whatever). However, that noticing of a failure is managed in such a way as to avoid a stark announcement that no action was taken: that is implicit in the reply, by being embedded in an account, '. . . but taking any action against them would have been taking our strength off our general purpose of keeping the whole crowd back'.

So these components are ways of managing noticings of failures, so as to avoid blame – implicative forms: but of course they mitigate blame in other ways besides that. It was mentioned that [Rebuttals] are designed to counter the presupposition in prior questions that witnesses *could* have taken certain action, *without* challenging the assumption that that action might have been appropriate. This is equally true of [Accounts], which are also formed to avoid disagreeing with the position in prior questions, that a certain action would have been expected or relevant or the proper thing to have done – though with the proviso, to which [Accounts] orient, 'if circumstances had allowed'. And of course these components are designed to show that circumstances did *not* enable that action to be taken. So while allowing that a certain course of action would have been appropriate or preferable if it had been possible – an allowance which is sometimes quite explicit, as in (7), '. . . not in a position to carry out the action I would have liked', and (14), 'A baton-charge to clear that street would certainly have been desirable if . . .' – [Accounts] are designed to exhibit the impossibility of that action.

[Accounts] are formed as *constraints* on witnesses, by citing localised factors which did not enable a given action to be taken: for instance, in lines 9–10 of (1), the witness cites the fact that 'We were under gunfire at the time', and elsewhere lack of manpower is frequently cited. However, perhaps by comparison with accounts produced in other kinds of sequences, in these blame sequences the constraints are made to appear as strong as possible.

(15) (ST:84,34H)
C: At this stage we had better be quite clear: at no stage during the course of that night did you take any action against any Protestant civilians?
W: No. The police were far too thin on the ground. We could not afford to do anything to antagonise this crowd which was not badly disposed towards us as the other crowd was. We were between the Devil and the deep, if I may use that expression: we just had no choice in the matter. To have tried to arrest any of the Shankill Road crowd would have taken more of my men, the crowd, I realised would have turned on us; they were fairly high at the time and we just had to act as best we could under very difficult circumstances.

(16) (ST:84,42C)
C: Did you not know the mob were liable to follow you on this occasion?
W: What I knew and what actually took place are two different things. I was powerless to prevent quite a lot of things that did happen. In fact we were just a drop in the ocean with so few a number. I realised certainly that there would be some of them following behind. I could not do anything to prevent that. I saw damage caused and tried to prevent it. I realised it was bashing my head against a brick wall really; we were completely ineffectual.

In cases such as these, the circumstances are described so as to make the witnesses' positions out to be as weak as possible, particularly by reference to how few police were available relative to the seriousness of the situation they faced. So in (15) and (16), statements of the impossibility of their taking certain action (e.g. 'We had no choice in the matter . . .', 'I was powerless to prevent quite a lot of things that did happen') are supported by references to the weakness of their position: in (15), 'The police were *far too* thin on the ground', and 'We were between the Devil and the deep . . .', and in (16) '. . . *we were just a drop* in the ocean with *so few* a number', and 'I realised it was banging my head against a brick wall really; and were *completely* ineffectual'. And in other cases cited more fully later, witnesses state that '*All* my force was *so small* I could not *under any circumstances* divide it up', and 'We just had not the police available to make *any* effort'. These display that the witnesses' positions were as weak as possible, particularly through the terms modifying descriptors of their positions, terms which have been italicised, as '*far too* thin' etc.

One point about the way in which the weakness of a witness's position is exhibited in an [Account] is that some contain descriptions of the party against whom it is being proposed action should have been taken, descriptions emphasising the difficulty of acting against them. We saw that *prior to* noticings of failures to take action, descriptions of other party's action are designed to minimise its seriousness. For example, in (3) the witness said that 'nobody went very far past me and no-one went on Divis Street from the Protestant crowd', and then 'No-one got more than a few yards past me'. But later in (15) – which occurs a little after (3) in the same sequence, concerning the same persons – he mentions that 'the Shankill Road crowd . . . would have turned on us; they were fairly high at the time . . .'. In his first reference to the other party, then, the threat posed by that crowd is minimised by selecting descriptions of a certain aspect of their movement, that is how far past they went: the opposite effect, upgrading the seriousness of their action, is accomplished in the later reference by selecting an alternative aspect, their 'mood'.

Thus [Rebuttals], and more particularly [Accounts], are designed to mitigate projected blamings for failures to take action, by invoking constraints which did not allow witnesses to take some appropriate actions: but they do so in ways which manage to avoid challenging the presupposition that such action was relevant or appropriate. In that sense they may be 'second best' strategies: where defence components pre-noticings of failures are designed to show that no action was

necessary, these may seem to give ground in allowing – or not disagreeing – that some action should have been taken. However, there is an
interesting way in which many [Accounts] are designed to hold on to
certain positions, against the ones in the prior questions, whilst still
avoiding disagreement with those. It may be noticed that in some of the
[Accounts] which have been considered, witnesses not only describe
constraints on their action – they also cite *other* actions which they *were*
engaged in. An instance is the witness's reply in (10).

   (10)   (ST:84,34B)
          C: In any event, when you mounted that second baton charge
               you took no steps to prevent the Protestant people
               following you?
          W: I was not in a position to take any steps. If I had taken
               any steps to prevent them I would have left more than half
→   my party and the other three or four of us would have had
→   no effect on chasing them from this fire that had been start
→   at the Sarsfield Hall.

Superficially, the constraint which appears to be invoked here is one of
an insufficiency of numbers to be able to prevent Protestants following
him. But that insufficiency is in a sense created by his engagement in
'chasing them from this fire that had been started at the Sarsfield Hall'.
For the moment, let us call the action being proposed in the question
'prevent(ing) the Protestant people following you', action X; it will be
recalled that that is the action which is occasioned by the threat posed by
these persons, in terms of their getting past the police to attack Catholics.
However, the witness now introduces another action, call it action Y;
that is, chasing persons from a fire – an action which is occasioned by a
different set of circumstances (or another party's action), involving the
burning of the hall. So to the action mentioned in the question, action X,
in his reply the witness cites an *alternative* action Y, itself formed as a
paired action on his part, occasioned by another party's action/incident.
Now, the [Account] is managed so as to treat action Y as *simultaneously
relevant* with action X. The reply is designed so as *not* to permit the
possibility of his first having taken action X, and then followed that with
action Y, which of course might be a way of handling alternative actions.
By not addressing that possible temporal ordering, two things are
achieved. Firstly, action Y is thereby treated as the witness's principal
aim: but secondly, that is managed without addressing the presupposition in the prior question that action X was of primary importance – and

by not addressing that, the witness manages to avoid disagreeing with
that presupposition.

Actions X and Y are treated as simultaneously relevant, by treating
the two episodes – the Protestants following and getting past him; and
the starting of a fire in the hall – as demanding his attention at the same
time, instead of allowing that he might have taken one action first and
then the other. This is achieved through the witness's reference to the
necessity of dividing his force if he were to have done anything to prevent
the Protestants following him, in 'If I had taken any steps to prevent
them I would have left more than half my party and the other three or
four of us would have had no effect on chasing them from this fire . . .' In
discussing the difficulty of thus dividing his force, he treats the issue as
being one of either doing both X and Y, or settling for Y. The simultaneous relevance of each ensures that the decision he faced is characterised
as one of doing *either* X or Y, but not both. The account for *not* doing X is
designed in terms of the importance of doing Y: again, that is emphasised
four replies later:

(17)   (ST:84,34D)
       C: And you did that despite your knowledge of what
           occurred the first time you made a baton charge?
       W: The second baton charge was dictated by the fact that
           there was a fire started in what I took to be a dwelling-
→   house and I thought it was imperative that I should get
→   down to that point to see what the situation was. I had
           no choice in the matter because I had no reinforcements.

However, whilst action Y is thereby treated as his principal aim, that is
managed without directly asserting the greater importance of Y. For not
only is the reply in (10) managed to avoid denying the *relevance* of X: it
also avoids challenging the question's presupposition of the *importance* of
action X, which might have been the effect of a more direct assertion that
action X was of comparatively less importance in the circumstances than
the action which he did take, action Y – though that is just the assertion
which might be projected from the earlier defence components minimising the seriousness of the incident taken to occasion X. Even the claim in
(17) that it was 'imperative' to deal with the fire which had been started
in the hall does not entail any direct comparision between that, and
preventing Protestants following, given that there is no reference to
action X in the prior question.

Thus the [Account] is managed so as to hold the position that it was

essential for the witness to take action Y, without addressing – but in
contradistinction to – the presupposition in the question that action X
should have been of overriding importance. Although that presupposition is implicit in the question, there is sequential evidence that that is
the basis in the questions for blaming the witness for a failure. The
evidence is, that subsequent questions are designed to demonstrate just
how serious was the other party's action/incident which occasioned the
necessity of some action X on the part of the witness, and hence to
display the *overriding* importance of action X. For instance, immediately
after the reply in (10), the counsel asks about the size of the Protestant
crowd,

>   (18)   (ST:84,34C)
>   →   C: Would the Protestant crowd at that time have numbered
>   →   100 to 150?
>   W: No. I did not look at them and I could not give an
>   accurate estimate really, but I considered that probably
>   60 or 70 came down after us.
>   C: Came down after the second charge.
>   W: Yes.

though a little later (following (15)) there is an extended exchange
concerning the degree of hostility shown by the Protestants, in which the
questions seem to be directed at emphasising that hostility. A case which
is similar to (10), in that the witness avoids addressing the implication in
the questions of the overriding importance of a given action, is this
sequence.

>   (19)   (ST:84,36E)
>   C: And at that stage you took all your force over to Percy
>   Street?
>   →   W: All my force was so small I could not under any
>   →   circumstances divide it up.
>   C: So you said yesterday. You took all the policemen over
>   to Percy Street?
>   W: Yes.
>   C: Leaving the bottom of Dover Street and Divis Street
>   entirely at the mercy of the Special Constabulary and the
>   Protestant civilians who had come down there?
>   →   W: Yes. There was a single unit in the area. I could only
>   →   do one thing at a time. I had to do it as the situation
>   developed and reports were received by me.

While this extract is discussed in more detail in a later section, we can see that a contentious issue is whether the witness should have moved over to Percy Street, and in so doing possibly failing to protect persons in Dover Street/Divis Street. In those replies, the witness only addresses the possibility of dividing his force (as in (10)), and therefore treats the two possible actions – staying put in Dover Street; or moving over to an incident in Percy Street – as simultaneous demands. Thus the [Account] is managed in such a way as to exhibit the constraint of having too few men available to be able to do action X (to stay in Dover Street/Divis Street, to protect people there), a constraint which results from the simultaneously relevant action Y (moving to Percy Street), which he thereby treats as his primary responsibility. Here it is evident that the position in the questions (see especially the last one in (19)) is that the witness should never have left Dover Street/Divis Street, because a primary aim should have been to protect people there. Once again, in his avoidance of that implication of the questions, the witness manages to account for his failure to take action X in terms of his having to do Y, though without disagreeing that X was relevant, and without directly asserting the greater importance of Y. Other cases already cited, in which in their replies witnesses similarly refer to a simultaneously relevant but alternative action to that proposed in a prior question, are these.[21]

(6) (ST:84,15A)
    C: While this was going on and you were carrying out these activities was the Protestant crowd staying back at that stage?
    W: Yes, they were quite good at keeping behind us. They did not try to go beyond us. Occasionally one or two would dart forward and throw something towards the Divis Street crowd and then would retreat back into the street again,
→   but taking any action against them would have been taking
→   our strength off our general purpose of keeping the whole
→   crowd back.

(15) (ST:84,34H)
    C: At this stage we had better be quite clear: at no stage during the course of that night did you take any action against any Protestant civilians?
    W: No. The police were far too thin on the ground. We could not afford to do anything to antagonise this crowd which

was not badly disposed towards us as the other crowd was.
We were between the Devil and the deep, if I may use that
→   expression; we just had no choice in the matter. To
→   have tried to arrest any of the Shankill Road crowd would
→   have taken more of my men, the crowd, I realised, would
    have turned on us; they were fairly high at the time and
→   we just had to act as best we could under very difficult
    circumstances.

To summarise: the [Account] components in the extracts we have just
been examining are formed in terms of a constraint which did not allow
the witness to take the action proposed in the question. However, that
'constraint' is achieved by invoking an alternative action which the
witness was engaged in, occasioned by some other circumstances, and
which is treated as relevant or necessary simultaneously with that
referenced by the counsel. Hence [Accounts] address twin possible
objectives; the action mentioned in the question is only considered
together with the alternative action which *was* taken. That latter action is
thereby treated as the priority (indeed, often in terms which suggest it
was the only conceivable choice), and as having required all the manpower etc. that was available. But these [Accounts] are managed so as to
avoid disagreeing with the presupposition in the question about the
relevance and importance of the action referenced there: and they
thereby also avoid addressing the implication in the question (an
implication for which there is often good sequential evidence) that *that
referenced action* (and *not* the alternative action cited by the witness) should
have been the overriding aim, given the seriousness of what is taken to
occasion its relevance.

THE DIFFICULTY OF PREVENTING AN INCIDENT

Finally, we should mention a third defence type, though it would
perhaps be unnecessarily repetitive to describe this type in such detail
because they share many of the properties of the types already discussed
– a consequence of their being sequentially intermediate, occurring
between descriptions designed to minimise the other party's action/inci-
dent, and Rebuttals/Accounts. This third type is very much less frequent
than those main types, but where it is used it occurs *prior* to noticings of
failures.[22] Some examples are these.

(20)   (ST:95,70C)
      C: Did you see them get out on to Divis Street?
      W: Yes.
      C: How did they get out?
→   W: As I said, there was a form of police cordon, not the
→   accepted form, but they did break out from where the
→   police position was and dashed forward.

(21)   (ST:84,33H) (This extract follows immediately from (3))
      C: No-one went very far past you, you say?
      W: No-one got more than a few yards past me.
      C: So some people did go past you?
→   W: I was hit in the leg by a stone and went down and that is
→   when they went past me.

(22)   (95,72B)
      C: Between ten and twenty. What did they do after they
          discharged their petrol bombs?
→   W: They disappeared in amongst the crowd again.
      C: They came back then into Percy Street?
      W: Yes.

In these objects, witnesses anticipate the issue of their failure to take certain actions, in replies designed to exhibit the *difficulty* of that action, and hence mitigate the failure. That is achieved through descriptions of the other party's action, as in (22); descriptions of the witness's own position, as in (21); or a combination of both, as in (20).

Whilst sharing with the first main type described earlier the property that they may consist of descriptions of the other party's action, the descriptions in *these* cases (i.e. in the third type) have a different effect: instead of minimising the seriousness of that action, here the descriptions are formed to display that the witnesses had little or no chance to take any appropriate action. These descriptions retain a compatibility with the earlier minimising strategy, but *not* upgrading the seriousness of their action, and by selecting an alternative aspect of the other party's action from that with respect to which its seriousness was minimised: generally this alternative aspect is the manner of their movement. For instance, where the witness had previously minimised the seriousness of a group going past the police to throw petrol bombs by emphasising how few there were in that group (see extract (12)), in (22) he describes the manner of their movement, as having '*disappeared* in amongst the crowd again'. Similarly in (20), a party's movement is described thus; '. . . they did *break out* from where the police position was and *dashed forward*' (involving the substitution of 'break out' in place of 'get out' in the question). These terms convey that persons moved in such a way, by 'disappearing', 'breaking out', and 'dashing forward', that there was no chance for witnesses to take action against them.

The difficulty, or even impossibility, of taking action exhibited in descriptions of the other party's action may be supported by descriptions of a witness's own position. For instance in (20), '. . . there was a form of police cordon, not the accepted form', invokes there being insufficient men available for there to have been an adequate cordon: and in (21), the witness qualifies his confirmation that persons went past him, by reference to when they went past, which was when he was 'hit in the leg by a stone and went down' – thereby displaying his inability to stop them going past. While such references to the witnesses' own positions might appear somewhat similar to those which occur in [Account] components, the way in which *these* descriptions are built in the turns manages to convey how the blameable incident (persons getting past them) could have happened – rather than as reasons for not taking action, as in [Accounts]. That is, whilst these descriptions could certainly be thought of as reasons why the witnesses failed to prevent people going past, they are actually constructed in the form of a narrative as to how it could have happened that they got past. In each case this is achieved by putting the descriptions of the witness's position in *first position* in the turn (e.g. 'I was hit in the leg by a stone and went down . . .'), so that the other party's action, reported in a subsequent position ('and that is when they went past me'), is formulated as having resulted from the witness's inability to stop them at that point (i.e. because he had been knocked down). The difference between this form and [Accounts] is, that in [Accounts] that ordering is reversed, with the other party's action/incident being reported in a first position (either a different turn, in the prior question; or in first position in the same turn), followed by an account as to why it was not possible to have taken action in connection with that incident. This ordering reflects the way in which accounts are designed to explain why, given some incident, a subsequent paired action was not taken: whereas these earlier defence components are designed to show how, given the witness's position (described in an initial segment), the incident could have occurred as a subsequent event – thereby attempting to forestall any later explanation for failing to take action.

So, unlike the first type of defence components designed to show that no action on the witness's part was necessary, because the incident was not sufficiently serious, this type of object attempts to avoid self-blame through citing facts concerning the witness's position, and/or the manner in which the other party acted, which display the difficulty in taking action against them. Such a difficulty is treated as having resulted in the incident (e.g. a crowd getting past, to attack the opposite crowd etc.), by contrast with the constraints cited in [Accounts] which are given as reasons for not taking action once the incident had occurred. Thus the third type of defence component, which occurs sequentially prior to [Accounts], and of course prior to noticings of failures to take action, seeks to forestall the issue of some failure on a witness's part subsequent to some incident. In other respects, these components avoid blame-implicative forms (e.g. the avoidance of direct confirmation that some people did get past him, in (21)), and avoid disagreement with questions (in most cases the questions which they are done in response to simply ask for information) in ways similar to those already discussed for the two main defence types.

THE DIRECTEDNESS OF QUESTIONING

An important feature of the way in which witnesses may recognise that questions are pre(blame sequence) items is that they may attribute to the questioner (i.e. counsel) knowledge of the answer to his question: that is, they may anticipate that the counsel already possesses the information which is asked for in the question. A feature of some of the questions which in conversation are treated by recipients as pre-requests, is that they are built to display prior knowledge of the answer, or as in (4) to include a possible (expected or preferred) answer to the question.

(4)   (US, 24)
→   M: Wuhddiyuh doing wh dat big bow-puh-tank. Nothing?
         (0.5)
      V: ((Cough))
      V: Uh-h-h
         (1.0)
      V: I'm not intuh selling it or giving it. That's it.

M's addition of 'Nothing' to his question here supplies a likely or expected answer, which can give that question its character as not just a disinterested enquiry. In this and other instances of pre-sequence questions, the questioner's overt anticipation of a certain answer (though in other cases, it may be that recipients detect the possibility that the questioner already knows the answer) may be a basis for recognising that the question is leading towards something else. Thus recipients can anticipate that the 'real' purpose of the question is not just, or even at all, to obtain the information which it apparently seeks, but to set up the subsequent intended action which in (4) was a request. In part, that relies on the recipient's recognition that the questioner is asking for information which he already possesses.

It happens in the Tribunal data that that possibility is provided by certain local features of the organisation of cross-examination, for example, that before their appearance witnesses produce written statements which are available to all counsel; that they first give evidence-in-chief, in which the 'unattached' Tribunal counsel asks questions which give the witness the opportunity to elaborate points in the written statement which are relevant to the Tribunal's present enquiry; that the information may have been given by an earlier witness, or by themselves during earlier cross-examination by another counsel; or that the information was given by the witness in some immediately preceding answers. Indeed not only may it be a possibility that a counsel already possesses the information requested, but it may be taken as an *expectation*, through treating as a requirement that witnesses give 'full' information at the earliest opportunity. Hence if it turns out that *new* information about some event etc. is elicited when the witness has already been asked about that event, that may be a noticeable matter – 'noticeable' in the sense not only that it may be commented on, but also that introducing 'new' information (having already had an opportunity for giving that information) may lead to inquiries about the possible inconsistencies in a witness's evidence (i.e. between what he is *now* saying happened, and his earlier version): it may further be grounds for finding that a witness has misled the Tribunal, possibly intentionally, or that at best a witness has been evasive.[23]

But the important point is that there is a general sense in which witnesses may be able to infer that counsel already know the answer to given questions; and it is partly this feature of questions which gives them their character as leading towards blame allocations. That is rather nicely illustrated in the following extract.

(19) (ST:84,36E)
     C: And at that stage you took all your force over to
          Percy Street?
     W: All my force was so small I could not under any
          circumstance divide it up.

➤   C: So you said yesterday. You took all the policemen over to Percy Street?

       W: Yes.

       C: Leaving the bottom of Dover Street and Divis Street entirely at the mercy of the Special Constabulary and the Protestant civilians who had come down there?

       W: Yes. There was a single unit in the area. I could only do one thing at a time. I had to do it as the situation developed and reports were received by me.

Here the counsel directly uses the fact that a particular answer was already given on an earlier occasion ('So you said yesterday'), in order to 'discount' that answer – thereby giving himself the opportunity of asking the question again (i.e. to get confirmation that the witness did move all his force over to Percy Street), as a lead into the blame-implicative upshot of that action (which was, that it left a Catholic area 'entirely at the mercy of the Special Constabulary and the Protestant civilians . . .'). So here the sense that the counsel already knew a particular answer to the question, because it was given on an earlier occasion, is quite explicitly involved in directing the questions in order to avoid the impact of the witness' first answer (which can attempt to forestall the blame assessment) and to lead to that accusation.

In other cases, witnesses' ability to recognise the directedness of questioning from inferring that counsel already knew the answers to the questions, is perhaps less overt – but nevertheless may be provided for in a more direct way than simply that a cross-examining counsel had earlier listened to a witness' evidence-in-chief etc. For in some cases, counsel may ask questions, the answers to which are explicitly or implicitly contained in immediately prior answers. For instance, we have seen that witnesses may construct replies which contain answers to projected next questions, especially by giving their reasons for not taking action, where such reasons have not yet been asked for: and very often counsel then go on to ask 'why' type questions, despite the fact that they have, effectively, already been answered. An example in which the counsel asks a question, the answer to which is implicit in an earlier question, is a continuation of (1).

(1)   (ST: 96,16C)

    8   C: What did you do at that point?

    9   W: I was not in a very good position to do

10		anything. We were under gunfire at the time.
11	C:	That shop of course could have been inhabited,
12		could it not, it could have been the residents in it?
13	W:	Yes.
14	C:	The living accommodation is upstairs?
15	W:	Yes.
16	C:	So far as you knew that could have been
17		people living there?
18	W:	Yes.
→ 19	C:	But you did not move towards it at all?
20	W:	You recollect we had our clearing operation.

We saw that the witness' reply in line 9, 'I was not in a very good position to do anything', presupposes that he did nothing (in relation to the petrol bombing of a newspaper shop). In line 19 the counsel uses that presupposition in the formulation of the question, 'But you did not move towards it at all?', in the sense that it displays an understanding of what the answer to that is, from the witness' earlier reply. Whereas the witness' answer in lines 9–10 can attempt to foreclose the projected sequence, by giving his reasons for not doing anything, the counsel manages the questioning so as to avoid that implication of the answer, thereby enabling him to draw explicit attention to the (blame-relevant) upshot from the earlier evidence (which is similar to (19)).

Of course, the questioning in (1) is managed in such a way that the counsel does not address the upshot of the witness' reply in lines 9–10 immediately after that reply. Instead those steps are separated by the *conditional* questions concerning whether the newspaper shop 'could have been inhabited' etc. (lines 11–18) – which, again, can be designed to avoid the implicativeness of the witness' earlier replies (to the effect that no action on his part was necessary or possible, for reasons elaborated earlier).[24] The sequential position of the question 'But you did not move towards it at all?' *after* the conditional questions which seek to establish the possible seriousness of the situation, is what gives the force of blaming the witness, a force it might not have had (or certainly not so evidently) had it been done immediately post the reply in lines 9–10. And the witness' recognition of that force, and hence of where the question is leading, is displayed in his production of a rebuttal in his reply in line 20, instead of a straight confirmation.

So, what is available to the witness as the basis for an analysis of the questioning – that is directed towards a blaming – is partly that the answer to the 'question' in line 19 is already contained (implicitly) in an earlier answer, which as was mentioned before is displayed in the format of the question: that is, its form relies on an understanding of the import of the reply in lines 9–10. Also, the witness may detect the directedness of the questioning through the way in which the conditional questions in lines 11–12 and 16–17 can be designed so as to avoid his own earlier attempts (in lines 5–7 and 9–10) to mitigate his not having taken action, and hence to forestall the projected blame sequence. Another kind of case in which counsel may be heard to avoid, or 'get around', the implicativeness of an 'awkward' reply ('awkward', that is, in the sense that it may jeopardise the intending blaming), is this sequence (which overlaps with (19)).

(23) (ST:84,36C)
      (The prior cross-examination has been concerned with the
      witness's handling of a Protestant crowd, referred to in the
      counsel's first utterance in the pro-terms 'those' and 'they'.)

1   C: If some of those, if, as Mr Allen has said (if he
2   did say it) threw petrol bombs, that would indicate
3   that they were in an extremely hostile mood?
4   W: They were obviously hostile.
5   C: After your second baton-charge you moved over to
6   Percy Street?
7   W: Yes.
8   C: Because of what you had heard was an attack on a
9   telephone pole?
10 W: No, I did not hear of any attack. I was told the
11   bulldozer had been commandeered and was being used
12   to destroy property.
13 C: A bulldozer was attacking the telephone pole or was
14   attacking property, that is what you heard?
15 W: Yes.
16 C: And at that stage you took all your force over to
17   Percy Street?
18 W: All my force was so small I could not under any
19   circumstances divide it up.

At two points in this extract, the counsel refers to the witness having moved his force over to Percy Street, in lines 5–6, and 16–17. In his reply on the first of those occasions, the witness merely *confirms* that he did so: but on the latter occasion, in lines 18–19, he produces an *account*, thereby displaying his understanding of the blame-implicativeness of the latter question. He might recognise that implicativeness in part through the way in which the reference to the fact that 'you *moved* over to Percy Street' in the former question becomes 'you *took all your force* over to Percy Street' in the latter. However something else occurs between these two question-answer pairs which may also be integral to the witness' analysis of the directedness of the questioning here.

Following the witness's confirmation (in line 7) that at some stage he moved his force over to Percy Street, the counsel produces a description of the circumstances which brought about that move (lines 8–9). There are two features of that description which are especially noticeable. Firstly, the inclusion of 'you had heard' can lend a certain indeterminacy to the report of the events which were going on elsewhere (i.e. in Percy Street), in the sense that that preface can mark the status of those events as not conclusively known to have happened but as something like 'hearsay' and possibly unsubstantiated, 'rumour', etc. The other feature is the description which the counsel constructs of the events which the witness 'had heard' about. The selection of terms in the description, 'attack on a telephone pole', can be designed to display the non-seriousness (or even triviality) of that event, by comparison with the situation – involving an 'extremely hostile' (Protestant) crowd – which he left in order to deal with the 'attack on the telephone pole'. So that, subsequent to a description of the situation in which the witness had been involved (lines 1–3), and the reference to his having moved from that setting (lines 5 and 6), is a description of the circumstances which caused the witness to move his force. Specifically those descriptions achieve a contrast in which the latter circumstances can be seen as 'less serious' in some respect than those which he decided to leave. Thus the witness may anticipate the ascription of blame for his having left a scene which was somehow 'more serious' than the one to which he moved. And already, in line 4, the witness *downgrades* the counsel's description of the mood of the (Protestant) crowd by the omission of 'extremely', so that 'they were in an extremely hostile mood' becomes, in the witness' 'confirmation', 'they were obviously hostile'.

However, the witness then *disconfirms* the counsel's description of the event which caused him to move to Percy Street.

```
 8  C:  Because of what you had heard was an attack on a
 9      telephone pole?
→10  W:  No, I did not hear of any attack. I was told the
11      bulldozer had been commandeered and was being
12      used to destroy property.
```

The witness designs this disconfirmation to manage the blame-implicativeness of both features of the counsel's version just outlined, the possibly unconfirmed or 'hearsay' character of the report of the event; and its being less serious than those which he left. In disconfirming that he 'heard of any attack', he substitutes 'I was told' for 'heard', where being 'told' can indicate the definiteness of the information reported to him. And then in place of the counsel's version ('an attack on a telephone pole') the witness substitutes descriptive terms so as to upgrade that event and thereby justify his action in moving his force; this is achieved through his introduction of the fact that a bulldozer was involved, which was being 'commandeered' to 'destroy property'.

Generally in examination, as in conversation, if a first speaker's statement is disconfirmed and corrected by the next speaker, then in his next turn the first speaker will acknowledge, or 'check', the correction, by doing a re-statement which contains the corrected (or repaired) version. The first speaker may repeat the 'corrected' version, even if he intends to go on to dispute that version: that step in the sequence may not necessarily indicate agreement.[25] So the structure for sequences in which disconfirmations occur is this:

A_1: Statement (contained in a question, report etc.)
B_1: Disconfirmation, with repair.
A_2: Re-statement with corrected version.
B_2: Confirmation.

The disconfirmation sequence in (23) is organised into something like this structure.

A_1	8	C:	Because of what you had heard was an attack on a
	9		telephone pole?
B_1	10	W:	No, I did not hear of any attack. I was told the
	11		bulldozer had been commandeered and was being
	12		used to destroy property.
A_2	13	C:	A bulldozer was attacking the telephone pole or was
	14		attacking property, that is what you heard?
B_2	15	W:	Yes.

Following the witness's disconfirmation in lines 10−12, corresponding with B_1, in which he corrects the counsel's version of what led him to move his force to Percy Street, the counsel's next utterance seems to be fitted with the slot indicated as A_2, that is the re-statement with the corrected version. However, he designs that utterance so as to avoid repeating the witness' correction verbatim. Instead he repeats some parts of that correction, whilst systematically *retaining* the crucial features of his own first version (crucial, that is, for the blaming), and omitting important aspects of the witness' correction. In particular, the counsel substitutes 'you heard' (which he had used in his first version) for the witness' 'I was told'. And he retains 'attacking', despite that being the thing which is specifically disconfirmed in the witness' prior utterance; although the witness had repaired the counsel's description of what was happening ('an attack on a telephone pole') to 'destroying property', in his re-statement the counsel drops 'destroy' and refers to 'attacking the telephone pole or was attacking property'. So the counsel holds onto the blame-implicative features in his first description of events in Percy Street, but in a way which successfully obtains the relevant next action by the witness (i.e. a confirmation), by 'disguising' those features by designing that turn in the form of a 'restatement with repair'. The witness may not, of course, be hoodwinked by that disguise: but an interactional difficulty facing him is that to have disconfirmed the 'restatement' might be made to appear pedantic, or as going back on the description just given in lines 10–12 (given that the counsel has included reference to the 'bulldozer' and to 'property').

Thus what is available to the witness as having happened between the two questions in which the counsel refers to the move to Percy Street (in lines 5–6, and then in 16–17), is that the counsel has managed the questioning so as to avoid his (i.e. the witness') own version of events upgrading the seriousness of the situation to which he decided to move his force (see also his attempt to downgrade the seriousness of the situation he left, by substituting 'they were obviously hostile' for the counsel's proposal that 'they were in an extremely hostile mood'). Thus he is able to analyse the questioning for the way it is directed towards a blaming, and to avoid his attempt to forestall that blaming. So that when his action in moving to Percy Street is referred to the second time, in lines 16–17, the witness treats that question as leading up to what has been the 'point' of the prior questions, in his production of an account for not having left some men behind to handle the 'hostile' Protestant crowd. It is noticeable how an account in *that* form still manages to retain a sense of the necessity of going to Percy Street, and of the precedence that has for the witness over remaining where he had been.

Thus the sequence in (23) may be described as follows: the counsel asks two very similar questions, in lines 5–6 and again in 16–17, the latter separated from the former (that is, not made in the immediately adjacent position) by questioning in which the counsel avoids the witness' version of the grounds for his action – a version aimed at displaying the correctness of that action. So the witness may analyse the question in lines 16–17, firstly for the fact that the counsel already knows the answer (from the confirmation in line 7), and secondly for the counsel's management of the intervening questions to avoid his (the witness') attempts to forestall further questioning towards a blame allocation. These aspects of his analysis are displayed in his reply in lines 18–19, where he does not give a simple confirmation, thereby attending to his already having confirmed that earlier; instead he gives an account which is an *alternative* to the reasons which he earlier gave for his action (in lines 10–11), thus orienting to their avoidance or rejection by the counsel. Replies such as this, and in line 20 of extract (1), frequently consist of *alternative* accounts to those which may have been given shortly before in relation to the 'same' action. These display witnesses' analyses that counsel already know answers to the questions, and that their earlier (first) attempts to describe or account for their actions have been avoided or rejected, often by conditional questions, as in (1) or by the way in which counsel hold onto their versions and explanations of events, even where those have been disconfirmed and corrected by witnesses, as in (23) – both techniques being very frequently used by counsel to side-step witnesses' attempts to forestall anticipated blame allocations.

WITNESSES' RESOURCES FOR SEQUENTIAL MANAGEMENT

Finally, we want to draw attention to witnesses' use of defence components, especially explanations, as resources for managing some control over blame sequences. It will be recalled that, in (cross)-examination, given the constraint which the pre-allocation system imposes on turns to talk, witnesses' speak post-question; because they are therefore expected to give answers, they have little opportunity for 'directing' talk themselves in the way in which participants in ordinary conversation may do. However, we have seen that replies may be designed to address (and even directly answer) *future* questions in projected sequences: such replies may attempt to gain a measure of control by ensuring witnesses opportunities to give replies to questions whose (future) production they cannot guarantee, and by avoiding giving their explanations, etc., in a sequential environment in which they would be especially likely to be rejected.

The initial observation, and a theme of this chapter, is that witnesses produce descriptions, explanations and the like, which may be heard as defence components although they are done *before* the counsel have made outright accusations or critical assessments of witnesses' actions. For instance, replies commonly contained 'reasons' (e.g. for not taking action), even though the prior question did not ask for an explanation; hence some replies consist, at least in part, of answers to as-yet unasked questions. As well as thereby *disaffiliating* themselves from the (blame-relevant) assessments which they might recognise are implicated in some information they are asked to give or to confirm – and thereby avoid concuring with or admitting information from which the faultiness of their action might be concluded – such replies manage the production of answers to questions which not only have yet to be asked, but which may *never* be asked. Clearly, as the pre-allocations of turns in examination ensures that only counsel have rights to ask questions witnesses cannot guarantee that questions will be asked which allow them the opportunity to explain their actions, or otherwise defend themselves. It is perhaps for this reason that on occasions the Chairman of the Tribunal interrupts the questioning in order to ask a 'why' question, and give the witness the chance to defend his action, where it might appear from the counsel's questions that he is not going to give the witness that chance. That happens in the following extract (where the Chairman's reference to 'the question (having) been asked hundreds of times before' is to the cross-examination of other witnesses: this witness has not yet been asked why he '(took) no steps to arrest anyone').

(24)   (ST:79,40F)
    C: Do you know of any persons being apprehended by any
          other party?
    W: I do not.
    C: Did you see petrol bombs being thrown?
    W: I did.
    C: Presumably the people who threw the petrol bombs at
          the property on the front of Divis Street must have
          carried them down either Percy Street or Dover Street?
    W: Correct.
    C: In fact, I do not want to go through the evidence in
          detail again, but Mr Allan said that he had got petrol
          bombs in Dover Street.
    W: If that is Mr Allan's evidence that might possibly
          be correct.

Ch: The question has been asked hundreds of times before
but I think it is only fair to put it to you. Here
you were in a situation of complete lawlessness on
both sides – petrol bombs, stones and later guns
→   were being used. Why did you, a senior policeman
→   in that situation, take no steps to arrest anyone?

W: We were containing two factions of the crowd. I had
such a small party that it would have been a waste of
manpower and futile to try to arrest anyone. I had
to try and contain both sides and that was the way I
assessed the situation.

The important point is, however, that the possibility that they may not
be asked questions which allow them to give explanations/defences is
available to witnesses and is a basis for their *not* waiting for 'why . . .'
questions to give their reasons. Instead, they may do so at an earlier
opportunity – especially, as we saw in the last section, in answer to a
question which is the same as or very like a question which has already
been asked. In this extract, the counsel's question 'All baton-charges
mounted by the police were mounted against the Catholics?' is a
reformulation of the information arising from the prior question-answer.

(25)   (ST:96,19C)

C: Finally a large number of baton-charges were made
on the night of the 13th and 14th by the police, is
that not right?

W: Comparatively speaking it was not a large number but
there were baton-charges made, yes.

C: Did you see any baton-charge made against any section
of the Protestant crowd at any time?

W: No, I did not.

→ C: All baton-charges mounted by the police were mounted
against the Catholics?

→ W: Yes, because of the fact that the attacks were being
– we had on the night of the 13th backed back until my
back was against the wall of Hastings Street police
station, I could go no further.
(Cross-examination ends)

Already in his first return where he downgrades the description of the
police action, the witness may be heard to anticipate some ascription of

fault. And then, although he need not have anticipated that the cross-examination would actually finish after that third 'question-answer' sequence, one possibility which is available to the witness, partly through the way in which that third question is in a statement form, as an upshot of the information confirmed in the prior question-answer pairs, is that the counsel is initiating the close of that topic sequence with the upshot,[26] and possibly without asking a 'why' question – and hence that he may not get the opportunity to give an explanation for his action. And we can see in the data that witnesses overwhelmingly give explanations, reasons, accounts etc. for their action to 'questions' which do *not* ask for such explanations. This suggests that witnesses may produce *accounts* (as distinct from the other descriptive work which may be bound up with defending action) in returns to questions which are *not* 'why . . .' questions, because techniques for managing the constraint that control the production of such questions are not in their hands, and they cannot therefore guarantee that they will be asked to give their reasons for their actions. Neither can they guarantee the future production of overt critical assessments of the faultiness of their action: it is always a possibility that the counsel may not go on to state the 'fault' explicitly, but may leave the Tribunal, public etc. (or in ordinary courts, the jury) to infer the blameworthy character of the witness' (defendants') action – thereby depriving the witness of an opportunity to give a denial, defence, or to rebut the charge etc. So the design of returns to include accounts and other defence components can be techniques through which witnesses can gain some control over the production of such objects as denials, defences, explanation, etc., which seek to deflect blame ascriptions – objects whose proper placement would otherwise be post accusations, post assessments of the 'fault' of an action, post requests for explanation, etc.

A further important feature of the design of replies to manage some control over projected sequences has to do with the *sequential placement* of witnesses descriptions, explanations etc. Although these may be heard as defences, an advantage of their being made before an accusation or critical assessment has been made is that witnesses thereby avoid doing such objects in a sequential position (i.e. post-accusation) in which their explanations are especially likely to be rejected. Instead, producing such components *prior* to a projected blaming can attempt to *minimise* the chances of having their accounts etc. rejected by the counsel. An action structure for sequences initiated by an accusation/complaint is:

A₁: Accusation/complaint

B₁: Defence (denial etc.)
A₁: Rejection/acceptance

That is, sequences which begin with an accusation may not close with
the recipient's defence: for the accuser may then go on to acknowledge
that defence by accepting or, more probably, rejecting it. (See, for
example, the counsel's rejection of the witness's defence in lines 73–5 of
(1) in the previous chapter.) An instance occurs in this extract from a
group therapy session cited in Chapter 2, in which T makes a complaint
against S.

   (30)   (BR:CM)

      T: Steve er::m (always) seems to make sarcastic comments
           en(s) things like (.) er:m its one of my:: yuhn the
           way I spea:k (.) en things like *th*a:,
           (1.8)
      T: Sor'a goes round sorta speaking (.) very very *posh*   (Complaint)
           °e(h)n
           (5.0)
      S: Alrigh' I'm s*o*rry I do tha', (.) but some(s)times   (Apology =
           its jus *my* way uva jo:ke un I know no- hardly   Defence)
           anybody likes my way (.) having jokes, =
  →   T: = ↑Its not *joke* it ↑a:ll its: . . . .   (Rejection
                                                                    of defence)

In response to T's complaint that S is sarcastic about his (i.e. T's) 'way of
talking', S makes an apology ('Alrigh' I'm sorry I do tha' . . .'), but then
goes on to make a *defence*, ('but sometimes its jus my way uva joke' . . .
etc.). In his next utterance, 'It's not a *joke* at a:ll', T initiates a *rejection* of
S's defence. It is, of course, no chance matter that a rejection is done by
the complainant in the above extract, for although the third action
component in the sequence has been described as rejection/acceptance
of the defence, these are by no means equivalent actions. 'Rejections' of
defences are, overwhelmingly, done by accusors in preference to 'acceptances' of the accused party's defence. Looking back to some of the
extracts cited in this chapter, in cases where a witness' utterance can be
heard as some sort of defence (though to an anticipated accusation),
what commonly happens is that in subsequent questions the counsel
challenges, questions or doubts the defence. Generally, therefore, defences are further investigated in later questions, and are not simply left

unexamined; counsels' investigations can be heard to be directed to undermining or rejecting the defence. Such rejections may be done explicitly, through counter-assertions by the counsel: for example, in response to the witness' account in lines 9–10 of extract (1) that he did not take action because 'We were under gunfire at the time', the counsel later says 'I am suggesting to you that you were not under gunfire at that stage at all': or they may be more implicit in the questioning. At any rate, the occurrence of rejections, challenges, and further questioning about proferred accounts, following defences, points to the *dispreferred* character (for the party making the accusation) of accepting recipients' denials, defences and the like. Other sequential evidence for that was discussed in Chapter 4; counsel may do considerable work to set up the grounds for an accusation, prior to making one, such that some possible and anticipated defence may not work. One further point supporting the accuser's dispreference for accepting a defence is that to do so can initiate a sequence in which counter-complaints may be made by the party originally accused about having been unjustly accused of unfounded allegations and the like – which can put the original accuser in the subsequent position of doing defences and/or apologies.

The preferred character of rejections over acceptances, following 'defences' (again, for the party who is the accuser) is in contrast to the sequence,

A   Accusation/complaint
B   Admissions (plus possibly, Apologies)
A   Acceptance/rejection

in which the 'admission' of blame or guilt is the thing which an 'accusation' can seek to achieve: thus 'acceptances' may be the preferred action in the third slot in the sequence. And it is noticeable that this may be oriented to by hearers, who may take A's non-production of an item which is hearable as belonging to the third slot in the sequence (e.g. a silence: 'non-commital' utterance: topic change, or whatever) to be a 'rejection', given that the preferred 'acceptance' would otherwise have been made explicitly. Moreover, such 'rejections' may be treated as special sorts of things, as indicating that for A the 'admission' does not go 'far enough', that it is 'too qualified', etc., and thus not a proper 'full' admission, for which an acceptance would otherwise be forthcoming.

For witnesses, of course, the preferred actions following accusations are ones which avoid the acceptance or admission of blame, that is denials and defences. But they can easily anticipate that, were they to wait for the accusation, their defences are very likely to be rejected by the counsel. The anticipated rejection is, then, a locally critical action component in the projected sequence, in the sense that it is an action which witnesses can attempt to avoid.[27] One way to do that is to produce their accounts, etc., *prior* to the accusation, thereby *avoiding* giving accounts in just the sequential environment where a rejection of the accounts is an anticipated outcome. This does not, of course, assure the acceptance of their justifications/excuses, explanations, etc., but it at least avoids making them in a position where rejections are highly probable. And it will be noticed that the design of replies in this way, as a strategy for avoiding rejections, can be nicely fitted to the way in which the distributions of *types* of turns ('questions' being asked by counsel; 'answers' by witnesses) operates as a constraint in cross-examination, in which the kinds of strategies employed by persons against whom complaints are made in other sequential environments in conversation are not available to witnesses.

We have, then, just briefly introduced some interactional aspects of witnesses' production of defence components, *prior to* accusations or critical assessments of their actions. We have noted that, because of the pre-allocation system for examination, witnesses cannot be assured of opportunities to give explanations for their actions, given that they have no control over the production of 'why . . .' questions. Nor may they have the chance to rebut or defend themselves against some charge concerning the inadequacy or inappropriateness of their action, given that counsel may not go on to state the 'charge' overtly but leave hearers to 'draw their own conclusions' about the blameworthiness of the witnesses' actions. Hence witnesses may give answers to 'why' questions apparently prematurely (before they have been asked), so as to ensure that they do get to give their reasons for actions – and thereby possibly rebut anticipated charges – despite whatever intentions counsel may have. Secondly, witnesses may manipulate projected action sequences, in order to avoid counsels' rejections of their accounts: thus replies are designed not only to deny the counsel the materials out of which an accusation may be built, hence forestalling anticipated blamings, but also to avoid producing accounts, explanations and the like post-accusation, that is in a sequential position where their defences are especially likely to be rejected.

6 The Data Base and some Analytic Considerations

1 IMPROVING THE DATA BASE

The exploratory character of the studies we have been able to do so far has been referred to at various points in the preceeding chapters, and it will by now be clear that it has only been possible to focus on a limited range of analytic concerns. Nevertheless, it is hoped that these will have served as an exemplification of the kind of research that may be entailed by adopting the approach outlined in Chapters 1 and 2, and to establish a case for pursuing such investigations further. In this chapter, however, we want to draw attention to some of the more obvious limitations of our studies, and to various ways in which future research (some of which is already under way) might improve on them, either by looking more closely at similar issues, or by investigating others which have yet to be considered. To this end we comment first on the data base and how it might be improved, before making some tentative suggestions about a number of technical problems to which further research might be addressed. These latter are, for the most part, additional to the issues considered in earlier chapters, and have been selected partly to illustrate how the availability of tape-recordings facilitates observations and analyses which could not be done with reference to the main data base used in the research to this point.

In noting that there were obvious shortcomings in the data base for the preceeding chapters, we have in mind at least two important ways in which it could be regarded as less than satisfactory. In the first place, it may seem that the particular types of court hearing from which much of the data was taken reflect somewhat obscure, if not downright eccentric, choices. Secondly, the form of data subjected to detailed examination (i.e. official transcripts and ones derived from notes taken in a public gallery) may appear to be hardly adequate in terms of our own introductory remarks about the advantages of recordings as a source of 'raw

data', which is not pre-organised by the researcher's descriptive practices prior to the start of any analysis. To the extent that these can be
construed as criticisms of our work, we are in the somewhat paradoxical
position of being prepared to agree with them in a general sense (and
especially as far as further research is concerned), but at the same time to
disagree that they can necessarily be forcefully made against our particular studies and the way they were presented. In this first section, then, an
attempt is made to clarify what we mean by this, and to show how there
may be nothing paradoxical or inconsistent about adopting such a
stance.

To the charge that a Coroner's Court and a Tribunal of Enquiry are
unusual hearings on which to base a study claiming to have a wider
relevance for the problem of court-room interaction, various defences
can be offered in addition to the accidents in our academic biographies
which originally led us to them.[1] Such a complaint, for example,
presupposes that sociologists should focus their research on 'more usual'
types of court hearings, meaning presumably those which are held with
greater frequency, or which deal with more regularly occurring routine
business. Alternatively, it might imply that we ought to have studied
'more important' court hearings, where the criteria for assessing relative
importance would have to be specified stipulatively, with reference
perhaps to assertions about certain social, political or economic
priorities. Either way, such a criticism would seem to involve the further
assumption that decisions as to analytic focus should be dictated by
things which members already know to be 'important' practical problems. And such a basis for making choices about the focus for research
can be seen, in the light of remarks made in Chapter 1, as a first step
towards the kind of unexplicated reliance on members' resources that
our approach specifically seeks to avoid. In other words, it would involve
asserting the primacy of members' practical concerns as grounds for
making research decisions. In the event, of course, it has to be admitted
that our choices were originally influenced by our concerns 'as members'
with what we knew in advance, and knew that others knew, to be serious
social problems (i.e. suicide, and the troubles in Northern Ireland). As
our interest in ethnomethodology developed, however, we had to come
to terms with the initially disappointing realisation that, contrary to
what our earlier training had led us to believe, traditional sociological
research methods were unlikely to do more than facilitate the construction of theories which were similar in form and content to those already
available to and used by members in their 'lay' attempts to make sense of
and/or resolve such problems (c.f. Atkinson, 1978).

Yet even though, in terms both of the constraints under which conversational analysts seek to work and of more traditionally revered notions of 'representativeness', the grounds on which these particular courts were selected may have been somewhat suspect, this does not necessarily also mean that analyses of data derived from them have no broader relevance for an understanding of the organisation of court-room activities. As far as we know, for example, *all* interactional sequences which can be recognisably described as 'court hearings' must be characterised by some organised resolution to the problem of providing for one speaker to speak at a time in such a way that his utterances can not only be heard by a next speaker, but can also be monitored by other parties present (who may or may not have rights to speak during its course). Moreover, the non-random co-ordination of spoken and un-spoken activity sequences would appear to be widely used in many different courts for achieving the necessary transition from pre-hearing circumstances in which the shared monitoring of a single sequence of spoken turns may not be possible (as well as for doing other things at different stages in a hearing). Similarly, as has been emphasised in various places from Chapter 2 onwards, examination is a massively predominant and prevalent form of speech exchange in most, if not all, types of court. So too is the pre-allocation of turns and types of turns (i.e. ones which are minimally recognisable as 'questions' and 'answers'), as are the kinds of actions done within such turns (e.g. accusations, denials, excuses, justifications, etc.). Thus, to the extent that such organisational properties are common to most court hearings (and perhaps also to a broader but as yet unspecifiable range of settings), there is little reason to suppose that the analytic issues considered in the present work are specific either to the types of court hearings, or to the particular instances of those general types from which much of the data was taken.

While the more general pervasiveness of the organised practices examined in previous chapters may provide some grounds for not taking too seriously possible criticisms concerning the lack of 'representative-ness' or 'typicality' of the court hearings from which our data were derived, we would certainly not wish to appeal to them in support of a continuing complacency about the possible further expansion of the data base. For precisely how such activities as we have described are organ-ised in different kinds of courts (and other settings too) remains an open empirical question, which is unlikely to be answered without a very extensive programme of further investigation. As yet, for example, little can be said about what variations there may be between civil and criminal hearings, between ones which involve juries and ones which do not, between higher courts and lower courts, between courts and tribunals, between 'adversarial' and 'inquisitorial' procedures, etc. And, as we have had occasion to note several times before, it also seems likely that there may be important parallels to be drawn between courts and other settings where similar organisational problems are a feature (e.g. meetings, classrooms, ceremonies, interviews, etc). There is also, of course, the question of how the organisation of activities in these various settings, about which there is still very little systematic knowledge, compares with that for conversations, on which a more extensive corpus of findings is already available. Some of the sorts of technical issues which, in the light of our work so far, seem worth pursuing in more detail are briefly summarised in Section 2 below, but for the moment it is enough to stress that the more extensive analytical programme we are proposing will require a much broader data base.

The second apparant shortcoming of our data referred to above is that we did not make much use of tape-recordings, even though such reproduceable materials were so highly commended in Chapter 1. The main reason was simply that we had no access to tape-recordings of court hearings until after the studies reported above had been completed. And, while we would have much preferred to have had tapes available right from the start, we would nevertheless defend the use of official (and 'do-it-yourself') transcripts with reference to the way we have used them. That is, we have sought for the most part to avoid investigating things which cannot be read from the appended transcripts.[2] This is not to say, of course, that the sorts of things which can be examined with reference to tape-recordings or transcripts derived from them (e.g. intonational variation, the serial placement and length of pauses within and between turns, overlaps, etc.) are insignificant for arriving at understandings of what is going on, and for analyses directed at providing for such understandings. But it does mean that some understandings can be arrived at perfectly well from official and other 'cleaned up' transcripts from which such details are excluded. Indeed, were it otherwise it is difficult to imagine what point there could possibly be in the production of court transcripts, a practice which is presumably based on the assumption that they are adequate for lawyers and others to understand for the practical purposes of submitting or deciding appeals. And that there may be differences in the kinds of understandings which can be arrived at from 'cleaned up' official transcripts, as compared with the more detailed ones derivable from tapes, is arguably a more serious problem for practising lawyers than it is for conversational analysts. Thus, for analytical purposes, it is not necessary to assume that the

displays of understanding discoverable from official transcripts correspond with participants 'actual' understandings at the time, or that no
analyses can be done without reference to features unavailable in the
transcripts (e.g. pauses, gestures, intonation, etc.), or indeed that no
alternative readings of the data might be possible. But for lawyers to
make similar assumptions would be to call into question the appropriateness of, for example, appeal procedures which are based on transcribed representations of the interactions leading to some earlier
decision.[3] Providing the analyst confines his attention to understandings
which can be arrived at from whatever data he has before him, however,
there is still much that he can do even without access to other interactional features. The inclusion of such features would certainly extend the
range of researchable topics, but would have no implications for claims
about due process and the accomplishment of justice.

While it is thus possible to offer a defence against criticisms addressed
to this second shortcoming in our data base, we would much prefer to be
in a position to study the broader range of issues which are opened up by
access to tape-recordings (both audio- and video-). This is not because
we think we have gone anywhere near to exhausting the analytical
potential of official or 'cleaned up' transcripts, for there is obviously
much that could be done with such materials. Rather it is because so
much of the work on conversations is based on tape-recorded data, and
has shown that details like gaps, overlaps, sound stretches, etc., can have
great significance for the sequential organisation of talk. Thus, in so far
as such studies are the major resource and reference point for our
attempts to explore the organisation of speech-exchange in court hearings, it is crucial that we should have access to directly comparable data.

As is already evident from the references to tape-recorded materials,
some steps have already been taken towards improving the data base,
though the situation can hardly be said (at the time of writing) to be
wholly satisfactory. In the first place, the only tape-recordings to which
we have been able to obtain access are of American criminal trials, which
were made available through the good offices of colleages with similar
research interests. But, as conversational analysis depends centrally on
the researcher's command over the natural language being used in the
settings studied, there is at least a possible problem as to how far our
understandings and analyses of court-room exchanges between native
speakers of American English will be affected by our status as English
native speakers of English.[4] Against the view that this poses a serious
problem, the same sort of argument can be presented as was outlined in
support of our use of official transcripts, namely that it is analytically

proper to proceed so long as the investigations are limited to readings of the American data which can be arrived at by us as English speakers of English. While this may facilitate a considerable amount of work to be done on American materials, however, it does nothing to ease the problems that are sometimes encountered in trying to make out what the American speakers are saying, either because words are obscured (to us) by regional pronunciation, or because certain usages are unfamiliar to English speakers of English. Added to this, an inferior knowledge (on our part) of the different legal rules of evidence and procedure which apply in different American states can lead to various confusions which would be less likely to arise were we to concentrate our attention on recordings of English court hearings.

Whether or not it will prove possible to remedy this problem is not clear at the time of writing, as negotiations about obtaining access to tape-recordings of English court hearings have only just begun. The analytical case for such permission to be granted will hopefully be clear from what has been said to this point in the book. But there is another reason why we consider that there should be no objections to the tape-recording (both audio- and video-) of court proceedings, which is simply that they are explicitly supposed to be open to the public. As such, it is very noticeable that it is easier for researchers to obtain access to tape recordings of extremely private and confidential interactional sequences (e.g. doctor–patient consultations, group therapy sessions, etc.) than it is to public ones. Thus, there is something ironic about the fact that summary reports of court proceedings based on scribbled jottings by researchers and journalists are not only perfectly permissible, but are also all that is available to a more general public than that which can squeeze into the limited seating accommodation in a particular court room. From the point of view of anyone who is sensitive to public reportage of hearings or criticisms based on it, of course, such a situation may have considerable advantages, for the enforced reliance on hastily collected extracts provides a continually available resource for repudiating reports and critiques. That is, it provides for any report or critique to be dismissed on the grounds that it was 'inaccurate', 'quoted out of context', 'biassed', etc. What else current restrictions on tape-recordings of hearings is designed to achieve, other than to create an impression that the authorities have something to hide, remains a mystery to us.[5] And, while we would want to argue strongly for courts to be public to the extent that anyone unable to attend a hearing could have access to recordings of it, our main concern as analysts is that the present situation is a very serious impediment to the development of rigorous empirical research into the organisation of interaction in courts.

II SOME NOTICEABLE FEATURES OF COURT ROOM TALK[6]

The discussion of future research possibilities which makes up the remaining sections of this chapter derives partly from the issues examined earlier in the book and partly from some preliminary observations on the collection of tape recordings of American criminal trials. As we did not have access to this improved data base until preparation of the final draft of this book was well advanced, the analytic remarks made about them are particularly tentative and provisional. And, while a major reason for including them was to provide at least a flavour of the differences between official transcripts and transcribed tape-recordings, it should also be noted that it has only been possible to touch on a few of the analytic possibilities they raise.

A central empirical focus throughout the book has been some of the features of court-room talk which appear to be noticeably different (to members and sociologists) from those exhibited in conversations, including particularly the co-ordinated sequencing of certain spoken and unspoken activity turns, and the pre-allocation of turn order and turn types in examination. Our main analytic interest has then been in various interactional tasks which are recognisably done within such sequential environments, and with explicating features of sequential organisation which could provide for the accomplishment of such tasks. At a fairly general level, this orientation points to two types of question. The first is that of what other kinds of interactional work are done within such sequential environments, and how they are accomplished. To what extent, for example, can methods usable in sequences which do not consist so exclusively of extended Question-Answer sequences operate within that more closely ordered environment? In other words, does the sequential organisation through which certain activities are produced in, for example, conversations require modification for them to be also done within utterances minimally recognisable as 'questions' and 'answers'? A second general issue centres on the extent to which forms of sequential organisation through which court-room activities are achieved are to be found producing similar actions in other settings, such as conversations, interviews, interrogations, etc.

While a focus on data drawn from a range of speech environments may thus be called for, this is not necessarily to imply that we already have enough systematic observations of features exhibited by court-room talk to be able to embark immediately on such comparative work. That is, we need to be much more specific about what appears to be distinctive or noticeable about the organisation of activities in court before it will be possible to do much in the way of careful comparative analysis. And an important way towards that goal seems likely to involve being able to say more about a number of distributional issues, some of which have already been raised in earlier chapters. Thus, perhaps the most obvious distributional point which can be made about the talk in court hearings is that sequences consisting of paired utterances minimally recognisable as 'questions' and 'answers' are overwhelmingly predominant. And to this it can be added that the co-ordinated sequences of spoken and unspoken activities appear to occur both relatively frequently, and at specific points in proceedings (e.g. at the beginning and ending of the hearing as a whole, of certain phases of the hearing, and of some turns of particular participants). It also seems likely that some kinds of actions involving explicit moral imputations (e.g. accusations, blamings, excuses, justifications, etc.) occur with greater frequency in court hearings than in many other speech environments and, in so far as these may have particular organisational implications, they would seem to be a potentially important focus for analysis and comparative reference.

But there are also various other noticeable features exhibited by court-room talk which may point to distributional differences in relation to talk in other settings, some of which have already been briefly mentioned. Several of the things which are noticeable in the following extract, for example, appear to be frequent and regular occurrences in tape recordings of cross-examination, but would appear to be heard less often in conversations (and perhaps also in examination in chief[7]). It is certainly not claimed that the list is exhaustive, and items are not listed in any specially significant order; it includes:

(1) The frequent placement of the continuation marker 'and' at the start of turns which are first parts of adjacency pairs.

(2) The placement of questions about the factual status of a description contained in an utterance early and late (and sometimes both) in the same utterance (e.g. 'isn't it a fact', 'is that right', 'wasn't it true', etc.).

(3) The occurrence of questions which set up a preference for an answer expressing agreement at the next turn.

(4) Frequent and relatively long pauses both within and between utterance turns.

(5) The relative infrequency of repairs.
(6) The inclusion of named references to the person whose turn it is to speak next, and the selection of a particular name form (i.e. title + surname).
(7) The selection of a categorisation of another person from a situatedly relevant collection of categories (i.e. 'defendent' from the duplicatively organised collection 'court room participants').
(8) Second position turns which are shorter in length (and frequently only one word) than those in first position.

Not all of these will be dealt with in the discussion which follows, but readers may like to check as to whether or not they too find them 'noticeable', and perhaps go on to consider for themselves what organisational significances may be involved.[8]

(1)   OU: 45,3A
C: And isn't it a *fact* (1.0) Miss Le Brette (1.0) where you (1.0)
      went to (1.0) on this evening (2.0) was at least *a* quarter of
      a mile (0.5) from the main highway?=
W: = I don't know
      (2.5)
C: Some distance back into theuh (.) into the wood wasn't it?
      (0.5)
W: It was up the *path* I don't know how far
      (4.0)
C: And during this dr*i:ve* up the pa:th (3.0) did you say anything
      to the defendent (1.0) (about Michael's Tavern) (0.5) where
      you were goin=
W: = No
      (11.0)
C: And the defendent dr*o:ve* (1.0) his c*a*r (1.0) along the dirt
      roa:d (.) and came to a st*op* (0.5) in an area known as Michael's
      Field is that right?=
W: = Yees
      (2.0)
C: Now wasn' it true whooah (1.5) Miss Le Brette thatuh (2.5) the
      area where that car st*opped* isuh (2.5) *some* distance from any
      house (0.5) isn that so?
      (2.5)
W: Yeh=
C: = There's a large (0.5) open area with some trees isn' it?

(2.0)

W: Mm huh

C: An the nearest house isuh some great distance away isn't it?
(2.5)

W: I don't know what you mean by great distance
(2.5)

C: Wasuh uh a fact isn't it uh Miss Le Brette that the nearest house (0.5) uh abuts theuh (.) uhh the Warwick turnpike? (0.7) Is that where the nearest house is?=

W: = I don't understand the question.

Before making any tentative remarks about the design of some of these utterances and their possible organisational significance, it may be as well to begin with a brief recapitulation of two fairly general issues which have already been introduced. The first centres on the idea that the turn-taking system for conversation cannot, without modification, provide for the orderly production of single sequences of utterance turns which are monitorable *both* by participants to the talk *and* by others who may be present though silent.[9] And the second suggestion was that part of the resolution to such problems is provided by the pre-allocation of turns and turn types (into ones minimally recognisable as 'questions' and 'answers'). A theme common to both of these is the idea that a way of minimising the probability of anyone present (rather than particular parties) starting to talk might be provided by the restricted availability of the 'next speaker selects himself' device, a restriction which is continually sustained by one party recurrently designing his utterances as first parts of an adjacency pair which projects a conditionally relevant next action *and* selects someone to do it. And an important implication of this is that utterances that are parts of a court hearing must be recipiently designed for a number of different parties. A turn which is the first part of a pair, for example, must be designed in such a way that the answerer can hear what is said, hear it as a question, and understand it in such a way as to be able to design a sequentially relevant answer at the turn's completion. But it must also be hearable in these ways by others who are *not* required to speak, such as the jury and members of the public, and by others who can sometimes self-select to speak (e.g. the judge, or opposing counsel). Such utterances, therefore, presumably have to be designed to be clearly audible to these various groups. In addition to audibility, however, there is also a potential problem of understanding for non-participants and infrequent participants as they, unlike the speakers, are excluded from being able to display their understanding of an utterance in the way that they do in conversations. That is, they cannot show that they understood what has just been said by designing an appropriate next utterance, the suitability of which may be confirmed or denied in the utterance of another speaker which follows it. Nor, if they are unsure as to what was meant by a particular utterance, are they able to initiate any kind of repair or understanding check at the completion of the ambiguous utterance. All they can do is to monitor the utterances of the speakers in order to assess how far their understandings concur with those being displayed by the active participants, and it may be noted in parenthesis that this could be a much more efficient way of assuring the non-speakers' continuous understanding of what is going on than some other possibilities, such as having to listen to a very extended single turn (e.g. a lecture).[10]

A general implication of this is that both clarity of enunciation and utterance design will be crucially important in court-room (and many other multi-party) settings if all those present are to be able to hear and follow (i.e. understand) what is going on. In a fairly gross way, then, it may be noted that the pre-allocation of turn types into questions and answers massively reduces the range of possible types of utterance for which an audience might otherwise have to monitor. The 'close ordering' properties associated with adjacency pairs, furthermore, also massively reduce the range of topics which might be talked about in second turn position, and therefore increase the scope for non-participants to assess the prospective implicativeness of a question for the kind of answer which is likely to follow, thereby easing the interpretive work required to make a sense of what is going on.

III   PAUSES, AND THE PRODUCTION OF CLARITY AND AMBIGUITY

More detailed aspects of the design of questions, however, may be oriented to such issues of audibility and understanding, and the presence of some of the 'noticeable' features in the data extract above can be seen as possible instances of that. The frequent and relatively extended pauses,[11] occurring within turns for example, can be seen to break up the questions into segmented parts which can be monitored in a 'piece by piece' way, so that the pauses appear to operate in a similar way to punctuation marks in written texts.[12] By phasing the delivery of an utterance, the chances of parts of it being missed (and the whole being misunderstood) by others present may thereby be greatly reduced. And, as far as a speaker of such an utterance is concerned, pauses may provide time in which to design further segments which do not include 'repair-ables'. In other words, the relative infrequency of repairs in these data (and in extracts not included here) could turn out to be organisationally closely linked to the occurrence of extended pauses within utterances.

Such pauses are not the only features of these questions which can be heard as being oriented to audibility and clarity of enunciation. Others which may work in a similar way include the stressing of particular words (e.g. '*fact*', '*a*', '*you*', etc.), and the stretching of vowel sounds (e.g. dr*i:ve*, pa:th, etc.), both of which occur immediately prior to a pause within several of the utterances in the extract. In some instances, then, a pause may be only the second indication that a segment of an utterance has been completed, the stress or stretching having already marked it and projected the imminent pause.[13] Issues such as these, however, have yet to be subjected to any detailed examination and it is clearly better to leave them for further research rather than continue with speculative suggestions here. But before leaving the question of what looks to be the slow and rhythmic phasing of utterances in these data, a possibly interesting point of comparative reference may be noted. Thus, recent research into language acquisition has given considerable attention to similar rhythmic features of 'baby talk' by adults to small children, and to its importance for learning how to talk. One suggestion is that it is a way of talking which is recipiently designed for small children, and may be local to adult-baby interaction.[14] That is, neither adults nor children (who are able to talk) routinely talk in this way. In drawing attention to a possible similarity between court-room talk and 'baby talk', then, we are not proposing that they are identical, or necessarily very closely alike. But we are suggesting that such rhythmically phased utterances may resolve similar organisational problems in that they can be heard as having been recipiently designed for hearers who may have difficulties in making out what is being said. It may not, therefore, be altogether coincidental that counsel sometimes sound as if they are 'talking down' to witnesses, 'treating them like children', etc.

While pauses during the course of 'question' turns may contribute towards both the audibility and understandability of such utterances as a whole, their inclusion in other sorts of utterances can often have a 'high risk' character as far as retaining the turn is concerned. Thus, as was elaborated at greater length in Chapter 2, the opening up of a gap may be seen as a possible turn transition point and, given the 'minimisation of gap and overlap' features of the turn-taking system, it is a place where another speaker may well self-select and start a next turn. Although

pauses within many utterances are frequently filled by another speaker,
however, that probability would appear to be greatly reduced when, as
in the present data, the type of turn in which the pause occurs is known in
advance of its completion, on account either of turn-type pre-allocation
or of an interrogative segment occurring at the start of the turn in
question (e.g. 'And isn't it a fact . . .', 'Now wasn't it true . . .', etc.). In
other words, if both parties are *prospectively* orienting to an utterance as a
question from the very beginning, the speaker can have greater confidence that the other will not start a next turn at least until enough has
been said for the utterance to be recognisable as a 'possibly completed
question', and before the next speaker has thereby been selected. The use
of pauses to partition utterances in this way, then, may be a device which
can only be used when it is already clear *before* the first pause has
occurred that an utterance will be of a particular type, and hence must be
recognisable as a completed instance of that type *before* a transition to the
next turn becomes a possibility.[15] Moreover, in the data extract cited
above, such an expectation appears to be made particularly clear and
unambiguous by the fact that two devices (i.e. turn-type pre-allocation
and interrogative first segments) are used simultaneously, and this would
seem to be the case much more generally in cross-examination sequences. In so far as pauses within a turn and the slow phasing of an
utterance can be done without interruption by a next speaker, given
advance knowledge that the utterance will have to be recognisable (at
least minimally) as a question, the question-answer format may have
additional advantages in providing for the monitoring of talk by parties
not directly involved in it, over and above the close ordering properties of
the adjacency pair structure mentioned earlier.

The emphasis in the foregoing has been on pauses which occur in the
course of a turn *before* a point when it becomes recognisable as a possibly
completed question. The reason for this is that, once an utterance is
recognisable as such, there may then emerge considerable ambiguity
with respect to whether or not the other party should start the next turn.
Thus it may be noted that the final pause in some of the questions in this
extract are followed by tag questions, as in:

(2)   OU: 45,3A
      C: Now wasn't it true whooah (1.5) Miss Le Brette thatuh (2.5)
           the area where that car st*opped* isuh (2.5) *some* distance from
  →   any house (0.5) isn't that so?
           (2.5)
      W: Yeh

C: Wasuh uh a fact isn't it uh Miss Le Brette that the nearest
      house (0.5) uh abuts theuh (.) Warwick turnpike? (0.7)
→   Is that where the nearest house is?=
W: = I don't understand the question.

And the final pause within these first utterances, it may also be noted, follows the first point at which each could be recognised as a possibly completed question. The tags can thus be heard not just as markers of that completion, but as being oriented to the fact that the answer has not yet started. In other words, while the earlier pauses in the utterance may have been counsel's, by virtue of its incompleteness as a question at those points, the last one (immediately preceeding the tag question) can be heard as being the witness's. When her turn does not start immediately it becomes a possibly noticeable absence, which can be heard to occasion counsel's use of a tag to mark the question's completion and prompt the recipient to start.

This would appear to have several interesting implications which relate to possible ethnographic readings of the activities of counsel and witness which may hinge on the occurrence and sequential location of the final pause and tag question. Thus, the reference just made to the witness's 'failure' to start her turn as a 'possibly noticeable absence' was intended to convey that it may not be regarded as such by all those present. And, depending on whether it is or is not regarded as a noticeable absence, different ethnographic readings seem to follow. If, for example, the pause is heard as the witness's, and the tag as orienting to her 'failure' to start *early* enough, then there may be grounds for thinking that the witness is 'reluctant to answer', 'evasive', etc. But if it appears ambiguous as to whether or not the question is complete, or reasonable to take such lengths of time before answering, the counsel's addition of the tag question may be heard as 'impatience' or 'bullying tactics' on his part. It can be noted, however, that the first of these possible readings (that the witness is 'slow to answer', etc.) depends for its sense on holding that the 'gap minimisation' constraint applies to the organisation of turn transitions in cross examination as well as in conversations, as otherwise there is no basis for seeing the next turn as 'late' in starting. But to see counsel's addition of the tag question after the pause as 'impatience' requires that the applicability of gap minimisation is at least ambiguous, and perhaps even suspended under the local circumstances of cross-examination; otherwise it is not at all clear how the tags could be regarded as manifestations of 'impatience'. Given that such a reading of some of counsel's utterances in the present data does seem to be possible, the question arises as to what it is about the talk that produces enough ambiguity about the gap minimisation constraint for that reading to be a posibility.

As a preliminary answer (which may be worth following up in further research) at least two tentative suggestions can be offered, both of which have to do with some of the earlier remarks about the way in which utterances in cross-examination can be seen as having been designed to be heard by various recipients other than the active parties to the talk. That is, the phasing of counsel's utterances into segments which are partitioned by pauses arguably sets up the possibility that any pause may be followed by yet another segment. But, while that probability may be reduced somewhat once a point is reached at which the utterance is recognisable as a completed question, it is unlikely to have been eliminated altogether. In other words, there is always the possibility of the speaker adding further segments after a *possible* transition relevance place; this may lead to considerable ambiguity with respect to whether or not the witness should start the next turn immediately.[16] And, even where there may remain little doubt that a question has indeed been completed, a second set of considerations may still provide for any delay in starting to be heard as perfectly reasonable. Thus, it was noted earlier that pauses within counsel's utterances may facilitate greater clarity in the selection and design of segments, and a reduction in the chances of repairables and self-repairs occurring before the end of the turn. The suggestion was also made that counsel's utterances can be heard to be recipiently designed for monitoring by parties other than those actively participating in the talk, for whom audibility and understandability may pose different sorts of problems. It seems unlikely, however, that counsel will be the only active party who orients to such recipient design considerations (though of course he may be more experienced at so doing), as the witness will presumably also attend to the requirement to design utterances in such a way that they can be heard by recipients other than counsel. Indeed, they are often explicitly reminded of this at an early stage in examination, as in the following examples:

(3)   CI:1
        W: I swear by Almighty God that the evidence I shall give
                 shall be the truth the whole truth and nothing but the
                 truth.
→   CO: Thank you. Could you just keep your voice up please.

(4)   OU: 46,1A

→ C: Would you please please state your name so the jury can
       hear/
       (0.5)
   W: Linda Lebrette
       (0.5)
→ C: Could you speak up a little bit more/=
   W: =LINDA LEBRETTE

And, at other stages in an examination sequence audibility may sink
to a level which prompts the non-examining counsel to initiate a repair:

(5) OU: 46,1B
     W: There was grass on the side I don – I don't know about
          the middle.
          (0.5)
→ OC: I'm sorry I can't hear it
          (0.5)
     J: She said there was (0.5) gra:ss on the side she doesn't
          know about the middle
          (4.0)
     C: An isn't it a *fa:ct* (0.5) Miss Lebrette . . .

Audibility and clarity for others present, then, must also be oriented to
by witnesses in their design of utterances, and it would be surprising if
they did not use some of the same methods as counsel in achieving such
ends. Thus, just as pauses within utterances can give counsel an
opportunity to design clear segments, so pauses may be similarly used by
witnesses in their turns. If a pause at the start of a witness turn is heard as
being used in such a way, then, the non-start of the utterance would not
be noticeably absent, but be perfectly reasonable. And that being so, it
becomes possible to regard counsel's continuation with a tag question as
'impatient', in that it can be heard to deny the witness's right to take time
to formulate an answer.

   While the witness's use of a pause at the start of a turn may be oriented
to similar organisational constraints as are involved in counsel's use of
them within turns, it is of course a high risk thing to do, given the
alternative possibility of its being heard as 'reluctance to answer',
'evasiveness', etc. In so far as witnesses must presumably be aware of
such possibilities, this raises a further interesting question about their
failure to use devices which are widely used in conversations to mark that
a turn has started even though there may be a delay in producing any

sequentially relevant content. Thus, while things like 'Uh', 'Um', 'Well uh', etc. frequently occur at the start of a turn and with no gap after the previous turn in conversations, they do not occur in the present data, and appear only very rarely in other data from court proceedings not included here. Or, to be more precise, such turn beginning markers are not a common feature of witnesses' turns (their use by counsel will be referred to briefly later). That they are not used by witnesses may also have to do with problems relating to turn pre-allocation and recipient design for various other audiences. Thus, in so far as there is little competition for the next turn (c.f. Chapter 2), part of the basis for the instant delivery of a turn beginning marker is not present, in that there is no necessity to 'claim' the turn. Recipient design considerations, furthermore, may render things like 'uh' and 'uhm' as inappropriate in the light of the audibility and clarity requirements. Indeed, given the volume at which parties have to speak as part of meeting such requirements, there may be a further sense in which 'uh' and 'uhm' might sound situatedly strange or inappropriate. That is, just as they are indistinct and indefinite with respect to the specific contents of an utterance, they may also be indistinctly spoken when they occur in conversations. Indeed, to vocalise 'uh' and 'uhm' loudly and clearly may well be hearable as 'strange', 'odd', 'satirical', etc., and the very concept of a clear 'uh' appears almost to suggest a contradiction in terms. If this is so, then, it may be that their use as turn constructional units may be troublesome in settings like court hearings where the requirements of audibility and clarity have implications for the sound level at which the talk is conducted.

To this point various remarks have suggested that the slow phasing of questions into segments partitioned by pauses may provide for clarity of monitoring by non-active parties to the talk, and at the same time for ambiguity with respect to when the next speaker should begin. In other words, it would seem that certain features of utterances which appear to be designed to resolve (or minimise) problems which may be faced by one set of recipients (i.e. those not currently involved in some present exchange), may simultaneously build up other sorts of problems for the recipient who will have to speak next. In a very general way, then, it may be that a rigorous understanding of the organisation of speech exchange in court hearings will have to pay special attention to the diverse and sometimes conflicting ways in which utterances in such settings have to be designed to be heard by several sets of recipients, few of whom will have rights to speak at any particular point in the proceedings. Thus some of the other observable features of data extract (1) above might be understandable in a general way with reference to such considerations (e.g. items 6 and 7). Also, of course, there are many things occurring in other sequences not included here which would facilitate a more detailed examination of utterances for the ways in which they may be recipiently designed for categories of persons other than witness, counsel, and 'other hearers' (e.g. opposing counsel, jury, judge, and even stenographers or transcriptionists).

IV   PAUSES AFTER ANSWERS AND THE PRODUCTION OF CONTINUITY

The above remarks focused on some possible organisational properties of pauses which occur within and at the end of questions. It should not be concluded from this, however, that all pauses, irrespective of their serial location, will necessarily be similar with respect to the interactional problems they may create or help to resolve. In Chapter 2, for example, it was noted that the automatic reversion of the next turn to counsel following a witness's answer (provided for by turn pre-allocation) gives counsel considerable scope for delaying the start of his turn, a practice which, it was suggested, can prompt various sorts of inferential work about the significance of the answer, the motives of the answerer, etc. But, while the opening of a gap following the witness's turn may have implications such as these, it can also simultaneously give rise to another sort of organisational problem, namely a potential break in continuity, which would seem to be another consequence of the packaging of the talk into sequences of recurrent Q–A adjacency pairs.

One important property of adjacency pairs which has been widely stressed in the literature of conversational analysis is the way they operate to resolve the problems of opening and closing conversations. The character of the closing problem, which is particularly relevant in the present context, has been summarised by Schegloff and Sacks (1974, pp. 237–38) as follows:

It may be noted that whereas these basic features with which we began (especially the feature of speaker change recurrence), and the utterance by utterance operation of the turn-taking machinery as a fundamental generating feature of conversation, deal with a conversation's ongoing orderliness, they make no provision for the closing of conversation. A machinery which includes the transition relevance of possible utterance completion recurrently for any utterance in the conversation *generates an indefinitely extendable string of turns to talk* (our italics).

Then, an initial problem concerning closings may be formulated: *how to organise the simultaneous arrival of the co-conversationalists at a point where one speaker's completion will not occasion another speaker's talk, and that will not be heard as some speaker's silence* (their italics). The last qualification is necessary to differentiate closings from other places in conversation where one speaker's completion is not followed by a possible next speaker's talk, but where, given the continuing relevance of the basic features of the turn-taking machinery, what is heard is not termination but attributable silence, a pause in the last speaker's utterance, etc. It should suggest that simply stopping to talk is not a solution to the closing problem: any first prospective speaker to do so would be hearable as 'being silent' in terms of the turn-taking machinery, rather than as having suspended its relevance.

In conversation, then, there is a problem of recognising some particular utterance as a possible final utterance after which no more need be said, and inspection of the closings of conversations reveals adjacently paired utterances (e.g. Goodbye – goodbye, thanks – you're welcome, etc.) to be widely prevalent occurrences at such points. How they work to locate the completion of the second pair part as the possible completion of the conversation as a whole is summarised by Schegloff and Sacks (ibid. p. 240) thus:

... by providing that transition relevance is to be lifted after the second pair part's occurrence, the occurrence of the second pair part can then reveal an appreciation of and agreement to the intendedness of closing *now* which a first part of a terminal exchange reveals its speaker to propose (their italics).

While Schegloff and Sacks (ibid.) and others (e.g. Davidson, 1978) offer much more detailed analyses of closing sequences, the important general point to note here is the status of second pair parts as possible terminators. For in sequences of recurrent adjacency pairs, such as are found in examination and cross-examination, the completion of any second pair part (i.e. an 'answer' turn) can be a possible termination point as far as at least two levels of organisation are concerned. That is, an answer could turn out to be the last answer of the present examination, or it could mark the termination of talk on some particular topic. Whether it is to be either of these, however, is largely (though not exclusively) in the hands of counsel, and there is an interesting way in which the problem of completing an examination (or a topic within an examination) seems not just to be different from that of conversation, but to be almost the direct opposite of it.

At the level of an examination sequence as a whole, for example, each possible completion point (i.e. answers occurring as second pair parts) is followed by the marker of yet another beginning (i.e. questions occurring as first pair parts). In so far as first parts thus keep on recurring *after* second parts, the status of the second parts as possible terminators (as they might well be in a sequence not otherwise made up so exclusively of adjacency pairs) is arguably massively weakened. In other words, while a conversation might continue indefinitely were first parts of adjacency pairs not introduced to project the suspension of transition relevance following the second part, an extended Q–A sequence is characterised precisely by the *non-suspension* of transition relevance following the second part's completion. In so far as the completion of the 'answer' turns will have been repeatedly followed by yet another question, an expectation that this will continue will have been established such that the recurrence of the Q–A–Q–A etc. chain could go on indefinitely were no specially designed indication of its termination to be introduced. In the data on examination and cross-examination inspected so far, this tends to get done by counsel delivering an utterance which (i) is not recognisable even minimally as a question, (ii) is an explicit announcement that his previous utterance was his last question, (iii) does not select the witness as the next speaker, but (iv) selects the judge, as in:

(6)   OU: 45,3B
      (1.5)
C: That's all the questions I have your honour
      (0.5)
J: Thank you.

The completion of a second part of a Q–A adjacency pair, then, can turn out to be also the completion of the examination sequence as a whole. This recurrently present possibility, furthermore, draws attention to the way in which second parts can be topic termination points too. Thus, each witness's turn that is recognisable as a sequentially projected answer marks a possible termination, which counsel may follow by the introduction of a new topic in his next turn. That this is so arguably sets up an ambiguity with respect to whether or not any next question will indeed involve a topic change, or will continue with the previous one, an ambiguity which may well be increased by the opening up of a long pause after the possible topic termination point. It may therefore be no coincidence that the two longest pauses which occur at such points in data extract (1) (of 4.0 and 11.0 seconds respectively) are both followed by counsel starting his utterance with the word 'and' which was referred to earlier in the list of noticeables as a 'continuation marker'. From the present remarks, the significance of describing them as such will hopefully be clear, as they can be seen to mark that the topic will be continued with during *this* turn, even though the lengthy pause might have given rise to a contrary expectation.

A general point which may be noted as being of potential interest and as a possible focus for further research, then, is the way this feature of topic organisation in an extended Q–A sequence contrasts with that in conversation. Thus, the suggestion here is that in the former sequential environment *continuity* between an answer and the next turn may be in doubt but can be resolved by placing a marker such as 'and' at the start of the subsequent question. In conversations, however, it is *dis-continuity* or *mis-placement* of a topic which is more likely to require this kind of explicit marking at the start of a turn. Prevalent examples of these are prefaces to utterances such as 'By the way...', 'Hey...', 'Look I'm sorry but...', etc., where a speaker can be heard to signal that what is about to be said is likely to appear 'out of place' at that particular point in the talk. As Schegloff and Sacks (1974, p. 258) summarise it:

> Misplacement markers ... display an orientation by their user to the proper sequential-organizational character of a particular place in a conversation, and a recognition that an utterance that is thereby prefaced may not fit, and that recipient should not attempt to use this placement in understanding their occurrence. The display of such orientation and recognition apparently entitles the user to place an item outside its proper place.

But in examination sequences, where answers may be heard as 'possible' terminators (especially if followed by an extended pause) it is a next question which *continues* a topic that may not fit, or be potentially 'out of place' in the sequence. Any such ambiguity can therefore be resolved by starting a question with a continuity marker which signals that what follows during the subsequent course of that turn is to be oriented to as being sequentially *in place*.

In so far as continuation markers are found with great regularity at the start of counsel's turns, another possible line of future research suggests itself, namely their occurrence in turns which may not otherwise appear to be topically linked to the previous one. That is, it is presumably possible to use them as a device to set up an appearance of greater continuity between a question and the previous utterances than might be warranted by a closer inspection of the details of those utterances.

V A NOTE ON OBJECTION SEQUENCES

The occurrence of objections was touched on briefly in Chapter 2, and sequences in which they occur would appear to be of considerable analytic interest. Work on these has only recently begun,[17] so no more will be done here than merely to mention some general points about their potential as a focus for further research, and to note some possible organisational significances that pauses may have in relation to them.

A first general point which is noticeable from an inspection of such sequences is that both objections by counsel and the judge's response to them seldom include any explicit reference to the legal rule of procedure which occasioned them. This is not, it should be stressed, a consequence of a careful selection of extracts with a view to establishing such a claim, but was noticed only after a considerable number of objection sequences had been listened to and transcribed. The frequent absence of any explicit reference to the legal basis for them may be of particular interest given that such sequences represent one of the relatively few places in the course of examination and cross-examination where specifically legal constraints are oriented to by parties to the talk in an explicit and visible way. Thus, any attempt to make the operation of the legal rules of evidence the main focus of analysis could give rise to considerable problems in locating precisely what rules were being invoked at particular points in the proceedings.[18] Indeed, even when discussions of legal technicalities do take place between a counsel and the judge, the details of these too tend to remain obscured to all those present other than the two parties concerned:

(7) OU: 45,3A
C: And (.) what did she do when she came inside?=
OC: = Well I object your honour
J: No you may uh have it
OC: Well may I approach the bench your⌈honour   ⌉
J: ⌊Yes certainly⌋
         ((Inaudible exchange between J and OC for 70.0 seconds))
J: Uhm (1.0) th*e* defence counsel has requested a preliminary
         instruction before the elicitation of more testimony from

this particular witness . . . ((instruction continues for
several minutes))

(8)   OU: 45,3A
C: Now he's older than thirty years old isn't he?=
OC: =Objection your honour=
J: = I'll strike the question
          (.)
OC: May I be heard on this your honour?=
J: = Yes you may be heard on it
          ((Inaudible exchange between J and OC for 120 seconds
          before tape runs out))

In both these examples, then, neither OC's initial objection nor the
judge's over-ruling of it contain any reference to the legal rule to which
their utterances were oriented and, while OC's second attempt to ward
off an answer is more successful, the detailed discussion of legal issues,
which is what presumably then takes place, is conducted at too low a
volume level for anyone else to hear.

A second general point is that objection sequences appear very
unfamiliar when considered in relation to conversation, particularly in
the way that a third party interrupts a two party exchange by initiating a
remedial insertion sequence (c.f. Chapter 2) which selects a fourth party
as next speaker (and arbiter as to the remedy). In so far as they thus look
like a highly specialised kind of other-initiated repair sequence (directed
to the repair of legally defined 'repairables'), further detailed study of
them may eventually provide for a more precise distinction to be made
between the *specifically* legal organisational features of examination, and
those of other extended Q–A sequences in multi-party settings.

A third general point concerns the way in which objections, although
usually designed to prevent an answer being started (and occasionally to
delete one which has already been started or completed[19]), they are also
recipiently designed for the judge. This rather obvious observation may
have interesting organisational implications for assuring the continual
attentiveness of the judge to the proceedings (over and above those
already discussed which appear to make for the attentiveness of everyone
else). Thus, almost any utterance could in principle occasion an objection from opposing counsel to which the judge would have to respond,
which makes it particularly important for him to be ready to speak if he is
not to be exposed as having been 'asleep', 'not concentrating as befits a
judge', etc.

Given that the turn projected for him by an objection is one turn further on from the utterance on which he must give a decision, and that (as will be seen from some of the examples below) there may have been a pause prior to the objection, the judge therefore has to be in a position to recall and offer definite comment on what may (in terms of time) be a rather distant last but one turn. In view of this, it may not be surprising that the judge's responses are sometimes delayed or hesitant:

(9) OU: 46,1A

   C: An (3.0) where di you first see Elaine?

   W: When she come back (1.0) she just come in (1.5) an she was cry:in an she was $\lceil$all (upset)

   OC: $\lfloor$Well I I object your honour

 →   (3.0)

   J: Yes its (.) not responsive to the question (.) where she first saw Elaine sh-she said that (.) she saw her come in and that may stand.

(10) OU: 46,1A

   OC: Well I-I object your honour

 → J: No:h uh th-that (.) that uh last comment must be stricken.

(11) OU: 45,3A

   W: The door was opened by a gentleman (0.5) that identified himself as Orwell's father
         (0.5)

   C: An (.) what happened then
         (0.5)

   W: I asked for the =

   OC: = Objection your honour

 →   (1.0)

 → J: Uh (1.5) uh (4.0) no what e asked will have to be stricken

Occasionally objections occur which appear to expose a possible lapse of attentiveness on the part of the judge.

(12) OU: 47,1B

   C: When you were having *in*tercourse with her the first time (3.5) you d'you recall saying anything to her then? =

   OC: = I object to that question
         (3.0)

→   J: I-I didn' understand the question (1.0)

C: During tha' first *act* of intercourse (1.0) what did you say to Elaine?

OC: Your honour I object to (.) this uh duh it's the question assumes *a* uh *a* fact which is uhh controversy here (0.5)

J: Well (.) she asked what if anything (.) I'll permit it=

OC: =Well she said during the first act of intercourse now this uhhh (1.5) that's *a* uh uh a question uhh when did you last stop beating your wife your honour there's no (1.5)

J: May I have the question (1.0) T*he* uhm (1.0) witness has testified in direct examination to two acts of intercourse you may have the question. (1.0)

W: Could you repeat the question again please?

In this extract, then, the objection is followed by a three second pause, whereupon the judge claims not to have understood the last but one utterance. Counsel's reformulated question is objected to again by OC who now spells out the grounds for his objection. By so doing, he can be heard to orient to the possibility that the judge may also not have understood the basis for his objection either. In rejecting the objection, however, the judge produces an interesting reformulation of the questions objected to ('she asked what if anything') which preserves features of *both* versions of the question. Thus, the 'what' had occurred in counsel's second try at the question and the 'anything' in the first, which suggests that the judge had heard the first one after all, even if he did not understand it. In rejecting the second objection, then, the judge refers to features of C's questions and ignores the grounds OC gave for his objection. OC then trys again by citing the standard text book example of a 'leading question' ('when did you stop beating your wife?'). The judge, however, then refers to an earlier part of the proceedings to show that OC's grounds for objecting are unacceptable in this case. Thus, even if his attentiveness had lapsed momentarily at the point where the objection sequence started, the judge is eventually able to demonstrate that it had nevertheless been continuous throughout earlier sequences, and perhaps more so than that of OC.

This sequence (12) is one of the relatively few in which the basis for an objection and the grounds for its being over-ruled are explicitly referred to in public exchanges between counsel and judge, and what occurs here may be suggestive of a disincentive against such a practice in addition to the fact that objections usually (though not always) have to be done promptly and quickly if some next utterance is to be successfully prevented.[20] Thus, where no such grounds are specified, it is left to the judge to 'see them for himself' as a prelude to sustaining or rejecting the objection. To draw attention to them, however, may be to imply that the judge has not noticed them and hence to call into question his legal competence. And, in so far as the citing of grounds by counsel presses the judge to provide grounds for his rejection, it may subsequently turn out that the judge has noticed things which counsel had not (as in the present case) with the result that it is then counsel's legal competence that is opened up for public scrutiny. A further point which is evident from extract (12) is that different segments of a question may provide different possible grounds for making an objection. In replying to OC's claim that the question assumes a fact which is in controversy, the judge takes it that what OC is orienting to is the assumption that the witness said anything at all. But, he points out, the question was 'what if anything', which leaves open the possibility that nothing was said, and is therefore permissible. OC immediately replies by saying that it was the reference to a 'first' act of intercourse that presupposed the controversial fact, but this too the judge is able to dismiss as an adequate basis for the objection, as the witness has apparently already testified to there having been two such acts. On both accounts, then, the judge is able to display OC's objection as improper and to expose flaws in his legal argument to public view. And that this can occur is presumably one reason why the introduction of grounds for an objection by counsel may be a high risk thing to do. The fact that a question may be 'objectionable' in more than one way, furthermore, could provide a more positive disincentive against being too specific about the basis for some particular objection, for it creates the ever present possibility that a judge may sustain an objection with reference to quite different reasons from those which occasioned it. In other words, the probability of an objection succeeding may be greater when the basis for making it are not made explicit.

It was noted above that objections usually, though not always, occur promptly after the turn to which they relate, and in the examples given so far they occurred either latched to (i.e. no gap and no overlap) or in overlap with the end of the previous turn. Both of these locations are arguably wholly expectable given that objections are designed to prevent a next turn (or delete a prior one), but that they sometimes occur *after* a post-question pause may initially seem somewhat surprising:

(13)   OU: 45,2B
C: How old's Mr (Chaplin)?
        (0.5)
OC: Objection

(14)   OU: 46,1A
C: An (.) d'you know how much she weighs now
        (.)
OC: W-well I w- I would uh uh ⌐object your honour
W: └about a hun

(15)   OU: 46,1A
C: An did you say anything to Elaine that night
        (0.5)
OC: Well I object your honour

In terms of the earlier remarks about the tendency of witnesses not to answer immediately, this possibility of inserting an objection after a post question pause may be more readily understandable. Thus, a first point to note is that there is often a space in which counsel can do an objection later than in overlapping or latched positions. A second is that the opening up of such a gap may on occasions prompt counsel to object. For, as was noted earlier, such gaps may be seen by participants as evidence that the witness is having difficulty in answering some question. Where counsel see a witness for their side of a case in such trouble, therefore, they can 'come to the rescue' with an objection. By so doing, what may until then have been heard as 'unreasonable delay' on the part of the witness can be displayed as having been perhaps not so unreasonable after all, and particularly if the objection is successful. That is, if there is doubt about the legal procedural propriety of the question just asked, then the witness's delay in answering can be shown to have been perfectly proper, and any discrediting inferences that might otherwise have been drawn can be thus mitigated.

Delayed objections of this sort, however, run the risk of not coming soon enough to avert an answer, as happens in the following sequence which is a continuation of extract (13) above:

(16)   OU: 45,2B
C: How old's Mr (Chaplin)?
        (0.5)
OC: Objection

W: I don't know
      (4.5)
J: The answer may stand she doesn't know (13.0)
      Uh (0.5) Miss Le Brette (0.5) when you hear the District
      Attorney object don't make any answer until I tell you
      you've to answer the question or not =
W: = Okay

In this instance, then, the witness's insertion of an answer between the objection and the judge's response occasions a specific instruction from the judge as to the proper turn order operative in such objection sequences.[21]

A suggestion in the foregoing is that pauses after questions may provide an opportunity space within which objections can be made, but it seems probable that this also applies more generally to pauses occurring in other locations (such as those discussed in section 3 above). In other words, the pauses which partition questions into segments (.) may similarly provide opposing counsel with time both to notice potential 'objectionables' and to insert objections. And, in addition to providing the speaker with time in which to design segments with a minimum number of repairables and some turn repairs, they thus also give him the chance to design questions with a view to avoiding or minimising the occurrence of objections. Viewed in these terms, then, the phasing of counsel's questions discussed earlier can be seen to facilitate more than just the possibility of continual monitoring by non-active parties to the talk. For such phasing also appears to work in such a way as to allow for both the insertion of objections by one counsel, *and* the other's (i.e. the currently speaking counsel's) attempts to keep them at bay.

VI CONCLUDING REMARKS ON FURTHER RESEARCH

A common feature of the analytic problems introduced in this section has been that almost all of them are issues which can only be examined with reference to tape-recorded data from court hearings and the kinds of transcripts which can be derived from them. The extent to which it will prove possible to consider such questions in relation to English courts and/or to different kinds of court will therefore depend on the extent to which it becomes possible to obtain access to tape-recorded proceedings.

There is, furthermore, a range of other issues which could be followed up in more detail with access to video-recordings additional to those that can be examined with reference to audio-tapes, some of which were discussed in Chapter 3. Some of these might also enable an expansion of themes focussed on in this section. What unspoken activities take place during pauses within and between turns, for example, and how they are co-ordinated with spoken activities would seem one obvious way in which some of these interests might be developed further. These could be particularly important given that counsel may often be referring to written materials in the course of examining a witness, and many pauses may be accountable with reference to the fact that counsel is looking at his notes.[22] Similarly, witnesses may sometimes delay answering when they see counsel standing up to make an objection, or they may await other unspoken signals as to whether or not they should go ahead and answer a question. It will not, however, be possible to subject issues such as those to detailed analysis without video-recordings of court proceedings.

Nonetheless, we hope that the discussion in this and earlier chapters will have provided a sample of some of the kinds of analytical work that is entailed by adopting the approach introduced in Chapters 1 and 2. At the very least, we hope to have shown that a rigorous understanding of the methodic bases of action and order in courts is unlikely to be arrived at independently or in advance of an adequate understanding of the organisation of verbal interaction. We also hope to have outlined some possible ways in which the analytical approach to the study of naturally occurring conversations developed by Sacks, Schegloff, Jefferson and their associates (and the findings which have resulted from such work) might be extended and applied in the study of another type of speech-exchange system. This is not to claim that our work has proceeded very far in that direction, but it is to suggest that it may have reached a point at which the case for pursuing it further has been established. If this is so, then there would by implication be a strong case for exploring the potentialities of conversational analysis in other settings which, like court hearings, exhibit noticeable organisational disjunctions and continuities when compared with conversations.

Finally, in so far as we have been able to display the logic of doing such work and how to do it, we hope that the book will have provided something of an introduction to one kind of ethnomethodological research for social scientists and others who may previously have had little or no familiarity with it. And if we have thus been able to arouse the curiosity of any such readers to a point where they might now want to look for themselves at the original sources we have attempted to summarise and use in this book, then another of its aims will have been achieved.

7 Postscript: Notes on Practical Implications and Possibilities

I THE CASE FOR CAUTION

A central theme in the emergence of ethnomethodology and conversational analysis has been that sociology has for too long allowed pressing social problems and the search for practical resolutions to them to dictate its subject matter and the terms of reference for its research programme.[1] In this book we have accordingly attempted to remain as analytic in our approach as possible, so that to consider the question of practical implications, even as a brief postscript, may seem somewhat inconsistent with the position taken so far. Yet if it is the case that research of this sort is, as has been proposed, capable of yielding findings about the hitherto unexplicated but systematic ways in which social order is accomplished, it would be rather surprising were it to have no implications whatsoever for practical debates about practical problems and proposed solutions to them. And, notwithstanding the exploratory character of our work, an impatience to have some practical implications spelled out is frequently a feature of responses to it by sociologists, lawyers and others with an interest in socio-legal studies.[2] While not wishing to deny that analyses done within the framework of those presented here have any practical implications or applications, we are reluctant at this stage[3] to do much more than hint at what these might be and how they might differ from the sorts of implications that are more usually expected from sociological research.

Before doing so, however, some preliminary *caveats* are in order. The first is that the most honest statement we could give at present would be that we simply do not know precisely what practical implications this kind of work may eventually be shown to have. And if this seems inadequate, it should perhaps be noted not only that it may be unreasonable to expect too much from an analytic approach which is still at so early a stage of development, but also that conventional sociology's persisting willingness to make ambitious claims on the basis of preliminary research may have been a major factor in limiting its past development and its current credibility as a scientific discipline. Indeed, it could be argued that sociology has still to learn one of alchemy's most important lessons, namely that if practical goals are given the most urgent priority, a systematic knowledge of what may or may not be practically possible may never be evolved. If there is anything in the claim that ethnomethodology and conversational analysis have provided a new starting point for sociology by introducing novel questions about social organisation and an approach to empirical research appropriate to its study, then it would be unwise to risk impeding progress by the premature repeat of one of alchemy's central mistakes. Once a corpus of soundly based studies has begun to accumulate, however, various practical limitations and possibilities entailed by them may become apparent (c.f. the record of chemistry as compared with that of alchemy). As this new approach to the study of social organisation may now be close to such a stage,[4] the time for cautious reflection on such questions may also be approaching.

When practical implications of sociological research are considered, it is usual to think in terms of 'recommendations' or 'proposals', whether these be for small changes in some present organisational arrangements or for the total transformation of society as a whole. It may, however, be more reasonable to focus instead on what practical limitations and possibilities might be entailed by research. Thus, 'recommendations' imply prescriptive suggestions as to how, for example, something that is currently claimed to be 'wrong' with courts might be improved or eliminated. But to embark on such a venture would be to retain a faith in sociology's continuingly unrealised (and unrealisable) dream of being able to decide moral and political questions on the basis of its research. Given that research in the natural sciences has done little or nothing towards the solution of such problems, however, great caution would seem to be called for in placing such demands on the social sciences. Indeed, it may be more useful to consider what lessons might be learned from the manifestly more successful natural sciences about the connection between their studies and the scope for organising the natural world that flows from them. And one thing which seems fairly clear about that relationship is that the state of systematic knowledge about natural phenomena current at any one time provides for the specification of practical limitations on what it may or may not be *possible* to do with them (e.g. iron cannot be transformed to gold, but it can be turned into steel). Such knowledge cannot, however, provide for specifications of what is or is not morally desirable.

When considering the practical implications of different approaches to social research, then, the most challenging question may be that of how far the knowledge of social organisation being accumulated points to practical limitations on what it may or may not be possible to do in the social world. For if such limitations could indeed be specified on the basis of a particular type of research, then it would arguably greatly strengthen any claims to the effect that its results are more rigorous and systematic than those of competing approaches. Moreover, to be able to identify even a few constraints on what is practically possible with reference to an empirically grounded knowledge of social organisation might eventually involve the addition of a genuinely new dimension to moral and political decision-making. In other words, rather than merely offering yet further additions to the stock of competing views about what ought or ought not to be done about this or that, researchers might be in a position to outline a set of minimal conditions which would have to be met by *any* proposed social reform. Viewed in these terms, the record of conventional sociology is by no means as impressive as is sometimes implied by demands that new approaches such as ethnomethodology should justify themselves with reference to their 'usefulness'.[5] For the sorts of recommendations and proposals usually made on the basis of sociological research tend to be no more than variations on existing ones already on the political agenda, which can be formulated easily enough by persons untrained in professional sociology. And, like these other proposals, sociologically derived recommendations are often unashamedly utopian, and unconstrained by any regard for the possibility that an adequate knowledge of the nature of social organisation might place practical limits on dreams of an ideal world.

A consideration of the extent to which research in ethnomethodology and conversational analysis may be suggestive of such practical constraints on proposals about alternative forms of social organisation could therefore become an important test of its claims to be an improvement on other ways of doing sociology. Some hints in this direction have already been implicit in some of the earlier analytic chapters, and the following section extends a theme which looks as though it might have the kind of practical implications just outlined. It should be stressed again, however, that the discussion is speculative rather than analytic, and is offered as a tentative example of one kind of practical implication that might be entailed by certain aspects of the work reported earlier.[6]

II SOME POSSIBLE CONSTRAINTS ON THE ORGANISATION OF TALK IN COURTS AND OTHER MULTI-PARTY SETTINGS

At various points in the book it has been noted that the turn-taking organisation for conversation requires modifications to be introduced if all parties to a multi-party setting are to be able to monitor a single sequence of utterance turns. This apparently obvious observation would appear to have quite far-reaching consequences for social organisation and for recommendations about change (and no change) which fail to take them into account. In order to illustrate the character of that generality it may be useful to show its relevance in understanding a setting other than a court, namely classrooms. Thus, while classrooms clearly exhibit differences from courts in the way that the turn-taking system is organised,[7] one organisational problem which they share is how to achieve and sustain the minimal conditions for everyone to be able to monitor one speaker speaking at a time in the face of the probability that the turn-taking system for conversations, if left unmodified, would provide for more than one conversation to take place at the same time (c.f. Chapter 3 above). Anyone who has been anywhere near a classroom cannot fail to have noticed that teachers spend a great deal of their time telling children to be quiet, stay in their seats, face the front, etc. And one thing that observers (both lay and professional) can do in response to such 'noticeables' is to see them as 'authoritarian' or 'oppressive' actions on the part of the teacher. These descriptions can then be put to work in the production of some more generalised story about the significances of such activities (e.g. they may be used to categorise teachers as 'agents of social control' working on behalf of the 'ruling class', in the interests of the political-economic *status-quo*, etc.). Similarly, they can be used to show how unpleasant an experience for children the educational process can be and, on the basis of these various purportedly 'objective' descriptions of the 'realities' of the classroom that can be constructed, recommendations aimed at the elimination of such 'unpleasant' features may be formulated.[8]

A problem in implementing proposals, however, is that the minimal conditions for achieving and sustaining shared attentiveness could very easily be put at risk; unless, of course, alternative procedures (which may or may not be available) were introduced to do the same thing. This, then, would appear to point to a fundamental limitation on the range of alternative organisational arrangements that would be practically possible if single speakers (whether teachers or pupils) are to have any chance at all of their utterances being heard and understood by everyone else who is present. And if this is so, the agenda for debates about how to eliminate (or minimise) what appear to be unpleasant features of classroom interaction would have to be confined to a list of those alternative possibilities which would not also have the effect of substantially reducing the opportunities for collective monitoring. Or rather this would be the case so long as ways of teaching that did not require relatively large groups to hear one speaker speaking at a time were unavailable. For that option to be a possibility however, facilities which would allow for one-to-one or a very small group teaching situation would presumably have to be provided. And under those circumstances the (unmodified) turn-taking system for conversations might become workable, and hence the elimination or drastic reduction of the 'non-conversational' (and possibly 'unpleasant') features of classroom interaction could become more of a practical possibility.

These kinds of general argument would seem also to be applicable to court-rooms and the vast majority of (and perhaps all) other multi-party settings where the monitorability of one speaker speaking at a time is a minimal requirement.[9] Clearly there will be considerable organisational variation between different settings according to, among other things, the number of people present, the number having rights to speak, the practical purposes of the gathering, etc., but the general point would seem to hold, namely that without some modifications to the turn-taking system for conversation, the minimal conditions for the collective monitoring of a single speaker turn or recurrent turns would be missing. If this is the case, critics and would-be reformers of court procedures must be alert to the possibility that their complaints may be occasioned by the ways in which structurally important modifications can be read, and that their proposals for change may thus be directed to the impossible goal of insisting that the talk should be organised in a manner that is totally insensitive to the contextual features of the setting.

As this may seem in one sense to imply a recommendation for no change, or to support a conservative view of the virtues of the present organisational arrangements, it should perhaps be stressed that it by no means closes down all possible options for 'humanising' court proceedings. That is, future research into the organisation of interaction may eventually yield findings which would be relevant to at least two dimensions which would appear to be crucial to any consideration of changes which would be practically (rather than 'ideally') possible. Thus, a close inspection of court-room interaction may be able to reveal *first* how it operates to meet certain general organisational requirements, and *second* how it is that observers (and, by implication, participants too) may interpret some of the particular methods used to that end as 'intimidating', 'oppressive', 'bewildering', etc. And in so doing it may of course turn out that there are also limits to the extent to which such 'unpleasant' features can in practice be eliminated, so that reforms might be more sensibly directed towards no more than their reduction or minimisation.

An example which may illustrate and support this point may be taken from the earlier discussion of the way in which features of counsel's utterances which may have organisational advantages in providing for non-active parties to monitor the proceedings may also set up difficulties for witnesses in answering, a type of problem which might be viewed as something to be eliminated. The problem of finding a practical way to do such a thing, however, would seem to be particularly acute so long as the *public* character of the hearing was to be retained, so that a first (and perhaps politically the most important) decision to be made might have to be on whether or not private small group hearings would be acceptable.

Considerations such as this, furthermore, would seem to be highly relevant to questions concerning the ecological arrangements found in courts. That participants may be required to sit or stand in certain places (e.g. judges on raised benches, defendents in 'the dock', witnesses in 'witness boxes' etc.), for example, has been a common focus for complaint by critics of many currently operative practices. But here again, the requirements of public audibility and understandability may impose important limits on how far all such features could ever be eliminated. Being able both to see and categorise who is currently talking would seem to be crucial if monitoring by all those present is to be a practical possibility. Things like locating different categories of persons in special places from which they face particular directions, the requirement that some speakers stand while talking, or when starting a turn, etc. may be recognisably describable as 'oppressive', 'unpleasant', or whatever, but they are also arguably very efficient methods for achieving and sustaining the conditions for continuous collective monitoring. Indeed, even things like the poor acoustics of some court-rooms and the substantial distance between speakers (i.e. substantial compared with that typically found in conversational settings), which have also featured as sources of critical complaint, may have similar organisational advantages. For they may serve as an added incentive both to speakers to design their utterances in such a way as to maximise audibility, and the audience to concentrate on the business of hearing.

While such ecological arrangements may be more or less efficient in providing for such minimal organisational requirements to be met, this certainly does not imply that any particular ones currently in use are in any sense the only or 'best' available ones. Conservative claims or recommendations to that effect are therefore just as likely to be based on a lack of awareness of practical possibilities as those of would-be reformers, and may involve an insistence on the retention of features which may have little or no importance for the organisation of interaction in courts. A possible example in this context is the wearing of situatedly specific clothes (e.g. gowns, wigs, etc.), an activity which appears to be hotly debated in at least some English legal circles. As has already been noted, there are good organisational reasons for being able to identify what category of person is speaking at any particular point in time, and 'uniforms' may be one of the ways in which legal personnel are recognised. But the provision for such identification in courts is arguably massively 'over-built' or, in other words, there may be several features working simultaneously to that end, of which special attire is only one. Others include the differentiated ecological locations in which particular categories of participants are positioned, the kinds of co-ordinated spoken and unspoken activities discussed earlier, and the types of turn done by different speakers. And there may of course be a range of other ways in which the necessary identificational work could be provided for, but which are not currently found in courts of law. Those who invoke other sorts of accounts (e.g. about the symbolic virtues of traditional clothing, etc.) in an attempt to defend the *status quo* should be alerted to the ways in which present procedures may be 'overbuilt', and that this very feature may be important in prompting critical interpretations of certain aspects of court-room organisation.[10] In short, conservative stories about the virtues of current practice may well be just as insensitive to the methodic bases of social organisation as may be the case with radical stories about the undesirability of present arrangements.

Some of these issues may be clarified with reference to the ecological arrangements to be found in Swedish courts, where reforms explicitly designed to 'humanise' the proceedings have been implemented. Prior to visiting them, English visitors are likely to be informed by their hosts that in Sweden attempts have been made to make courts more informal and less intimidating for participants. In the words of one lawyer, 'We've tried to make them as much like seminars as possible'.[11] And on attending hearings, it is noticeable that the judges do not sit on a raised platform, defendants are not confined to a dock but sit beside their advocates at a table, there is no requirement to stand while speaking, and lawyers do not wear wigs or gowns. But, as can be seen from the sketch plan below (Figure 1), the judges sit behind a desk facing outwards, prosecution and defence sit facing each other across a distance of five or six metres behind tables which are set apart from the public.

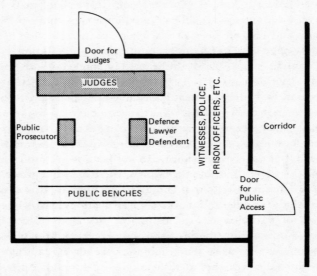

FIGURE 1: *Sketch plan of ecological arrangements in a Swedish Court*

The arrangements thus provide for the active parties to see and monitor each other and for their actions to be seen and monitored by everyone else. But enough 'noticeables' remain for potential use by critical observers in constructing ironic descriptions of the arrangements. They might well suggest, for example, that the distance between prosecution and defence is too great (on the grounds that defendants and witnesses may not be 'used to' speaking across such a space), a complaint which could possibly be met by placing the opposing parties around a single small table in the middle. But the shorter distance would then have implications for the volume of speakers' utterances, in that speaking loud at such close quarters might be just as difficult for participants, and could give rise to a further range of critical inferences (e.g. a person who 'shouts' at another at close range is very likely to be seen as 'angry', 'rude', 'hostile', etc., unless the hearer is known to be hard of hearing). Speaking in a manner which would be sensitive to that shorter distance between active participants, therefore, would simultaneously be totally insensitive to the minimal listening requirements of everyone else in the court-room. Yet further solutions may therefore be considered, such as crowding everyone closer together, arranging the seating around a single large table (as in Scottish Juvenile Panels), or exploiting the technological possibilities provided by microphones, earphones, amplification, etc., bearing in mind of course that each of these may also give rise to various other inferential possibilities as to their 'unfamiliar' or 'unpleasant' character.

The extent to which the problems of organising talk in multi-party settings are very general ones may be further illustrated with reference to two other examples, one of a particularly large gathering, and one from a society which is economically, culturally and ideologically very different from Britain and Sweden. The first of these is the Westminster Parliament, the proceedings of which have just begun to be recorded and broadcast (sound only) at the time of writing. A noticeable feature of these which has aroused comments from listeners, and which was precisely one of the reasons for the long-standing reluctance of many MPs to agree to the broadcasting of parliament, is the apparent rowdiness of the proceedings. Thus speeches are often punctuated by heckling, boos and cheers, utterances which some observers are quick to interpret as evidence of 'rudeness', 'animal-like behaviour', 'setting a bad example to the young', etc. Yet in terms of the present discussion, it is fairly clear that considerable organisational problems will inevitably be involved in a setting where single speaker turns have to be distributed between up to six hundred or more co-present parties. Given that the chances of all but a few of them getting a turn to talk in the course of a sitting will be very remote, it is arguably not surprising that alternative ways of expressing agreement and disagreement with a current speaker are used. That they are permitted, furthermore, may be an important way of providing for the continuing attentiveness of members to the proceedings. Thus, were they prevented from cheering and booing, their incentives to monitor speeches might be greatly reduced, for those who will not get a turn to talk are already cut off from the opportunity of displaying their understanding of previous utterances in the design of a turn of their own (which is how co-conversationalists display their understanding of each other's utterances). Any such display of understanding (whether it involved agreement or disagreement) would therefore have to be deferred perhaps indefinitely and, in the face of such a prospect, a readily available response is to opt out from continual monitoring altogether. The tradition of heckling, booing and cheering, however, arguably works against, or at least reduces, such a possibility by providing MPs with scope for responding immediately to any current turn, a condition of which is that they will have to monitor the talk closely enough to be able to identify 'cheerable' or 'booable' items. In other words, a danger in any proposed attempt to eliminate what can be read as 'rowdy' or 'disreputable' conduct on the part of members of parliament might also eliminate what may be an important way of accomplishing and sustaining shared attentiveness to the proceedings.[12]

A somewhat different example is provided by village meetings in Tanzania.[13] While the official rationale for these is grounded in a socialist-collectivist ideology, it is noticeable that they exhibit some of the same features which have prompted the kind of ironic or critical accounts of Western court proceedings discussed in Chapter 1. Thus, a chairman is set apart from and faces the other co-present parties, who have to raise their hands if they wish to have a turn to talk. When selected to do so by the chairman, they stand up to speak and sit down again at the end of their turn. These 'noticeable' activities could no doubt provide sociologists or other observers with all they require to produce critical stories about the 'intimidating', 'bewildering' or 'oppressive' character of such procedures. Indeed, the scope for irony is probably even greater than it is when such things are noticed in Western societies where a 'fit' can be claimed to exist between these manifestations of 'oppression' at the 'micro-level' of organisation and the more 'generalised oppression' associated with the 'macro-structure' of such societies by many sociologists. The occurrence of 'oppressive' activities at the micro-level in Tanzania, however, could be contrasted with the collectivist-socialist claims of President Julius Nyerere, and displayed as a 'basic contradiction' in Tanzanian social organisation, or as proof of his willingness merely to 'pay lip service' to such ideals. And no doubt, similar stories could be built up from such observations in any other society, where it be China (ancient or contemporary), Nazi Germany or the Soviet Union. That is, such stories can be plausibly told so long as observers pay no attention to the organisational problems which arise in *any* setting where a minimal practical requirement is that more than a few people should be able to hear and/or participate in a single sequence of talk. With an awareness of this requirement, however, turn-mediation by a chairman can be seen as something other than the oppression of would-be speakers. Similarly, in so far as standing up to speak can contribute to the identification of a speaker, which in turn is important to understanding of his talk, this too would appear to resolve a basic problem of organisation, irrespective of whether or not it may also be describable as oppressive, unpleasant, etc.

So far, the main emphasis in this section has been on how various organisational arrangements which differ from those operative for conversations may be necessary to facilitate the production of talk that can be monitored by all parties to a multi-party setting. But, while they may be more or less efficient in providing conditions for continuous shared attentiveness, these modifications to conversational organisation are also noticeable and accountable as such, and are thus simultaneously open to interpretive assessment by participants and observers. Other aspects of court-room interaction share these dual features, and a brief consideration of one further example may serve to illustrate the inextricable connectedness between them.

A focus in earlier chapters was on how the actions of participants in court proceedings are conducted within the framework of extended sequences of turns that are minimally recognisable as 'questions' and 'answers'. And such sequences would in general seem to be extremely efficient for doing certain sorts of activities, which include controlling what topics get to be talked about, eliciting information, checking understanding, comparing competing versions of an event or set of events, assessing the consistency of a particular version, gauging 'accuracy', 'truthfulness', etc. Given that it is difficult to imagine how the law could operate without some methods for accomplishing such tasks, it is hardly surprising that question-answer sequences are massively prevalent in the work not just of courts, but of the legal process more generally.[14] Their efficiency in providing for such ends to be achieved would appear to derive from the close-ordering properties of adjacency pairs, and the constraints thereby exerted on the type of turn to be done following a first pair part. For, as was elaborated in more detail in earlier chapters, the occurrence of an absent, delayed or dispreferred second part is not merely noticeable, but that very noticeability provides a basis for inferences to be made about the motives and moral character of the speaker who failed to do a projected second turn. Were this not a recurrently present possibility, it is not clear either that there would be any constraints on speakers to answer questions, return greetings, respond to accusations, etc., or how question-answer sequences could work at all efficiently in doing the kinds of things referred to above.

An obvious implication of this would seem to be that it would be impossible to eliminate the scope for making moral inferences (either positive or negative) about speakers that is a built-in feature of question-answer sequences without also doing away with such sequences themselves. Furthermore, in the unlikely event of an attempt to implement this proposal, the morally implicative character of *all* communicative activity would assure the survival of plenty of scope for deriving moral inferences from how people talk and what they say. And it would also raise the more particular practical question as to what alternative organisational arrangements would be capable of facilitating the sorts of interactional tasks for which question-answer sequences are so effective and so widely used.

III CONCLUDING REMARKS

This chapter began with the suggestion that, rather than being viewed in terms of specific policy proposals, the practical implications of social scientific research might be more fruitfully considered with reference to the extent to which its findings point to limits and possibilities of social organisation. An attempt was then made to show how the research reported earlier is suggestive of ways in which certain features of court-room interaction that may have organisational advantages in facilitating the accomplishment of a court's work simultaneously provide a basis for moral assessments to be made about particular speakers and about the character of hearings more generally. Various devices which work to enable all those present to monitor the proceedings can be identified as modifications to or departures from conversational organisation and, as such, they may be regarded by some participants as strange, bewildering, oppressive, etc. Similarly, the fact that the truthfulness, reliability and responsibility of speakers will be decided on the basis of an analysis (by others present) of how questions are answered is something to which witnesses and defendants continually have to attend. Given that observers are also able to identify such pressures, and may deem them to be 'unpleasant', 'undesirable', etc., their possible reduction or elimination may become a central focus for discussions of procedural change.

One implication that our research would seem to have, however, is that arguments about the scope for change and no change are likely to be exaggerated or unrealistic so long as certain features of social organisation remain unexplicated and unconsidered. Thus, conservative claims about the virtues of present arrangements tend to underestimate the range of alternative possibilities that may exist for achieving similar practical ends, and hence to idealise the currently operative constraints. Conversely, radical critiques would appear to underestimate the extent to which some minimal constraints may be essential, and to idealise alternatives which may or may not be practically possible. And both positions arguably share common ground in a failure to appreciate the inextricable ways in which the organisation of communicative activity and the making of moral assessments are inter-connected. This is not, it should be noted, to suggest that an improved understanding of that inter-dependence could ever lead to any definitive resolution of such debates, or prevent protagonists from adhering to 'extreme' views about the virtues and vices of court procedures. But such a knowledge of social organisation might at least alert opposing sides to a range of problems with which, sooner or later, they may have to come to terms. Some of these have already been touched on at various points in the book and a few concluding remarks will suffice, it is hoped, to indicate the sorts of general issues that seem to be involved.

In Chapter 1 it was noted that the law provides practical ways of achieving what is impossible in principle. That is, it has various methods for deciding between truth and falsehood, fact and fiction, vice and virtue, guilt and innocence, etc., notwithstanding the fact that such matters have remained obstinately resistant to the analytic efforts of philosophers and others who have tried to find a definitive 'principled' way of deciding between them. But that no such definitive solution is likely to be forthcoming is, of course, unsurprising if it is accepted that a crucial feature of any utterance in any setting is that it provides a possible basis for a range of moral inferences to be made about the speaker by those who hear it. And this feature of talk is a crucial resource without which the law would be unable in practice to reach practical decisions about the truthfulness of testimony, the blameworthiness or otherwise of particular persons, etc. At the same time, various procedural rules are designed to restrict the sorts of utterances which can be used in arriving at such decisions (e.g. responses to some leading questions, hearsay evidence, details about a person's past criminal convictions, etc.), and that this is so may be held to be a virtue of some current set of procedures. Yet in addition to the few types of utterances affected by these rules, there is an immense range of other features of the talk that takes place in court hearings which is left wide open to interpretation by participants. As was suggested in Chapter 6, even an occurrence like a pause between turns, which may on the face of it appear unimportant, can readily give rise to inferences about the 'evasiveness' of a witness, and subsequent assessments of the relative truthfulness of the testimony as a whole. And the probability of such inferences being detrimental to the moral credibility of a speaker may be no less than is the case with other occurrences (such as references to a criminal record) that may be prohibited by a procedural rule.

A central dilemma facing staunch defenders of existing court procedures, then, is that any claims they may be tempted to make about
having found near-perfect or even the best possible methods for resolving
the ('in principle') insoluble problems referred to above are bound to be
exaggerations. It is inevitable that any set of procedures will be massively selective with respect to the features of verbal interaction that are
singled out for special control, and the basis for including some and
excluding others may well be obscure. Why, for example, participants
are permitted to make what they will out of the occurrence, location and
duration of pauses, but are not supposed to have access to (let alone
make anything of) 'hearsay' may not be altogether clear. What is more
certain, however, is that the retention of considerable scope for making
moral inferences about what is said and how it is said during the course
of a hearing will be essential if participants are to be able in practice to
reach conclusions about truthfulness, blameworthiness, etc.

To the extent that courts must thus allow a great deal of scope for the
exercise of members' common sense methods of practical reasoning,
there is an Achilles heel to claims about the ultimate purity and fairness
of existing legal procedures and their success in transcending or resolving 'problems' associated with ordinary discourse. For critics will always
be able to expose the limitations of such assertions by drawing attention
to the scope for inferential work that is unrestrained by the legal
procedures, to the ways in which the constraints do not do what they are
claimed to do, or other 'unpleasant' consequences they may appear to
have. In so doing, however, critics tend to ignore the way in which the
potential for making moral inferences is a built-in feature of all communicative activity (including their own observational work), and hence
are likely to over-estimate the extent to which that potential can be
controlled in practice. By attacking the alleged virtues of existing
procedures on the grounds that what happens in practice fails to
correspond with the conservative's 'rhetoric of justice', critics may fall
into the same trap of proposing that some alternative, but equally
idealised, correspondence between some other rhetoric and proposed
methods of implementation is practically attainable. In other words, if
critics are correct in pointing out that conservative defences of current
procedures involve exaggerated claims about the extent to which certain
principles are actually put into practice, then they will presumably be
just as mistaken to invoke a contrasting set of principles together with the
proposal that they should be put into practice instead. For this would be
to pretend that methods for implementing principles in other than a 'for
practical purposes' *ad hoc* manner were also available, and hence that the

alternative procedures would be immune from similar critical comments about the presence of inconsistencies between the principles and the way they work in practice.

In short, a central problem in assessing existing procedures (whether critically or supportively) with reference to the estimated size of the 'gap' between a version of what they are supposed to achieve in principle and how they apparently work in practice is simply that the gap could never be closed. And this feature of practical reasoning is something with which a systematic knowledge of social organisation must presumably come to terms if it is to be able to elucidate the ways in which moral inferences are produced and managed in the real world, and the limitations on the scope for controlling such things that may be entailed.

In so far as any feature of any talk may provide a basis for making moral inferences about speakers, at least four related and troublesome questions appear to be at the heart of practical debates about procedural design and reform. The first concerns what features of talk are to be selected from the infinite range of possibilities for special control, which will depend on some assessment of the differential moral implicativeness of different features, and their potential for facilitating the practical work at hand. A second question is that of what devices could be introduced which might in practice come close to exerting the type of controls required. And a third question then would concern the further scope for making moral inferences that would be introduced by the new controls themselves. Finally, some assessment may be required as to the relative desirability of these possible effects of the new controls and those which they were designed to eliminate. In other words, it may turn out that the revised procedures generate more or worse problems than the ones which prompted their initiation in the first place. To have too many controls, or controls of a particular type, might make it impossible for proceedings to proceed at all. And they may also of course be seen as intimidating, bewildering or oppressive to some participants so that, if the elimination or minimisation of such possible effects is also given high priority, reformers may be faced with a grave practical dilemma. Thus, the wholesale elimination of procedural rules might make judicial proceedings more like conversations, and hence more interactionally 'comfortable' for participants, but the cost would be the elimination of other procedures which could in the longer term make life for some a good deal more 'uncomfortable'. As was suggested earlier, to close the court-room doors to the public might be a necessary condition for being able to do without certain ecological arrangements, slowly phased questions, etc. The gains in interactional 'comfort' possibly entailed by this, however, might be deemed less important than the considerable losses that could so easily follow once the doors were closed. And this is not simply a veiled reference to the scope for physical torture that would be made possible, though clearly this would be an important consideration. For in conversational settings there is immense scope for getting people to say things on the basis of which moral inferences can be derived, even without having to resort to clubs or electric shocks. It is, for example, well enough known that putting a person at his ease can be an extremely effective prelude to extracting a confession. Viewed in these terms, then, decisions about how far reforms should be directed towards easing the 'interactional comfort' of participants may have to pay very serious attention to the possible consequences of other interactional arrangements, which may at first sight seem preferable.

Finally, it should be stressed that conclusions as to what arrangements would be preferable or desirable will always be moral and practical ones, and will never be simply decided by research either within the framework adopted in the present book, or by any other. It does seem however, that approaches to the study of social organisation which view the organisation of communicative activity and moral implicitiveness as separable, rather than inextricably interdependent, are likely to lead to recommendations which tacitly assume that communicative arrangements free from all potential for moral inferences are a realistic and viable possibility. That the elimination of one set of problems will give rise to other different ones may not be news to inhabitants of the real world in which practical decisions are made, but it may be news for researchers who believe that the moral order can be understood and manipulated independently of a systematic understanding of the organisation of communicative activity.

Notes

CHAPTER 1

1. One reason for this is that, while there appears to be a growing interest in ethnomethodology within sociology and related disciplines, much of the debate has been conducted at a highly abstract and programmatic level. Critiques of such work have tended to focus mainly on 'theoretical' and 'epistemological' questions and to pay little or no detailed attention to empirical developments, and particularly those associated with the study of naturally occurring talk (a notable recent exception to this is Phillips, 1978). Ethnomethodology is also one of the few fields in contemporary sociology which has not spawned a plethora of introductory text books, although several useful edited collections have been published in recent years (e.g. Douglas, 1971; Sudnow, 1972; Turner, 1974; Schenkein, 1978; Psathas, 1979; *Sociology*, 1978). For the most part, however, these contain research papers, and the absence of much in the way of an explicitly introductory text can make it difficult for newcomers to the work to learn about the theoretical and analytic concerns which direct it. As our own analyses have been conducted within a framework which may still be more or less unfamiliar to many readers, it seemed essential to provide a relatively extended introduction to ethnomethodology and conversational analysis.
2. An exception to this is the paper by Frake, 1972.
3. The suggestion here is that ordinary language philosophy and Hart's version of jurisprudence may have argued themselves into a position where the next logical step would be to engage in systematic empirical research into how language is used. Such a step, however, would have involved them in a programme of work very different from traditional philosophical scholarship, and for which they may have felt more or less ill-equipped. In any event, there is an important sense in which the currently growing interest of social scientists in the study of naturally occurring talk can be seen as an empirical sequel to the philosophy of Wittgenstein, Austin and Hart.
4. On the relationship between the notion of 'competent membership' and 'mastery of natural language', Garfinkel and Sacks (1970: 342) note the following:

> We do not use the term ('member') to refer to a person. It refers instead to mastery of natural language, which we understand in the following way. We offer the observation that persons, because of the fact that they are heard to be speaking a natural language, *somehow* are heard to be engaged in

the objective production and objective display of commonsense knowledge of everyday activities as observable and reportable phenomena. We ask what it is about natural language that permits speakers and auditors to hear, and in other ways witness, the objective production and objective display of commonsense knowledge, and of practical circumstances, practical actions, and practical sociological reasoning as well. What is it about natural language that makes these phenomena observable-reportable, that is *accountable* phenomena? For speakers and auditors the practices of natural language somehow exhibit these phenomena in the particulars of speaking and, *that* phenomena are exhibited is thereby itself made exhibitable in further description, remark, questions, and in other ways for the telling.

5. The ways in which mastery of natural language has provided both the *topics* and analytic *resource* for sociological research has been a major theme in the emergence of ethnomethodology. See especially Garfinkel and Sacks, 1970, and Zimmerman and Pollner, 1971.

6. It should be stressed that these remarks are included for heurisic purposes only. In particular, it is not intended to suggest that this *really* is '*the* actual' origin of law (let alone that such origins could indeed be definitively located), even though this particular version may be just as plausible as most other competing claims. It must also be emphasised that, for reasons to be clarified later, the use at this point of terms like 'ordinary ways of talking' is not meant to imply that there is a clear and specifiable 'objective' difference between 'ordinary' and 'other' (e.g. 'legal') ways of talking, nor that it is sensible to treat all contexts which might be described as 'ordinary' as belonging to some objective homogenous type of setting. But, while such distinctions may not be verifiable in any absolute or decontextualised manner, the point to be noted is that members can and do make use of them for particular practical purposes (e.g. designing, recognising, evaluating, etc., 'legal' procedures).

7. The preference here for saying 'recognis*able*', rather than some phrase which might imply the existence of some sort of binding factual consensus (such as, for example, 'are recognised') is quite deliberate, as is the addition of 'for practical purposes'. That is, the claim is neither that such decisions are 'really' or 'universally' recognised as definite, final and legitimate in some objective way that is independent of the contexts in which such recognitional work gets done, nor that members must necessarily agree on the moral desirability of the particular procedures used and the decisions thereby reached. Rather it is that some methods and procedures *can be* recognised by members as usable for arriving at decisions which are definite and final for all practical purposes and until further notice.

8. Anyone can write in his own words a last will and testament which may be legally acceptable but, as a practising solicitor put it to one of the authors (JMA), 'the great thing about writing them in legal jargon is that every word has been tested in a court of law'. That may, of course, be no guarantee that past usages will never be overturned by a subsequent court decision, but the point is that their use will provide for a lower probability of dispute than is the case with words which may or may not have been so tested.

9. That is, a central principle of ethnomethodology is that there is no escape for sociologists from a reliance on their everyday members' competences, but that

a long-standing mistake has been to leave that reliance largely *unexplicated*. The challenge facing social scientific researchers, then, is to find a way of doing analysis which comes to terms with the inevitability of that reliance.

10. On the systematic ways in which descriptions and categorisations get to be selected and recognised as 'possibly correct' in specific contexts, see especially Sacks, 1972a, 1972b and Schegloff 1972a.

11. For example, while the sociological theories of Durkheim and Marx are typically contrasted as opposites, there is agreement in the writings of both that ordinary members' descriptions and explanations of the social world are inadequate. Thus, Durkheim's (1897) classic study of suicide begins with a rejection of everyday conceptions of suicide and attempts to substitute a 'scientific' definition. And the Marxist account of why proletarian revolutions do not always occur, even though the material conditions of production may render them inevitable, hinges on the notion of 'false consciousness', which requires the assertion that the non-revolutionary proletarian is operating with an 'incorrect' description of social reality. That 'scientific' analysis can come up with 'correct', or 'more adequate', descriptions, then, is a common assumption of both Durkheimian and Marxist sociology, though their respective 'correct' descriptions are, of course, very different.

12. What is being suggested here is that, by the time an understanding of ethnomethodology began to develop in Europe, several styles of work had emerged. Thus, in contrast with those who had been involved in the work from the start, mostly in Southern California, those who came to it from a distance encountered a range of approaches to ethnomethodological studies, between which comparisons could be made. This was reflected by the two sociology departments which were the first main British centres of ethnomethodological interest in the early 1970s. At one (Goldsmith's College, London) the influence of Cicourel, and subsequently Blum and McHugh seems to have been paramount, while at the other (Manchester University) the major focus was on the work of Garfinkel and Sacks.

13. Also, of course, they have important implications for all other sociological methodologies. The main focus here is on ethnography (or participant observation) because it has been employed by ethnomethodological researchers, as well as by sociologists and social anthropologists more generally.

14. The way in which having been to some particular place provides speakers with a warrent for speaking authoritatively about it has been touched on by Schegloff, 1972a, pp86–87).

15. In so far as the methodic procedures used to organise and make sense of our everyday activities must presumably be general enough to enable us to cope with anything which we encounter in any setting, the danger in selecting 'exotic' features for report is that what may be of *least* organisational importance will be singled out for attention. At the risk of implying that such estimates could ever be made, one can reflect on what the implications for sociology would be if ninety-five per cent of what is constitutive of any social setting were general to all settings, with only five per cent being peculiar to the setting being studied. In that case, we would have a sociology which could only report on a large number of different 'five per cents', and on little or nothing of the 'ninety-five per cent' that is constitutive of social order wherever it is found. In other words, that which Harold Garfinkel has referred to as 'the

whatness' of social organisation would be more or less totally ignored. And the collection of diverse examples of the contextual peculiarities associated with various settings would provide no basis for the development of a cumulative body of systematic knowledge of the more fundamental and general 'ninety-five per cent'. Thus, so long as sociology insists on a division of academic labour between 'exotic' areas (e.g. the sociology of development, education, crime, deviance, law, medicine, etc.) it may never develop much in the way of cumulative knowledge, and practitioners from the different specialisms may never have very much to say to each other.

16. A very obvious legal illustration of this point is the problem of deciding the point at which a person becomes describable as 'the accused', rather than 'suspect', or 'someone helping with inquiries', during the course of police investigations.

17. The qualification 'at least on one level' here is included because the examination of such data subsequently suggests further grounds for selection. Thus, in recent years, conversational analyses have focused increasingly on the study of collections of action sequences taken from a range of conversational settings.

CHAPTER 2

1. Even those who might generally favour the examination procedures used in courts sometimes refer to the possibility that the effect of cross-examination may be to distort the truth. Thus Frank – one of the most notable critics of judicial procedure, and for whom the ability of counsel to control the production of information is part of the 'inhumanity' of cross-examination – quotes Chief Justice Taft:

> Counsel and court find it necessary through examination and instruction to induce a witness to abandon for an hour or two his habitual method of thought and expression, and conform to the rigid ceremonialism of court procedure. It is not strange that frequently truthful witnesses are . . . misunderstood, that they nervously react in such a way as to create the impression that they are either evading or intentionally falsifying.
>
> (Taft, quoted in Frank, 1949, p. 81)

2. The stages of court proceedings which are listed here are those which normally occur in the course of, for instance, a criminal trial at a Crown Court: they clearly do not occur in the proceedings of all courts, and there are other stages which are not found in criminal courts, but which are particular to more specialised courts (eg to the Court of Appeal). So types of court can differ with respect to which of these and other stages are included in their proceedings. However, *examination* occurs in the proceedings of all types of court from which data discussed in this book is taken, Coroners' Courts, Tribunals of Inquiry, and an American Criminal Court, though in the first two only witnesses may be examined, since there are (formally at least) no defendants.

3. Throughout this section reference is primarily made to the paper by Sacks,

Schegloff and Jefferson, 1974, because it is perhaps the most systematic and formal statement of their work into the organisation of conversation. Other published papers which include consideration of turn-taking phenomena, and particularly of the adjacency pair format of utterances (which is discussed later), are Schegloff and Sacks, 1974, and Schegloff, 1972 and 1977. These are some of the published products of continuing work into conversational analysis, prompted by Sacks's investigations conducted over the past ten years or so. Some of Sack's (unpublished) lectures which have been particularly used for this section are Lectures 1–5, Spring 1972 (these lectures are presently being indexed and edited for publication by G. Jefferson and E. Schegloff).

4. Hence the possibilities for detecting that, where more than one speaker is talking, then more than one conversation is taking place in the same setting – though that may entail the condition that the utterances of participants in one conversation are not related to those in the other. This general issue is raised again in Chapter 3.

5. Sacks notes, for instance, that it can be imagined that a rotating order for the speakers could be established for each conversation, so that single-speaker turns and speaker transitions would be handled by each speaker knowing his place in the order, – the consequence of which would be certain interactional difficulties:

> Then you'd have something like A-B-C-D, C-D-A-B or whatever, each such unit constituting a Round in which every party talks. And the Rounds could be built in such a way as to reproduce themselves (A-B-C-D, A-B-C-D), or to provide only that nobody who has already talked in a round talks again until that round is over. That seems awfully simple and possibly very neat. If one begins to think of how it would work, one could begin to derive sorts of problems with it; i.e., difficulties that would emerge if that were the way that a conversational system worked. Imagine, for example, a situation in which 'A' speaks and asks a question, and then 'B' speaks and says in effect 'I didn't hear the question'. Now under a Round system with, say, three or four speakers, 'A' could not go and repeat or clarify the question, but would have to wait until after 'C' and 'D' spoke in order to get a chance to do a clarification.
>
> For the way in which our conversations operate, that is plainly a kind of troublesome feature; that you could not, in your utterance, address the last speaker and get the last speaker to put an answer to your utterance, unless you were at the end of a round. The last speaker in a round, but only the last speaker could pick anybody. (Sacks, Lecture 1, April 4th, 1972)

6. One can find sequences which appear to contradict this, in which the first speaker's utterance can be designed to have the floor returned to him following the recipients turn, thus building up action sequences of three or four turns in length (these are discussed briefly in Chapter 5). However, it turns out that such multi-turn sequences are operated through adjacency pairs: on the completion of each pair, the first speaker self-selects and initiates a new pair.

7. A speaker may anticipate that what he has to say will last beyond a point at which his turn might be treated as complete – and therefore at which he might be interrupted. In order to avoid that, a preface may be made which contains instructions about when this turn will be complete, prefaces such as 'well, I've

got two points to make. . . .' On the use of such instructions to free a turn to tell a joke – a joke which is built as a story – see Sacks, 1974.

8. (O:r what) is contained in brackets here because a completion could be projected before or after its production. In many cases the next speaker does not begin exactly at the turn transition relevance place, but starts just a little before (for example *in* the word which is anticipated as the last in the present speaker's turn) or shortly after, there being a delay between the transition relevance place and the next speaker's start.

9. The possibility of a same speaker continuing if no-one else self-selects following an initial completion of their turn can also result in overlaps, as in the following extract:

> (TW: Ta, 27)
> Mother: Well they're learnin' how to cross th' road
>   (3.2)
> Mother: ⌈(   )
> Child: ⌊Why's .hh how have they (   ) hats
> Mother: Well (.) its a party.

The mother's initial utterance does not appear to allocate the next turn to the child (the mother and child being the only persons present). The 3.2 second pause which follows the completion of her utterance may be the product of the child's failure to exercise the option of the second rule, the self-select; and the mother then continues, following the provision of the third rule that a current speaker may continue after a transition-relevance place, if no-one self-selects. However, simultaneously with the mother's continuance the child does self-select, the resulting overlap being minimised by the mother giving way.

10. One very important aspect of overlaps which is not discussed here has to do with one speaker's *interruption* of another, which can be designed specifically *not* to allow the first speaker to complete the turn. Attempts by one speaker to cut off another occur in a variety of sequential environments, including (strong) agreements and (strong) disagreements, challenge and complaint sequences, and where the first speaker is complimenting the interruptive speaker. The structure and scope of these cannot be dealt with here.

11. In extract (5) it is unclear whether A completed what she had to say in the untranslated part of her utterance, or whether she cut off her utterance to give way to M.

12. Schegloff describes this as the nonterminality of summons-answer sequences:

> By nonterminality I mean that a completed SA sequence cannot properly stand as the final exchange of a conversation. It is a specific feature of SA sequences that they are preambles, preliminaries, or prefaces to some further conversational or bodily activity. They are both done with that purpose, as signaling devices to further actions, and are heard as having that character. This is most readily noticed in that very common answer to a summons 'What is it?' Nonterminality indicates that not only must something follow but SA sequences are specifically preliminary to something that follows. (Schegloff, 1972, p. 359)

13. For a more detailed explication of this, see Schegloff, 1977.

14. Again, see Schegloff, 1977, for an analysis of an empirically occuring
    misunderstanding.
15. Schegloff, 1972, gives a very clear outline of these and other aspects of the
    conditional relevance of a second pair part following a first.
16. This is very often complicated by the format in which the clarification is done
    by the speaker who first asked the question. For example, in this extract M's
    clarification formulates a particular sense of his initial question which has the
    effect of slightly altering the question:

> (AA, CA, 2)
> M: What=so what did you *do* did you have people – did
> M: Morag (.) come (.) down with the car ag⌜ain (   ) or what
> A: ⌞When last year
> → M: Mmm how did you man⌜age to s*hif*t it back and forward
> → A: ⌞Last year I don't know ho:w I managed it
> A: I got it a::ll in (0.8) two suitcases. . .

In his clarification M not only confirms A's 'when last year' with his 'Mmm',
but goes on to reformulate the question. That can mean that A might begin, as
she does, to address the 'new' question: that is the answer is constructed
without reference to some of the content of M's initial question. Insertion
sequences like this have the result that the recipient of the initial question may
indeed answer, but answer the reformulated questions, which are often quite
different from the original ones.
17. Another sequence in which the recipient of a request uses a 'delay' question is
    this:

> (US: 9)
> M: *Li*sten. The *mi*rrors.
>   (0.7)
> → V: Yeh, The mir*rors* I don' know. Like – yihknow
>   whaddiyou want them fuh the livin room?
> V: ⌜I'll
> M: ⌞Now I don' wannum in the⌜re
> V: ⌞*If yer* intuh
> V: one *I'*ll take one too=
> M: =Yeh.

In his turn which is arrowed, V treats M's noticing of 'The mirrors' as a
request to have them, and responds with a 'non-commital' component ('I don'
know') which defers or delays a decision, followed by a question about what M
wants them for. Thus his question (possibly like the mother's in (21), but it is
clearer in this extract) does not seek any clarification about the request in the
way that R's question in (20) does. Such questions as this are differentially
susceptible to being treated as seeking more information, or 'merely' delaying
(and therefore possibly being evasive).
18. 'I think' (and other equivalent units such as 'I mean') are used to 'soften'
    other dispreferred utterance types, such as disagreements:

A: That game's the most boring game I've ever come ┌across
→ B: └I think its
      a great game

19. Appreciation components may be done in Acceptances, but then they are
    placed in a *later* position in the turn (not serving to cushion a subsequent
    component): hence the Acceptance is done in the initial position, followed by
    an Appreciation, as in this extract, which is taken from Pomerantz, 1975:

      (DA: 4)
      B: Would yuh like t'come ovuh *here*? Or eh wih- will yer
            friend b-pick you up in the morning?
            (0.8)
→ A: Ah, *yes*.
→ A: I *would* like to *very* much.

20. See for example extract (21) and the one reproduced in footnote 17 above, in
    which a rejection, and a modified acceptance, are witheld sequentially by the
    'delaying' insertion sequences initiated by recipients of requests. Other places
    besides Pomerantz, 1975, especially Chapter 3, where preference organisa-
    tions are discussed are Schegloff, Jefferson, and Sacks, 1976, Sacks and
    Schegloff (forthcoming), Pomerantz, 1978, and Wootton (forthcoming).

21. The party who is being examined may, of course, from time to time ask
    questions; but they are subject to the considerations mentioned earlier, that is
    that they should be properly requests for clarification. This is discussed in
    more detail below.

22. Objections may also be placed after the completion of an answer, for instance
    on the grounds that the answer is non-responsive. In such cases the counsel
    objects to the answer, whereas the type of objection we are referring to here,
    and which is illustrated in (23) is objections to questions.

23. In these extracts, the following speaker indications are used:

      | Counsel conducting the examination | C |
      | Other (non-examining) counsel | OC |
      | Judge | J |
      | Chairman (eg of Tribunal) | Ch |
      | Witness | W |
      | Defendant | D |

24. See for example Linton, 1965.

25. See footnote 8 for points which bear on the precise positioning of the start of
    W's turn in (26).

26. An example occurs in this extract from a case in which the witness being
    cross-examined alleges she was raped by the defendant.

      (Ou: 45,3)
      C: You were out in th*e* woods with the defendant at
            this point isn't that so
            (1.0)

```
  W;   Yeah
→      (7.0)
  C:   And the defendant (.) took (.) the ca:r (1.0) and backed
       it (1.0) into some trees didn'e
       (0.5)
  W:   Mm⌐hm
  C:      └underneath some trees (1.5) Now Miss Lebrette this
       time did you make any mention about turning around.
  W:   No
→      (11.0)
  C:   An it was at this point that you say that the defendant. . .
```

The positioning of the two long pauses (7.0 second, 11.0 second respectively) can be heard to be used by the counsel to give special weight to the
answers which they follow, which perhaps does not need elaboration.

27. Clearly, issues to do with pauses are only introduced here, and there are
    many other aspects of their use which are not mentioned. Among the more
    noticeable pauses (and this appears to be very different from conversation) are
    those which occur *in* a counsel's turn, in the construction of a question: such
    pauses are discussed further in Chapter 6.

28. See, for example, Cross and Wilkins, 1971.

29. A notable example is that leading questions are not permitted in examina-
    tion-in-chief (except in certain circumstances), but are allowed in cross-
    examination. For other differences in the kinds of questions which may be put,
    and the admissability of certain kinds of evidence, between direct and
    cross-examination, see Cross and Wilkins, 1971, pp. 60-78.

30. This is simply to point to a condition concerning the use of *all* rules, that not
    all the relevant circumstances or factors bearing on the application of a rule
    can be specified in advance, Thus a rule's use is not strictly delimited, but is
    subject to judgements concerning the fit between present circumstances and
    the conditions specified in the rule. For a discussion of the flexibilities of rule in
    a legal context, see Hart, 1961; and for a more general discussion, Heritage,
    1978.

31. It is important to distinguish here between blame, and more formal notions of
    guilt. Witnesses who are in no formal sense accused of anything may nonethe-
    less find themselves facing questions which can implicate that they were to
    blame for something, for example for some aspects of the defendant's be-
    haviour, or, as in the case of the Tribunal material analysed in later chapters,
    for actions or events about which an investigation is being conducted (where
    the respect to which they may be to blame may not formally constitute a crime
    etc). Hence witnesses may detect blame implications in questions, even
    though they are not charged with an offence.

32. For example in some interviews (which share a similar turn-allocational
    system with examination) it may be recognised that 'blame' is at issue, either
    attached to the person being interviewed, or to a third party, without the
    interview being thought of as an 'examination'. We are thus not wanting to
    deny the fact that talk in examination may be particularly concerned with
    blame or offences; but we are questioning whether that feature together with
    the turn-taking organisation for examination is definitional, in the sense of

being necessary and sufficient conditions for determining that the talk is examination. For a notable attempt to define litigation, see Frake, 1969. Frake attempts to identify the components or structural dimensions of the talk through which litigation is conducted, there being no other way of defining litigation, given that it is not marked off by any formal indications such as distinctive settings, court-rooms etc.

33 Witnesses may find themselves being blamed in a variety of situations, but especially in the Tribunal of Inquiry from which some of the data extracts analysed in later chapters are taken. In that Tribunal, police witness routinely found themselves being blamed (for taking inappropriate action, or for sectarian bias etc), as did some civilian witnesses (e.g. for not taking action to stop youths throwing missiles, for not helping the police, for engaging in riots, etc.).

34 An example is T's complaint in extract (22), which occurs in a therapy session, a complaint which is clearly not built to elicit information through questioning the person against whom it is made, though that person's defence does occasion a series of question-answer sequences which can be heard to be directed to rebutting the defence.

35 This extract is considered in more detail in Chapter 5.

CHAPTER 3

1. This work is part of a multi-disciplinary programme of research into the social organisation of judicial procedures, which is one of a range of projects involving social scientists and lawyers at the (British) Social Science Research Council's Centre for Socio-Legal Studies.

2. Throughout this chapter 'conversational analysis' is used to refer to research conducted within the framework established by Harvey Sacks and his co-workers and which was introduced in Chapters 1 and 2. Given how much of the inspiration for this present study was derived from that work, it would have been difficult to have provided precise bibliographical citations whenever they became due without cluttering up the text with references. However, it is hoped that my debts even to studies not mentioned will be evident in what follows.

3. Given that this chapter focuses increasingly on a specific problem in the organisation of turn-taking in courts, it may be as well to note in passing that legal rules of evidence and procedure relate to a good deal more than turn pre-allocation. There are, for example, various (mostly exclusionary) rules of evidence which are designed to control topic coherence and relevance. Thus, one problem with which lawyers are confronted and have to resolve is what they refer to as the 'multiplicity of issues' problem, which appears to be almost synonymous with what is referred to in ethnomethodological writings (e.g. Sacks, 1963; Garfinkel, 1967; Garfinkel and Sacks, 1970) as 'the etcetera problem'. In short, the potentially infinite extendability of talk is one of the various problems to which courts must find a practical solution.

4. It will be noted that the term 'unspoken activity' is used throughout this chapter in preference to other descriptors such as 'non-verbal activity' which

are perhaps more usual in social psychological writings. One reason for this is that the latter term tends to be associated with things like glances, winks, gestures, etc., and as these do not provide the topic here it seemed as well to make some sort of explicit distinction. Another reason is that to differentiate between 'utterances' on the one hand, and 'non-verbal activities' on the other, is to risk implying that utterances are not (or are something other than) activities, which is a suggestion we would wish to avoid.

5. A very preliminary consideration of these problems (Atkinson and Heath, 1976) led to the conclusion that an *a priori* solution is unlikely to be found in the abstract and without reference to empirical data.

6. There would seem to be a variety of ways in which unspoken activities may be tied in with the sequential ordering of talk. In the data examined in this chapter they appear to feature as turns in the opening sequence of the hearing. At later stages in a court's proceedings, however, standing up and sitting down occur before and after utterance turn beginnings and endings respectively.

The grouping of those present at most points in time into some who are standing and some who are sitting also coincides with their grouping into speakers involved in the current sequence of talk and those who can only listen to it (some of whom may never get a turn to talk at all: e.g. members of the public, jury, etc.). The only exception to this is the judge, who remains seated whether he is talking or not, but this is arguably wholly consistent with the 'active parties'/'hearers only' distinction just noted. For, in so far as all utterances are addressed to the court, the judge is an 'active party' to all the sequences that make up a particular hearing. If judges were not exempted from the 'active parties stand' requirement, then they would have to remain standing all day and every day of their working lives. There would thus be, among other things, serious physical obstacles to their inclusion under the auspices of such a rule, particularly in England, where they can continue working well beyond the normal retirement age.

7. A further combination which occurs in the data considered here, but which is not analysed in much detail, is an utterance which projects *two* second parts, one spoken and one unspoken. Thus, 'That's it' at line 15 of Transcript version (3) presumably acknowledges the proper completion of the unspoken activity (taking the book) projected earlier in the same spoken turn as that which also projects the next utterance. That is, the utterance at line 13 projects *both* sorts of activities as conditionally relevant next turns. Interestingly, the two activities done together (i.e. holding the book and reading from the card) are recognisable as another single activity, namely 'swearing an oath'. At that level of analysis, then, the sequence looks like a more familiar example of an adjacency pair, with one first action ('oath elicitation') projecting one second ('swearing the oath').

8. The collection of the data examined here was made possible by the award of (British) Social Science Research Council Grant HR 1496/1: 'Community Reactions to Deviance'. With reference to Coroners' Court Hearings, it should perhaps be noted that they are the final stage of the procedures for deciding the causes of sudden deaths in England and Wales. Not all such deaths get that far in the process, but categorisations of accidents, suicides, and one or two other types of death can only be done at a Coroner's inquest. The procedural rules operative at these hearings are markedly different from those of most other

English courts in that, for example, the normal rules of evidence do not apply, and the 'adversarial' format is noticeably absent. (For a more detailed account of how the coroner system works, see Atkinson, 1978.)

9. This abbreviated form is used throughout to refer to the whole of the first utterance: 'Be upstanding in Court for Her Majesty's Coroner'.

10. By this is meant that, in terms of the ecological arrangements, the Coroner's Officer was the only person currently on the raised platform and was separated from the various clusters of people in the court-room by a considerable distance. Without wishing to be stipulative about there being some minimal number of yards within which parties to a sequence of talk must be positioned for their verbal exchanges to be regarded as 'a conversation', it may be noted that he was far enough away from everyone else for it to have been very equivocal as to whether his utterance could be recognisably describable by observers as 'conversational'. The possible implications of such ecological matters are considered further in Chapters 6 and 7.

11. These and other observations of Swedish courts reported later were made possible by the award of a Council of Europe Criminological Fellowship which facilitated a three week visit to the University of Stockholm in November 1976. I am grateful to Professor Knud Sveri and Ingemar Rexel of the Institute of Criminology for having given me so much help in finding my way around some of the courts in Stockholm.

12. For supplying me with this example, I am grateful to one of the participants at the International Institute in Ethnomethodology and Conversational Analysis, Boston University, 1977.

13. The close ordering implications of requests which have the syntactical form of an imperative (as opposed to a question) and which occur as first parts of a U–A pair may well have much to do with the accomplishment and recognisability of 'politeness'. Consider, for example, the following sequences:

Example (A)	Child:	Pass the cornflakes
	Parent:	What's the little word
		(Pause)
	Child:	Please
		((Parent passes cornflakes))
Example (B)	A:	Could you pass the salt
		((B passes salt))
	A:	and the pepper
		((B passes pepper))
	A:	and the mustard
	B:	Who do you think I am – your slave?

In both these examples, the business of completing U–A sequences appears to be a highly delicate matter. Once they cease to be babies, children find that the summons parts of summons-answer pairs require more careful design than was the case with their cries and screams of the past, if they are to get others to do unspoken activities for them. For, as is illustrated by Example B, recipients of first parts may find, as the sequence unfolds, grounds for making a complaint. Yet this could easily have been avoided by A had he, for example, prefaced his second or third utterance with an apology and thereby displayed a recognition of the way in which his actions might be seen as inconsiderate, demanding, etc. In short, the design and sequential ordering of spoken parts in U–A sequences could well be a promising starting point for research into the accomplishment and recognisability of politeness and impoliteness.

14. There is a suggestion here (which cannot yet be supported with reference to data) that, where an utterance is heard as the first part of a U–A pair there may be a preference for the projected unspoken activity twin to follow immediately and *before* any spoken turn. If this is so, then a spoken turn would be oriented to as being out of place in the sequence, one kind of evidence for which would be the occurrence of misplacement markers (c.f. Schegloff and Sacks, 1974) in utterances occurring prior to the completion of the unspoken turn. Other evidence which appears to support such a view is provided by the frequent occurrence at such points of utterances which display an orientation to the delayed start or completion of a projected unspoken activity turn. This can be illustrated with reference to the example cited earlier:

A: Have you a light
B: Yes
A: Can I have one then

Here it is A who displays an orientation to the non-occurrence of the projected unspoken activity turn in second position, but in other variants of the sequence B might display a similar orientation as in:

A: Have you a light
B: I'm sorry I don't smoke

In this example, B apologises and gives an account for the non-occurrence of the unspoken part, while other instances can readily be imagined where searching through pockets or handbags is accompanied by utterances oriented to the delayed beginning of the projected turn (c.f. the ubiquitous 'just a minute').

15. See, for example, the discussion of how to repudiate the authority of courts by Bankowski and Mungham, 1976, pp. 110–39, and the way such actions are recommended as ways of achieving such a goal. Would-be rebels, however, should be alerted to the fact that simply not doing a sequentially projected action may not be enough to secure their identification as rebels, as misplaced actions can also be read as failures to display understanding. Thus, unless they make it clear that they *know* that what they are doing is indeed misplaced, rebels run the risk of being viewed as being unable to understand, silly, or even mentally ill. Somehow or other, then, the rebel who wants to avoid any such imputation has to display both that he understands what would be in place at the particular point in the sequence, and that his not doing that is quite deliberate. This is probably easier said than done, and there may be many more practical obstacles to the successful accomplishment of such rebellious actions than are even hinted at by radical sociologists.

16. Such situations would appear to be characterised by a considerable amount of close co-ordination of spoken and unspoken activities, and point to another data source relevant to the issues being discussed here.

17. A more general point being hinted at here is that in settings where unspoken activities requiring close monitoring are taking place there may be a preference for silence. Thus, just as it is extremely difficult to monitor talk while talking (e.g. even professional simultaneous interpreters can only work effectively for periods of a few minutes at a time), so also may talk interfere with the monitoring of certain sequences of unspoken activities. Conversely, to talk during an unspoken activity being done by another party may be to fail to exhibit an understanding that the activity in question requires the full concentration of the party who is doing it. People may therefore complain at being 'interrupted' while doing some unspoken activity, or the 'interruptors' may preface utterances made at such points with apologies, where such an apology can be heard to orient to the fact that this is a delicate moment at which to talk.

18. This point about the relative ease with which two party sequences can be monitored as compared with, for example, a very extended turn by one party (as in a lecture), is developed further in Chapter 6 below.

CHAPTER 4

1. See, for example, the study by Burgess and Holmstrom, 1975, of the processes by which alleged rape cases come to court, and some of the features of, and issues raised in, such trials.
They comment that:

> Technically only the man is on trial. But as the drama of the courtroom unfolds, it becomes clear that in people's minds the victim is as much on trial as the defendant. Certainly it is his reputation against hers, his word against hers. (Burgess and Holmstrom, 1975, p. 27–28).

The possibility that a 'victim' somehow contributed to the action for which the defendant is accused is often likely in some cases involving violence against the person, e.g. murder, though for that there is no possibility of a victim giving evidence. But of course witnesses other than victims may sometimes find themselves implicated in some 'faulty' action, even if not the action for which the defendant is accused, and generally not in the sense of being implicated in some statutory offence. That raises the distinction between a legal sense of culpability, and a more general sense in which someone's action may be thought to be faulty. Thus witnesses may recognise that their action is being impugned in some way, without that implicating them in a chargeable offence (otherwise separate charges should have been brought against the witness).

2. This includes the possibility of designing questions to blame a party other than the person presently being examined. Hence witnesses appearing 'on behalf of' a defendant may similarly recognise the implicativeness of a question (i.e. as having the effect of blaming the defendant), and thus seek to avoid that in various ways.

3. The Royal Commission of Tribunals of Inquiry (the Salmon Commission)

reported in 1966 and set out a number of 'cardinal principles' to be followed in order to protect persons giving evidence to Tribunals, which were:

(i) Before any person becomes involved in an Inquiry, the Tribunal must be satisfied that there are circumstances which affect him and which the Tribunal proposes to investigate.
(ii) Before any person who is involved in an Inquiry is called as a witness he should be informed of any allegations which are made against him and the substance of the evidence in support of them.
(iii) (a) He should be given an adequate opportunity of preparing his case and of being assisted by legal advisers. (b) His legal expenses should normally be met out of public funds.
(iv) He should have the opportunity of being examined by his own solicitor or counsel and of stating his case in public at the Inquiry.
(v) Any material witnesses he wishes called at the Inquiry should, if reasonably practicable, be heard.
(vi) He should have the opportunity of testing by cross-examination conducted by his own solicitor or counsel any evidence which may affect him. (Summarised in Cmnd 5313, para. 17.)

Government acceptance of these principles, though with some circumstantial provisos, was outlined in a report entitled 'Tribunals of Inquiry set up under the Tribunals of Inquiry (Evidence) Act, 1921', which was published in 1973. The report proposed certain modifications to the original (1921) Act, though the qualifications expressed there (see for example paragraphs 18–37) led to the recommendation that the principles listed in the Salmon Commission be treated as 'guidelines to be followed wherever it is practicable to do so'.

4. From transcriptions of the evidence to the Tribunal of Inquiry into Violence and Civil Disorder in Northern Ireland in 1969, Government of Northern Ireland; Day 91, 22 October 1970. Tribunal counsel (C) cross-examining a witness, the Royal Ulster Constabulary Deputy Commissioner for Belfast (W).

5. The point that the grounds for an accusation may be set up through questions and answers *prior* to the actual accusation needs qualifying, of course, in the sense that a defendant stands accused at the outset of the trial. Even here, however, the formal charge can be seen as the end product of investigation and the accumulation of evidence against the defendant. The point here is to draw attention to the *interactional* accumulation and management of evidence supporting a blame ascription during the court hearing.

6. Those and other aspects of participants' formulations of talk are considered more generally by Heritage and Watson (1979).

7. No matter how much detail is included in a description of an object, person, etc., there is always more information which in principle could be added; so what is included in a description does not exhaust what could be said about what is being referred to. Most of the time any further detail may be deemed to be irrelevant for practical purposes, so that whatever might in theory be added is bracketed away for the present. Thus the theoretical indefinite extendability of descriptions results in their (again, theoretical) incompleteness, though that incompleteness may become a matter of practical import and even dispute. To

say that a description is incomplete is not to doubt descriptions as inadequate or the like, but is only to underline that a description is *in principle* incomplete, and hence necessarily a *selection* from what could have been said. Sacks and Schegloff (1979) discuss the remarkable economy with which reference is done, by generally using only a single category or description, as in many of the cases cited in the text here. For instance, in referring to persons, the descriptions 'This *friend* . . .', 'I'm waiting in the *electrician*', etc. may be used, or an identification – especially a proper name – which can allow the recipient to recognise the person referred to, whenever it is possible to use a recognition-al (i.e. whenever the recipient might be expected to know, or to know about, that person). So despite the detail which could be included in a description, empirical descriptions are formed with some economy, with a single category. However, philosophers have been concerned for some time with the problems which the indefinite extendability of descriptions poses for the definition of concepts, given that in principle one cannot be sure that a description of the circumstances of a term's use has included *all* the features which might be relevant, and which might therefore be criterial. This kind of problem, discussed extensively by Wittgenstein, 1972, is often referred to as the problem of verification (see Waismann, 1951), but has very widespread implications for the definition and use of words, the application of rules, etc., issues discussed in Garfinkel and Sacks, 1970, Heritage, 1978, and Wootton, 1975.

8. Named 'place of origin' is a far from trivial resource in descriptions of scenes, because, for example, it can be used to accomplish the 'common identity' of crowds in referring to what appear to be separate crowds (judged by their present location, rather than their location of origin), by demonstrating that the crowds only appeared to be separate at that particular moment in the sequence, and that 'in fact' they were part of a single, larger crowd which has split ('As I say some of the Divis Street crowd appeared from out of Ardmoulin Avenue, and some appeared back along Percy Street from Divis Street end. I would not have thought the first ones coming out of Ardmoulin Avenue, I would not suggest they were in hundreds at that stage'). Thus, without going into detail about it here, named place of origin can be used to provide for the monitoring of the movement of groups in a way when other location formula-tions including named places may not.

The particular place names used, 'Sandy Row', 'Shankill Road', etc., are *accomplished identifications* of some location of origin, and not the literal only, or 'most natural' way of identifying the place of origin. That is to say, we should not assume that the way in which 'Shankill Road' performs a referring task is the same on each occasion of its use: sometimes it may refer to where members of the crowd are resident, on other occasions to the place where they gathered, and on others to some location which for some purposes can stand 'instead of' the names of streets to which it is adjacent, or to which it is close. The latter sort of cases indicate that members may hear a location term as adequately or appropriately referring to some place, collectively, etc., even though it may not, by a correspondence test, be accurate. Thus routinely in this data and elsewhere, collectivities are identified as 'coming from' Shankill Road or wherever, without speakers seeming to find any discrepancy that in so doing they are referring to, or including, persons 'from' *adjoining* streets, streets *in the vicinity of* the named street, etc.

9. Watson instances the use of category-mapping procedures in an analysis of a person's claim to entitlements to facilities, treatment, and privileges due to her over and above black people. He suggests that the speaker's claim may be seen to involve mapping the categories 'established residents' and 'newcomers' on to 'white' and 'black' respectively, so as to set up the special rights due to 'established residents' in contrast to 'newcomers'. (Watson, 1975).

10. For instance one finds disputes about whether *all* Catholics were 'disloyal' (i.e. supported the integration of Ulster with the Republic of Ireland); whether the Civil Rights Association was a 'Catholic' organisation, and/or a Republican organisation. The 'synonymity' of one category with another is very commonly a matter of (political) disputes. For instance, many of the speeches made by Unionist politicians and by members of the CRA, from about October 1968 onwards, can be heard to make certain claims about the nature of the organisation of the CRA (who its members were, who directed its policies, whether the granting of 'civil rights' was only an ostensive reason for its existence, etc.), and thus addressing the issue of whether or not the CRA was 'synonymous with' Catholicism and/or Republicanism.

An example where the lay distinction between 'Catholics', 'Republican', 'the minority community' etc., and common-sense notions of the selective relevance of using one rather than another of these categories to refer to a particular population, is used as a resource for sociological analysis is Wright (1973). Wright identifies two different Protestant ideologies about the Catholic minority, the fundamentalist 'Protestant', and the 'Loyalist' perspectives, each of which displays the relevance of different categories (i.e. 'Catholic' and 'Republican' respectively) to describe the same population.

11. The basis for this account of Sacks's work on membership categorisation devices is in his 1972 paper, which is a refined and more formal version of his earlier work on calls to a suicide prevention agency. A question which informed that work was: how do callers demonstrate that they are calling because they have no-one else to turn to for help, that for them persons who might be expected to give help (friends, husbands/wives, relatives etc.) cannot actually do so (Sacks, 1966, 1972).

12. It is, perhaps, possible to misunderstand the category-boundedness of activities as the basis for ascribing activities to persons in a setting. It would be incorrect to read Sacks as proposing that speakers simply invoke a pre-existing or determinate list of activities matched against categories of persons by whom the activities are properly done. Thus when inferences are made about someone who is asserted to have done some action, by invoking an identity of who might normally or typically do such a thing (e.g. in claims that someone is behaving like a fool, an old woman, a guilty man, a hooligan, a schizophrenic) this can be heard to *occasion* the boundedness of certain activities with 'fools', 'old women', 'guilty men', etc. The recognisable sense of such claims derives, then, from members' production of a tie between some activity and some category, a production which may be reflexively ordered in the text. Very often though – and the analysis of this data will demonstrate this point – additional work may be done to occasion the relevance of an activity to a certain category.

13. The identification of one party as 'Catholic' and the other as 'Protestant' may *not* need to be done independently. Their co-selection may be achieved through the identification of *one* of the parties, which can then provide for the

relevance (according to the consistency principle) of the other paired category. Hence, a 'positive identification' may only be needed for one party, for the identity of the other to be deduced.

14. The 'sectarian group' device is discriminative in a number of ways, giving it rather widespread possibilities for accomplishing a variety of tasks. Whereas the device 'Christian' may be accountably extended beyond the two categories, and within which various denominations of the Protestant faith may be relevant (e.g. Church of Ireland, Methodist, Presbyterian; Barritt and Carter, 1962, provide figures for nine distinguishable Protestant denominations or sects in Northern Ireland), the device 'sectarian groups' may be conventionally regarded to consist of just these two groups. If one wants to assess the effect of religious divisions on the everyday life of people in Northern Ireland, one counts the number of *Protestants* in a particular Trade Union, employed in the shipyards, employed by local government, who are judges, who enter further education, who are elected to Stormont, who benefit in certain ways from the Social Services, and who are allocated council houses by a local authority, (and *not* numbers of Methodists, Presbyterians, etc.), in order to compare these figures with the number of Catholics who are employed in local government and the rest – a common-sense counting operation which can be used to evidence discrimination, divisions in education, social and political life, etc., and nicely illustrated in Barritt and Carter's study of the divisions in Northern Ireland. Also the categories in the 'sectarian groups' device can be treated as coterminous with paired categories from other devices, like majority-minority, Loyalist-Republican, etc., a purpose for which the device 'Christian' may not do. Finally, we have instances such as this advertisement appearing in a newspaper (cited by Barritt and Carter): 'WANTED – Reliable cook-general, Protestant (Christian preferred)'. But the more serious and general point about the device 'sectarian groups' is that it is a *contrastive device*, with just two categories. Contrastive devices, consisting of two categories, are commonly constructed for identifications (and for the consistency of identifications) of parties in conflicts (e.g. male/female; Church/State; 'town'/'gown'; 'left' wingers/'right' wingers, etc.).

15. Thus certain areas may be widely known as the stronghold of the Rev. Ian Paisley's supporters. This point is also nicely illustrated by the way in which division between Republicans on ideological or policy issues may be held to be co-incident with territorial divisions.

16. See Sacks, 1972: 334–5. We owe some aspects of this interpretation of Sacks' notion of duplicative organisation to R. Watson (see especially Watson, 1975, Chapter 5). It must be emphasised that the duplicatively organised property of a device is entirely an occasioned accomplishment, and is not a 'natural' property of the device; so different speakers may be heard to orient to alternative formulations of a device's organisation on a particular occasion, or the same speaker may be heard to invoke that property of a device on one occasion, but invoke an alternative organisation of the same device on other occasions. Thus it may happen that claims are constructed that all political parties should 'work together', for example to solve Britain's economic problems.

17. However, while the question of whether their action is the result of some plan is an investigable matter for the interactants, it should be noticed that treating

activities as organised through this particular relationship between categories in a device does not entail a speaker's proposing an overt plan or conspiracy among persons so categorised: so throughout the word 'organised' is meant to indicate the ordered or structured nature of social activity, but leave open the precise *basis* of that order.

CHAPTER 5

1. Elsewhere in the data, questions such as that in line 8 (and they sometimes occur in just that form) are routinely treated as having to do with the Tribunal's task of trying to piece together an overall picture of events from the observations of various witnesses, some of whom may have seen only a part of the events, or may be unsure about the exact time or location of an incident. So enquiries are often made in the examination about when a witness arrived on the scene, what his movements were, what he saw and did at various times and locations, and when he finally left that scene. Hence a question such as 'What did you do at that point?' may be treated as serving some narrative purpose, and answered with a report of what was done *subsequent to* that point, rather than with an explanation. An instance where a witness answers such a question with a 'narrative' description occurs in the following extract.

(ST:84,34E)

C: And some of the civilians went past you?

W: Yes, they went past me, but not very much. No-one went on to Divis Street, as far as I can remember.

C: This was the time when you were hit with a stone?

W: In the leg, yes.

C: And you went down. Were you down for long?

W: No.

C: You got up again?

W: Yes.

→ C: And what did you do?

→ W: I went back and called my men back and we occupied the position at Ardmoulin Avenue junction across the road.

C: What did you do so far as the Protestant civilians who had gone past you were concerned?

W: By the time I got up they were back and certainly I took no action against anyone.

In reply to the question, 'And what did you do?', the witness reports what he then did at a next stage in the sequence of events – though as it turns out from the Counsel's next question, 'what did you do?' was intended to refer to what he did about 'the Protestant civilians who had gone past you', and therefore to tie back to the first question-answer pair in this extract. The point is, then, that witnesses' treatment of such questions as 'What did you do then' is variable; they may be recognised as referring back to some previously mentioned incident ('what did you do about X?'), or as enquiring about subsequent moves/actions.

2. As does the counsel in the following extract: in response to the witness's challenge that the counsel was 'suggesting that I was conspiring with the extreme Protestants about firearms', the counsel rebuts that interpretation of the question by saying that 'I do not think any reasonable person could possibly so interpret it. I hope, my lord, that my phraseology is a little more accurate than that.'

    (ST:91,31D)

        C: Let us examine that for a moment. Did you not know that there were arms in extreme Protestant hands?

        W: I probably would have presumed that they may have a few arms,
→   but where they were I do not know. If you are suggesting that I was conspiring with the extreme Protestants about firearms

        C: Now, listen, Mr. Bradley. Did you think my last question amounted to a suggestion that you are conspiring with extreme Protestants?

        W: A couple of questions before that, you made a very strong suggestion that there had been a Protestant crowd at the bottom of Percy Street and that I was asking them very nicely to go home. It seemed to me that you were under the impression that I was biassed with regard to religion. I, my lord, would resent that very much.

        C: We had better not carry on cross talk about this, but did you interpret my questions as suggestions that you had been conspiring with extreme Protestants?

        W: I did.

        C: To get back to the question which I asked you . . .

        Ch: Mr McSparran, you had no intention of making such a suggestion?
→   C: Not the slightest, my lord, and I do not think any reasonable person could possibly so interpret it. I hope, my lord, that my phraseology is a little more accurate than that.

3. See, for example, Scott and Lyman (1968).
4. These are just a very few of the objects which accounts may be done along with, but they give some idea of the interactional and 'reparative' work which they can be aimed to do with respect to dispreferred actions.
5. That may be conveyed, for instance, in many examples Emerson gives of the accounts delinquents give for offences in a juvenile court: Emerson (1969, Chapter 6).
6. Sacks discusses pre-sequences in a number of his unpublished lectures, and notably in those dated 31 October and 2 November 1967. See also Schegloff (forthcoming). The question format, rather than statement, is particularly relevant for packaging pre-sequence items, given the speaker's interest in securing a response from the recipient which will indicate whether or not to go ahead with the intended action. And questions, because they are first parts in adjacency pairs, 'demand' a response from the recipient in a way statements may not.
7. It is for that reason that V's response, 'I'm not intuh selling it or giving it. That's it', can be heard as 'abrupt': that is, what V does not do is give an answer about what he is doing with the tank, or what he intends to do with it,

in order to indicate to M that a request would not be granted – thereby giving M the chance to not make the request. This way, the request is treated as having been put, and gets the (dispreferred) outright rejection. It is noticeable that it is treated by these participants as abrupt, partly in M's 'Dat wz simple' followed by laughter; but also V gets defensive about why he isn't willing to let M have it, in the immediately following sequence not reproduced here.

8. In (4), of course, following V's rejection, M does not claim that he was not asking for it, which he might have done if he had thought V 'misinterpreted' him. And actually a little later he says: 'Buh I din say giving it. If yer intuh selling it, I'll take it man.' And of course in (5), A's last utterance acknowledges that he was going to invite B over, in 'I was just gonna say come out and come over here an' talk this evening . . .'.

9. Similarly, in the following fragment the reply 'Nothin' can be selected with a view to the anticipated invitation, to encourage it, without it needing to be literally true that B is doing 'nothing' (whatever that might be) at that very time.

   (7) (JG: CN: 1)
       A: Whatcha doin'
    → B: Nothin'
       A: Wanna drink? ((go out for a drink))

10. 'Discourage' and 'encourage' are used in a technical sense here, to refer to the sequential consequences of given replies – that some replies may leave the next slot free for first speaker to do the intended action (e.g. invitation), whilst others may result in the non-production of that action. So the terms may have nothing to do with personal propensities, or inclinations towards, and outcomes of, future invitations.

11. A number of sequence shapes can be associated with pre-sequences. Where the recipient's response encourages first speaker to go ahead with the intended action, say a request, the full sequence may run.

   A_1: Pre-request question
   B_1: Answer
   A_2: Request
   B_2: Acceptance

And if the turn shown as B_1 discourages the request (as B's discourages the invitation in (5)), then A's second turn would be unlikely to be a request, but may acknowledge the import of B's reply, or simply continue on topic. However, if as in (4) the turn B_1 is designed directly as an Acceptance/Rejection (and it would more likely be the former), then A's second turn becomes an acknowledgement of some kind – probably an expression of gratitude. Thus the 'Request' turn is omitted, the sequence being 'collapsed' to

   A_1: Pre-request question
   B_1: Granting (often formed as Offers)/Rejection
   A_2: Acknowledgement (expression of gratitude, if B_1 is a granting).

12. By repeating a question, counsel may treat the previous 'answer' as unsatisfactory, in the sense of it avoiding, or not answering something in the question. In the following extract, the counsel draws explicit attention to the way in which the prior reply answers a 'next' question, by giving a reason for which he has not yet been asked.

> (ST: 90,10C)
>   C: This is going back to the point which Mr Nicholson made a moment or two ago but it is an important point. Did you make any attempt to persuade the Catholic crowd to go back before you baton-charged them?
>   W: I do not see how you could persuade them to go back.
> → C: Never mind that, just answer the question first and then give your reason. Did you make any effort to persuade the Catholic crowd to go back before you baton-charged them?
>   W: No.
>   C: Why not?
>   W: I doubt if they could even hear me.

13. Some transformations in blame sequences in conversational data are reported by Pomerantz (1978). She points out that, where a first speaker reports an 'unhappy' or untoward incident in an unelaborated form, and without mentioning an actor-agent, the next speaker may transform the referent-events from 'incident that happened/is happening' into 'action performed by action/agent'. The effect of the second speaker's transformation is to locate an actor/agent responsible for the untoward event announced by the first speaker, and hence to treat that event as subsequent to, and a consequence of, a prior action.

14. In (7) the action asked about is whether the witness *observed* that incident. In the answer, that becomes some other unnamed action. But in the following extract, in which again the witness explicitly attends to a possible failure on his part, the issue of what he 'knew' in the question becomes what he could do (or not do) to prevent it.

> (ST:87,65G)
>   C: You knew from your experience of the first baton charge that the Protestants would come down behind you again?
>   W: I felt that there was nothing I could do to prevent it.

15. In (6) that sequential ordering is achieved within a single turn. An interesting feature of (6) by contrast with the others, is that the report of the other party's action is done by the witness himself. While the prior question refers to 'the Protestant crowd', it is the witness who first draws attention to that party whose actions are treated as implicating his own inaction, that is the 'one or two (who) would dart forward and throw something towards the Divis Street crowd. . . .': and then later in the reply he gives reasons for not 'taking action against them' (though again, the implication that he did not do so is embedded in that explanation). So that whereas in other extracts the report of the other

party's action/incident is sequentially separated from the turn in which a witness embeds a noticing of his failure to take action in an explanation for that inaction, in (6) the 'report' and the 'noticing' are combined by the witness in a single turn, though retaining the same relative positions ('reporting' in first, and the 'noticing' in a subsequent position).

16. The basis on which witnesses might anticipate blame being ascribed to them for failing to take action is important here, because of course not any conceivable inaction may be treated as blameworthy. That basis appears to be that the actions/incidents which are reported in the first part of the sequence involve some kind of 'offence'.

17. Pomerantz (1975 and forthcoming) analyses features of the organisation of turns in which disagreements are done, which exhibit their dispreferred status.

18. A case in point is the following, in which the witness first accepts (and himself uses) the descriptor 'invasion' to describe the actions of Protestants. But later, as the questioning turns to the results of that 'invasion', and thus possibly implicating the results of his not having stopped Protestants from 'invading', the witness disavows that descriptor, and instead uses the term 'incursion', which diminishes the event's seriousness, whilst avoiding overt disagreement or disconfirmation forms.

> (ST:95,50G)
> C: And you did not pay any regard, I take it following that answer, to any possibility of invasion from the Protestant area into the Catholic area?
> W: I certainly did not take into consideration that there would be an invasion.
> C: Do you agree now that in fact there was an invasion?
> W: I must accept that.
> C: That was something which you took no account or consideration of on the morning of the 14th?
> W: On the morning of the 14th I did not consider that was a possibility. That is my own view.
> C: And there was an invasion which resulted in the wholesale destruction of Catholic property?
> → W: Well, I said I accepted it, but it is the word 'invasion'. Again, I did not see this, my lord, but I accept there were incursions. 'Invasion', is a strong word to me and I do not know whether it is advisable or not, not having seen it.

19. That is, the first defensive effort is through one of these objects; so that the first (defence) positions in these sequences are generally (indeed, it appears are always) filled by instances of this first type – though these objects do, occasionally, occur subsequent to accounts. When they do, a feature is that they tend to 'renew' the sequences, which then progress to further accounts.

20. Direct confirmations are sometimes given in response to a statement of a failure in the prior question – but, as in (15) below, where such direct forms are used, they are generally post *repeats* by questioner of an already stated failure.

21. Other such cases are line 20 of (1), the reply in extract (16), and the following instance.

> (ST:84,41H)
>
> C: When they were participating in that charge had you posted any guard or taken any steps to prevent Protestants coming into Ardmoulin Avenue behind you?
>
> W: No.
>
> C: Or into Percy Street or down Percy Street behind you?
>
> W: No. The matter of posting guards was out of the question;
>
> → I had too few men to do it; we were working as a unit.

22. It may help to follow the ordering of the three types of defence objects to reproduce the sequence from which (3), (10) and (21) are taken. For clarification, the objects which describe the other party's action so as to minimise it are labelled A; the [Rebuttal] + [Account] which occurs post the noticing of a failure is C; and the third, intermediate type, which occurs after the A strategy, but prior to the noticing, is marked as B.

> C: How far did you drive the Catholic crowd at that time?
>
> A→W: I stopped in Dover Street and nobody went very far past me and no-one went on Divis Street from the Protestant crowd.
>
> C: No-one went very far past you, you say?
>
> A→W: No-one got more than a few yards past me.
>
> C: So some people did go past you?
>
> B→W: I was hit in the leg by a stone and went down and that is when they went past me.
>
> .
> .
> .
> .
>
> C: In any event, when you mounted that second baton charge you took no steps to prevent the Protestant people following you?
>
> C→W: I was not in a position to take any steps. If I had taken any steps to prevent them I would have left more than half my party and the other three or four of us would have had no effect on chasing them from this fire that had been started at the Sarsfield Hall.

It is noticeable that where these three objects are done in the *same* turn, in (6), that ordering is retained. So the first strategy used consists of the description 'Occasionally one or two' (minimising frequency and numbers); the B strategy is 'would dart forward . . . and retreat back'; and the [Account] begins 'but taking any action against them . . .' etc.

> (6) (ST:84,15A)
>
> C: While this was going on and you were carrying out these activities was the Protestant crowd staying back at that stage?
>
> W: Yes, they were quite good at keeping behind us. They did not

try to go beyond us. (A) Occasionally one or two (B) would
dart forward and throw something towards the Divis Street
crowd and then would retreat back into the street again,
(C) but taking any action against them would have been taking
our strength off our general purpose of keeping the whole crowd
back.

23. This is well illustrated in the following exchange between the Tribunal
Chairman, and the witness who had admitted to seeing 'more than missiles' at
a certain location: it turns out that he saw petrol bombs there.

> (ST:95,35C)

C:	How were the petrol bombs laid down?
W:	I cannot remember; I do not know how they were laid out, but there were petrol bombs there.
→ Ch:	What I do not understand, Mr. Cushley, is why you did not tell us about the existence of these weapons when you were giving your direct evidence and giving us the impression that this was not a very dangerous crowd.
W:	Certainly, my lord, there was not any intention of misleading the Tribunal. I said I volunteered this information.
→ Ch:	You volunteered it a little late in cross-examination, but we will not go into that. But speaking for myself, I was misled. I had no idea that you had seen any weapons of war behind this crowd which you assessed as being, in the circumstances of that night, not a dangerous crowd, but now I realise that this is a crowd which, however unaggressive at the time, was in possession of weapons of war.

24. 'Conditional' questions are similarly used in other speech settings, to 'get
round' a prior speaker's answer which would otherwise inhibit or forestall the
present speaker's intended action. The following extract occurs in a group
therapy session.

> (GTS: MH: L)

G:	Well with people s*i*ttin round on the same *ta*ble as me (1.0)
G:	I thought well I'd *better* eat it else I'm going to show meself up (.) or something (1.0)
G:	Whi:ch I've managed to kee- *push* it down.
→ Dr:	Were you upset after:wards?
→ G:	No. (1.0)
G:	°No
→ Dr:	So you ate at t⌈he convalescent home *some*thing you knew:
G:	⌊°Rome wasn't built in a day
→ Dr:	that n (.) would normally upset you. What was tha'

The doctor's first question in this extract, 'Were you upset afterwards?' can be
heard to be designed to get a confirmation, and thereby to provide material out

of which to make some formulation of George's 'problem'. What it actually gets from George is a disconfirmation. Despite that, the doctor designs some statement of an upshot which can step round the disconfirmation, with the formulation that, though what George ate did not make him ill *that* time, nevertheless he ate what he knew would *normally* make him ill.

25. Exchanges in court data, in which witnesses etc. have disconfirmed something the counsel has proposed, clearly follow the structural pattern outlined here, even though the sequences contain indications that the counsel do not agree with or believe the witnesses' corrected versions. In this extract from a case of alleged rape, the 'victim's' correction 'No we started talking' elicits the repeat of the correction by the counsel, who then goes on to repeat that correction again, and ask further questions about how long it was before the defendant began kissing her – all of which can display his scepticism of her version, especially in view of his use of 'You say' in his first question, thereby attributing this information to the witness herself.

```
   (O: 43.5)
        C:   An it was at this point that you say that the defendant (2.0)
             started to kiss you is that right
        W:   No we started talkin'
             (.)
   →    C:   You started talking
        W:   Mm hm
             (1.5)
   →    C:   Didn't kiss you right away
        W:   = No
             (3.0)
        C:   An (.) about how long did you say you ta:lked before ⌈(this was      )
        W:                                                        ⌊I don't
             remember
        C:   (started ta kiss(h)a =
        W:   = I don't remember
```

26. On the use of formulations of upshots as topic or conversational closing relevant objects, see Heritage and Watson (1979).

27. Jefferson and Schenkein (1977) analyse some aspects of the design of utterances so as to secure control of a position in a projected sequence, the incumbency of which may allow that speaker to 'disarm' the co-participants 'victory' over an 'embattled issue' (p. 97). Such positions in the sequence are therefore 'locally critical action components' because they afford speakers the opportunity to control contested outcomes.

CHAPTER 6

1. This is a reference to the fact that neither of the authors originally collected data from these particular courts with a view to doing analyses of the kind presented here, let alone writing a book on the organisation of verbal interaction in courts.

2. The qualifier 'for the most part' is included here because some of the observations made in Chapter 3 (e.g. those concerning the location and activities of the Coroner's officer, policemen, etc.) were not available from the transcript.

3. That is, in so far as features of court proceedings not reproduced in the official transcripts may have been important in reaching a decision that is appealed against, appellate courts may not be as well placed to assess how the earlier decision was made as might idealised views of their procedures imply. Nor are they as well placed as would now be technologically possible.

4. These various points are referred to as a 'possible problem' because it is a domain about which there is still relatively little systematic knowledge. Native British speakers of English would appear to have few difficulties in understanding analyses of tape recordings and transcripts of conversations between American speakers of English, though problems can arise in attempting to produce detailed transcriptions thereof. To the non-American ear, for example, it is sometimes difficult to identify stressed and stretched sounds in American English, and we suspect that Americans might experience similar problems in transcribing British English. Given the importance which stressed and stretched sounds can have in projecting same turn repairs, turn transition points, etc., difficulties in identifying and distinguishing between such sounds could be considerable impediments to analyses of American data by British analysts and *vice versa*. In short, there would appear to be good technical reasons for preferring the form of spoken English that is most familiar to the researcher. And it may be noted more generally that a more precise comparative understanding of the organisational properties of American English and British English is unlikely to be arrived at in advance of more extensive empirical investigations.

5. The restrictions on filming trials in Britain appear to date from the early days of photography when the taking of indoor pictures required explosions and various other elaborate forms of lighting which might have interrupted the proceedings in highly visible ways. Yet, in spite of advances in video-recording technology which make such things redundant, the restrictions remain. A recent BBC news programme featured an item on the televising of extracts from trials in Florida, and the American politician interviewed made much the same points as are made here about the public/open character of courts. In response to these, Sir David Napley, a well known English lawyer conceded that this was so, but invoked two lines of argument against doing the same thing in Britain. One of his suggestions was that people could easily get the wrong idea when exposed only to selected extracts. When the interviewer pointed out that this applies equally to current trial reporting arrangements, Napley introduced a second theme, namely that it would be a terrible thing were trials to become a form of entertainment. He did nevertheless concede that he could see no objection to such video-recordings being used for 'educational purposes', though he was not explicit as to whether or not these would include research.

6. Many of the points in Sections 2–5 of this chapter emerged during data analysis workshops held at Wolfson College, Oxford in the Michaelmas Term 1977. While it is impossible to record either who came up with which particular observation, or the level of consensus reached on each, thanks are

nevertheless due to the regular participants, notably Robert Dunstan, Roy Harris, Talbot Taylor and Jeremy White. None of them, however, has any responsibility for the errors that remain.

7. While it will clearly be an important future task to study both examination and cross-examination, attention here is confined mainly to the latter.

8. Two additional points of possible interest which have been noted by many of those who have heard the recording are first that the witness is 'clearly' the alleged victim in a rape case and second that she is at this point being 'difficult' or 'evasive' in her answers.

9. See the discussion in Chapter 3.

10. A very general point being touched on here is that incentives to pay attention may be greatly reduced where turn distribution is limited to only a few co-present parties. The possibilities of falling asleep during lectures, speeches and sermons do not merely provide materials out of which jokes can be built, but are arguably oriented to both by speakers and their recipients. The problem is compounded by the well known fact that a hearer who does not understand an early segment of some such (extended) turn, and who is unable to solicit clarification there and then (as can be done in a conversation), may be unable to understand much of what follows for the next hour. Evidence for the view that extended Q–A sequences may be more effective in providing for continual and successful monitoring by recipients who are excluded from obtaining a turn to talk is provided by the broadcasting media's overwhelming preference for interviews and panel discussions over formal statements and speeches by persons in the news.

11. Given that much of what follows is concerned with the preliminary observation that pauses are frequent and extended, it should perhaps be noted that it is in relation to utterances in conversation that they are frequent and extended, and that this is one of the particularly obvious and noticeable ways in which court-room talk differs from conversational talk.

12. This is not intended to mean that pauses tend to coincide with where punctuation marks would appear in written versions of the talk, nor that they work only or exclusively in the same way as punctuation. The point is merely that one of the things they do is to break up the talk into temporally bounded segments. In this context it may be noted parenthetically that one of the features of many public speeches that are read from a script is that the pauses are by no means confined to those places where punctuation marks would have appeared in a text. This appears to contrast with certain other forms of 'reading aloud' (e.g. broadcast news reading), in which there is a greater coincidence between pauses and punctuation. It seems probable that the placing of pauses has much to do with the varying 'effectiveness' of public speaking such that, for example, staying close to the punctuation in the manner of a news reader may be a way of displaying 'detachment' from the contents of the talk.

13. This and the previous remarks about the relative absence of repairs may be closely related. Thus, there is evidence that the stretching of sounds and pauses within a turn are often precursors of immanent trouble in that utterance. Reparables and same turn repairs may often follow, though sometimes of course the sound stretch or pause may be enough to ward off the occurrence of the trouble (these points were reported in a seminar given by

Emanuel Schegloff in the series 'Language as Social Interaction', University of Oxford, Trinity Term, 1978). This suggests that, while same turn repairs by counsel may be relatively infrequent (compared with their occurrence in conversation), they are headed off by the use of commonly occurring conversational devices (i.e. sound stretches and pauses).

14. Consider, in this context, the following comments on Baby Talk (BT) by Jerome Bruner (1978, pp. 11–12):

'Formats obviously have utility for the child, providing a simpler, more predictable bit of the world in which and about which to communicate. But they also have an important function for the mother in the mutual task of speech acquisition. Everybody working on BT (or 'Motherese' as it is sometimes called) notes that in addition to slower rate, broader intonation spectrum, less complex grammar, etc., BT virtually always starts with 'here and now', within the format where the two are operating. It permits the mother to calibrate her talk to the child's capabilities.

15. These remarks, it may be noted, are relevant to many types of turns other than 'questions' in examination, and also provides for how it is possible for public speakers, lecturers, preachers, etc., to get away with pauses in some of their pre-allocated turns (e.g. speeches, lectures, sermons) without fear of losing their turn.

16. As was noted with reference to data fragments 25–26 in Chapter 2, a witness's utterance may sometimes start in overlap with counsel's.

17. Work on objection sequences is currently being done in conjunction with Robert Dunstan, Pat Syms and Jeremy White at the Centre for Socio-Legal Studies.

18. This point, of course, means that it is extremely difficult for the social scientist to explore some of the sorts of issues a lawyer might expect him to study. These might include, for example, questions concerning the 'effectiveness' of legal rules, how far the proceedings are constrained by them, how vigorously they are enforced, etc. For the analyst, however, the relative infrequency with which particular rules are explicitly referred to by participants places a serious obstacle in the way of making their operation the central topic for study.

19. Objections occurring after answers are typically aimed at deletion of the answer or part of it, as in

```
OU: 46,1A
C:    Whadid you do then
      (1.5)
W:    I broughder in the ba:throom (0.5) an I gave her a
      douche
      (2.0)
C:    An
      (2.0)
→  W:    I got hys:: I got so hysterical I didno
      what to do
→  OC:   Well I I object your honour
J:    No: uh th that (.) that uh last comment must be
      stricken.
```

20. In other words, this constraint would appear to exert considerable pressure against the inclusion of the grounds for an objection in the course of the objection turn.

21. This sequence is interesting in other ways too, in that an answer is allowed to stand, while the question to which it was an answer is stricken. It is possible that the particular line of questioning, which is seeking to characterise the alleged rape victim's boy friend (who is not the alleged rapist) in such a way that various moral imputations about her orientation to sexual activity could be made, would cast doubt on her claims not to have consented to intercourse in the present case. In so far as the questions might arouse very damaging suspicions on the part of the jury, the judge may be seeking to eliminate any such hints by allowing the answers (which deny any association with a boy friend who is either 'a member of a local motor cycle gang' or 'more than thirty years old') to stand, and ruling the questions out of order.

22. There is also a physiological constraint that would appear to have an important bearing on the frequent occurrence of pauses within turns designed to be heard by all parties in a multi-party setting. Thus, the requirement to speak more loudly than in a conversation means that more energy is used to produce the necessary volume of sound. Under such circumstances, control over breathing will be more of a problem for speakers and frequent pauses may result. Thus, if our earlier observations about phased utterances being easier to monitor are valid, there may be an interesting way in which physiological constraints are finely tuned to the production of talk which is situatedly appropriate to a multi-party setting.

CHAPTER 7

1. It should not be thought that this and following remarks about the practical interests of sociology refer only to so-called 'policy-oriented' research. For the discipline's emergence was itself prompted primarily by a concern for the practical problems associated with social change and upheavals in the nineteenth century. And the earlier dreams of being able to develop theories which will facilitate the explanation and amelioration of current social problems still persist in various guises. Were that not so, then it is doubtful whether government and other agencies would continue to spend so much on sociological research, particularly given the apparently increasingly frequent 'finding' that, for each social problem, 'society is at fault' and hence nothing can be done without its total transformation. And on a more localised level, optional topics in sociology degree programmes still tend to reflect the primacy of contemporary social issues (e.g. race, deviance, education, stratification, etc.) as central organising principles for the discipline.

2. This observation is made largely on the basis of responses to oral presentations of parts of the work reported in this book.

3. One reason for reluctance 'at this stage' is simply that the sort of research which might facilitate a more reasoned assessment of possible practical implications has yet to be carried through. Such work is, however, currently being planned (by J.M.A.) in conjunction with colleagues at the Centre for Socio-Legal Studies.

4. A difficult problem is, of course, that of knowing how much research would have to be done for it to be said that such a stage has been reached. The view that it may be close is thus a purely subjective view derived from an assessment of the growing body of findings about the organisation of conversations and the scope for speculation about broader implications they provide.

5. That is, such demands seem to assume that the 'usefulness' of other sociological approaches is not in question, even though there is arguably little in the way of positive evidence for such a view.

6. It should be stressed that the issues addressed in this chapter are no more than a selection, and there may be others which eventually turn out to be more important. So far, however, those engaged in this kind of work have given relatively little attention to the question of broader implications (at least in published form), and it would thus be surprising if more than a few limited reflections could be offered in the context of this early attempt to air some of the possibilities.

7. Thus, while classrooms are also multi-party settings in which turn pre-allocation and a reduction in opportunities for self-selection are features, the patterns of turn-taking clearly exhibit differences from those found in courts. Thus, while the predominant form in examination is ABABAB etc., speaker change in classrooms tends to involve a greater range of speakers in second turn position, with first turns returning to the teacher, an idealised form of which might be characterised thus: ABACADAE etc.

8. Viewed in these terms, teachers are easy prey to critical observers, as their efforts to sustain the minimal conditions for shared attentiveness make it possible for them to be described as being 'obsessed with keeping order', 'more interested in keeping the children down than letting them express themselves', etc. Issues such as these have, of course, been central to recent moves towards 'more progressive' teaching methods in various countries, particularly in the area of infant and primary schooling. It may therefore be a sobering thought for some to discover that such reforms may be based on what may be a very narrow and one-sided view of the organisational problems that may be involved.

9. There are, of course, many multi-party gatherings where this is not a minimal requirement (e.g. cocktail parties, bars, coffee lounges, etc.), as well as others where no one speaking at all, or everyone in unison, or each of these in sequence, may be a feature (e.g. academic examinations, church services, ceremonies, etc.).

10. By 'over-built' is meant that there may be several features of an utterance or sequence which do similar interactional work, when fewer might be enough. Thus in Chapter 3 it was suggested that the efficiency of 'Be upstanding in Court . . .' in bringing about silence may be a consequence of there being a number of features of its design working to that end. Similarly, there seem to be several which work to provide for the recognition of which category of person is now speaking. Witnesses and defendants for example do not wear robes, may be located in a dock and do second turns in examination sequences, and the procedures for recognition may thus be 'over-built' in the sense that any one of these could well be enough for any competent person present to know who is speaking. To insist on the retention of them all may therefore be to imply that those present are less than competent, and hence may be seen as

unduly offensive, oppressive, etc. If evidence were required that not all are necessary for the identification of speakers to be assured, then it may be of relevance to note that no one who has so far heard extracts from the tape-recorded trials has had any trouble whatsoever in recognising which category of person is speaking, even though they are cut off from seeing who is standing or sitting where, who is wearing a robe, etc. When it comes to talking in terms of practical reforms, then, there may be something to be said for the view that some features of court hearings may involve the use of a procedural sledgehammer to crack an organisational nut.

11. These materials on Swedish Courts were collected under the auspices of the Council of Europe Fellowship and with the help of the colleagues in Stockholm referred to earlier (Chapter 3, Note 11).

12. Tape recordings of parliamentary proceedings are currently being collected and analysed by Robert Dunstan at the Centre for Socio-Legal Studies.

13. These remarks on Tanzania result from watching a BBC television documentary on life in that country. A subsequent TV programme showed that similar points could be made about the various meetings involved in Yugoslavian workers' self-management.

14. This includes, of course, consultations between lawyers and clients, police interrogation of suspects, etc. The broader implications of Q–A sequences and the adjacency pair organisation (of which they are an instance) would seem to be much more extensive than is indicated here, and could well provide an important focus for further reflection. Work on adjacency pairs, furthermore, may provide an interesting basis for considering the organisation of the law more generally, as they appear to be basic units across a range of legal activity. Consider, for example, the centrality of offer-acceptance to the law of contract, plaint-defence in civil proceedings, and charge-defence in criminal proceedings.

Appendix: Symbols used in the transcription of conversational extracts

(These symbols are adapted from those which are commonly in use for conversational analysis, and which have been developed particularly by Gail Jefferson.)

1. T: =↑Its not *joke* it ↑a:ll its⌈:
   G: ⌊Look. Can I
      ⌈finish what I'm trying' ta say
   T: ⌊Ah mean I *do:n lau*:gh when you do it do I

The *extended straight brackets* indicate the point at which a current speaker's talk is overlapped with the talk of another speaker. In some extracts, *double oblique lines* are used at the point (in the word) at which another speaker's talk is initiated, thus:

   M: Well I w'z gla//d you came
   A: 'N yer friends'r so darling

2. H: H*war*yuhh=
   N: =F*i*:ne how'r you.

The *equals signs* at the end of one speaker's utterance, and at the beginning of the next speaker's indicates no discernable interval between the first speaker finishing and the next starting, but where the next speaker does not start in overlap.

   P: Rome wasn't built in a da:y (.) *Try*ing to keep myself
       a*wake* = Trying to keep myself from

When the equals signs *occur in a single speaker's turn*, they similarly indicate no interval – but here it is not interval between words (or sounds) in the same speaker's talk.

3.   P: Saying that *he* wants to go home and eats *ba*:con fuh
a:nd t(h) ((clears throat))
(3.5)
      P: *I* think he should be at home doin' it.

Numbers in brackets indicate time gap, to the nearest tenth of a second which could be recorded. This may be the gap between utterances of the same speaker (as above); between the turns of adjacent speakers; or between the parts of a single speaker's utterance in a turn, as here:

    C: Hello = is eum: (0.3) Lh Ilene there?
    I: Ye ::*h* this is Ile: ne
    C: Ch hi, = this is *Char*lie about th' trip tih *Syr*acyse?

Discernible gaps – again between a same speaker's utterance, between adjacent speakers' turns, or within a single speaker's turn – but gaps which cannot be timed (i.e. are generally less than a tenth of a second, but are 'larger than normal') are indicated as micro-pauses with a *dot inside brackets*, (.), as in:

    C: Alrigh' I'm s*o*rry I do tha', (.) but some(s)times its
jus *my* way uva jo:ke un I know no- hardly anybody likes
my way (.) having jokes,=

4. *Punctuation markers* are not grammatical symbols, but mark intonation patterns:

    M: H'l*lo:*
    A: *Hi* is Mary*a*nne there?
    M: Thi:is Maryanne,
    A: Hi how*a*areyou.

Generally, *commas* indicate upward intonation at the end of the word it is placed after. *Question marks* indicate upward intonation on the whole word after which it is placed. And a *full-stop* indicates downward intonation, either over the course of the word, or at the end of the word.

Margy: = cu⌐z he- *I::* bet hasn' *u*sed it since hh*hh Fa*:ll(f)
Edna: ⌊*Y*e::::ah.   n*y*ouknow=
Margy: = mayb⌐e *twi*::ce.
Edna: ⌊ee *Y*e:::ah.

Colons indicate prolonging or stretching of the sound of the prior letter or syllable: the degree to which the sound is stretched is marked by the number of colons included.

5. M: Who's *thi*:s? *A*:LA :N!hh
  A: hhhn – hih – hih

The intonational features of stressing either by pitch or volume may be indicated by setting word or letters in *italic* or for very high volumes *capital letters*.

Dr: So you ate at t⌐he convalescent home *some*thing you knew:
P: ⌊°Rome wasn't built in a day
Dr: that n (.) would.

The *degree symbol*, °, on the other hand indicates very soft tone or low volume.

T: = ↑Its not *joke* it ↑a:ll its:

Upwards arrows indicate sharply upward intonation in the letter following the arrow. *Downward pointing arrows* indicate sharply downward intonation, as here:

Margy: = ↓*Oh*::: : it wz:

6. C: I was um: (0.3) I wan' u- (.) I spoke t' the gir- I
    spoke to Karen.

The *dash* indicates a cut off of the prior sound or word.

7. C: An she's wh::m She's caught he ma:n 'hh and she wanted
    (.) Uhm the same ( ) en she's laughin cos you know her
    daughter. ˙hh (.) It's like Sw- er: Swan Lake or
    somethin'. =
  D: enhh hhhh ˙hh
   =
  B: ((cough))

The ˙h indicates audible breathing: a dot in front of it indicates an inbreath (the number of h's corresponding to length of breath), and placed after it indicating an outbreath.

Single brackets, with no words contained in them, thus (   ), indicates that the speaker made some sound (e.g. said a word), but that it could not be heard sufficiently to transcribe.

Double brackets, as ((cough)), or ((door slams)), indicates features of the audio material which may be verbalisations but which have not been transcribed; or sounds other than speakers' verbalisations.

Bibliography

Atkinson, J. M. (1976), 'Order in Court: Some Preliminary Issues and Analyses'. Paper presented at the I.S.A. Research Group on the Sociology of Law Conference, Balatonszeplak, Hungary.

Atkinson, J. M. (1978), *Discovering Suicide: Studies in the Social Organization of Sudden Death*. London: Macmillan.

Atkinson, J. M., Heath, C. C. (1976), 'Problems in Analysing Video-taped and Other Observational Data'. Paper presented at the Annual Conference of the British Sociological Assocation, Manchester.

Austin, J. L. (1961), *Philosophical Papers*, London: Oxford University Press.

Bankowski, Z., Mungham, G. (1976), *Images of Law*. London: Routledge and Kegan Paul.

Baritt, D., Carter, C. F. (1962), *The Northern Ireland Problem*. London: Oxford University Press.

Barnard, D. (1974), *The Criminal Court in Action*. London: Butterworth.

Bauman, R., Sherzer, J. (eds) (1974), *Exploration in the Ethnography of Speaking*. Cambridge: Cambridge University Press.

Bittner, E. (1965), 'Police Discretion in Emergency Apprehension of Mentally Ill Persons', *Social Problems*, 14, pp. 278–92.

Bittner, E. (1967), 'The Police on Skid Row: A Study of Peace Keeping', *American Sociological Review*, 32, pp. 699–715.

Blumberg, A. S. (1967), 'The Practice of Law as a Confidence Game', *Law and Society Review*, 1, pp. 15–39.

Bottomley, A. K. (1970), *Prison before Trial*. London: Bell.

Bruner, J. S. (1978), 'Acquiring the Uses of Language', Mimeo, Department of Experimental Psychology, University of Oxford.

Burgess, A. W., Holmstrom, L. L. (1975), 'Rape: the Victim and the Criminal Justice System', in Drapkin and Viano (eds) 1971, pp. 21–30.

Campbell, C. (1974), 'Legal Thought and Juristic Values', *British Journal of Law and Society*, 1.

Carlen, P. (1974), 'Remedial Routines for the Maintenance of Control in Magistrates' Courts', *British Journal of Law and Society*, 1, pp. 101–17.

Carlen, P. (1975), 'Magistrates' Courts: A Game Theoretic Analysis', *Sociological Review*, 23, pp. 347–79.

Carlen, P. (1976a), *Magistrates' Justice*. London: Martin Robertson.

Carlen, P. (1976b), 'The Staging of Magistrates' Justice', *British Journal of Criminology*, 16, pp. 48–55.

Carlen, P. (ed.) (1976), *The Sociology of Law*. University of Keele: Sociological Review Monograph, 23.

Cicourel, A. V. (1968), *The Social Organization of Juvenile Justice*. New York: Wiley.

Cross, R. (1974), *Evidence*. London: Butterworths.

Cross, R., Wilkins, N. (1971), *An Outline of the Law of Evidence*. London: Butterworths.

Davidson, J. (1978), 'An Instance of Negotiation in a Call Closing', *Sociology*, 12, pp. 123–33.

Dell, S. (1970), *Silent in Court*. London: Bell.

Denzin, N. K. (1971), 'Symbolic Interactionism and Ethnomethodology: a Proposed Synthesis', in Douglas (ed.).

Douglas, J. D. (ed.) (1971), *Understanding Everyday Life*. London: Routledge and Kegan Paul.

Drapkin, I., Viano, E. (eds) (1975), *Victimology: a New Focus* (Volume 3: *Crimes, Victims and Justice*). Massachusetts: Lexington Books.

Dressler, W. (ed.) (forthcoming), *Current Trends in Text Linguistics* Berlin: De Gruyter.

Durkheim, E. (1897), *Le Suicide*. Paris: Alcan.

Emerson, R. M. (1969), *Judging Delinquents*. Chicago: Aldine.

Filstead, W. J. (ed.) (1970), *Qualitative Methodology: Firsthand Involvement with the Social World*. Chicago: Rand McNally (Markham).

Frake, C. O. (1972), 'Struck by Speech: the Yakan Concept of Litigation', in Gumperz and Hymes (eds) 1972, pp. 106–129.

Frank, J. (1949), *Courts on Trial*. Princeton University Press.

Goffman, E. (1959), *The Presentation of Self in Everyday Life*. Garden City, New York: Doubleday.

Garfinkel, H. (1956), 'Conditions of Successful Degradation Ceremonies', *American Journal of Sociology*, LXIV, pp. 420–4.

Garfinkel, H. (1967), *Studies in Ethnomethodology*. Englewood Cliffs, New Jersey: Prentice Hall.

Garfinkel, H. (1974), 'The Origins of the Term "Ethnomethodology"', in Turner (ed.), pp. 15–18.

Garfinkel, H., Sacks, H. (1970), 'On Formal Structures of Practical Actions', in McKinney and Tiryakian (eds) 1970, pp. 337–66.

Gumperz, J. J., Hymes, D. (1972), *Directions in Sociolinguistics: The Ethnography of Communication*. New York: Rinehart and Winston.

Hacker, P. M. S., Raz, J. (1967), *Law, Morality and Society: Essays in Honour of H. L. A. Hart*. London: Oxford University Press.

Hart, H. L. A. (1961), *The Concept of Law*. London: Oxford University Press.

Heritage, J. (1978), 'Aspects of the Flexibilities of Natural Language Use: a Reply to Phillips', *Sociology*, 12, pp. 79–103.

Heritage, J., Watson, D. R. (1979), 'Formulations as Conversational Objects', in Psathas, (ed.).

Hood, R. (1962), *Sentencing in Magistrates' Courts*. London: Stevens.

Jefferson, G., Schenkein, J. (1977), 'Some Sequential Negotiations in Conversation: Unexpanded and Expanded Versions of Projected Action Sequences', *Sociology*, 11, pp. 87–103.

King, M. (1972), *Bail or Custody*. London: Cobden Trust.

Linton, N. K. (1965), 'The Witness and Cross-examination', *Berkeley Journal of Sociology*, 10, pp. 1–12.

McBarnet, D. J. (1976), 'Pre-trial Procedures and the Construction of Conviction', in Carlen (ed.), pp. 172–99.

McBarnet, D. J. (1978), 'The Police, the Courts, and the Right to Silence', paper presented to the Conference on Legal Reasoning and Legal Procedures, Centre for Socio-Legal Studies, Wolfson College, Oxford.

McKinney, J. C., Tiryakian, E. A. (eds) (1970), *Theoretical Sociology: Perspectives and Developments.* New York: Appleton-Century-Crofts.

Napley, D. (1970), *The Technique of Persuasion.* London: Sweet and Maxwell.

Northern Ireland Government (1972), *Violence and Civil Disturbance in Northern Ireland in 1969. (Report of the Tribunal of Inquiry: The Scarman Tribunal).* Cmd 566, Belfast, H.M.S.O.

Phillips, J. (1978), 'Some Problems in Locating Practices', *Sociology*, 12, pp. 55–77.

Pomerantz, A. (1975), 'Second Assessments: a Study of Some Features of Agreements/Disagreements', unpublished Ph.D. dissertation, University of California at Irvine.

Pomerantz, A. (1978a), 'Compliment Responses: Notes on the Cooperation of Multiple Constraints', in Schenkein (ed.) 1978.

Pomerantz, A. (1978b), 'Attributions of Responsibility: Blamings', *Sociology*, 12, pp. 115–21.

Pomerantz, A. (forthcoming), 'Agreeing and Disagreeing with Assessments: Some Features of Preferred/Dispreferred Turn Shapes', *Semiotica*.

Psathas, G. (ed.) (1979), *Studies in Language Use: Ethnomethodological Perspective.* Boston: Irvington.

Ross, H. L. (1970), *Settled out of Court.* Chicago: Aldine.

Royal Commission on Tribunals of Inquiry (the Salmon Commission) (1966), H.M.S.O. Cmnd. 3121.

Sacks, H. (1963), 'Sociological Description', *Berkeley Journal of Sociology*, 8, pp. 1–16.

Sacks, H. (1966), 'The Search for Help: No one to Turn to', unpublished Ph.D. dissertation, Department of Sociology, University of California at Berkeley.

Sacks, H. (1966–72), Unpublished lectures. University of California at Irvine. (Where reference is made to these in the text, the date of the lecture is cited.)

Sacks, H. (1972a), 'On the Analysability of Stories by Children', in Gumperz and Hymes (eds), 1972, pp. 325–45.

Sacks, H. (1972b), 'An Initial Investigation of the Usability of Conversational Data for Doing Sociology', in Sudnow (ed.), 1972, pp. 31–74.

Sacks, H. (1974), 'An Analysis of the Course of a Joke's Telling in Conversation', in Bauman and Sherzer (eds), 1974, pp. 337–53.

Sacks, H., Schegloff, E. (1978), 'Two Preferences in the Organization of Reference to Persons in Conversation and their Interaction', in Psathas (ed.), 1979.

Sacks, H., Schegloff, E., Jefferson, G. (1974), 'A Simplest Systematics for the Organization of Turn-taking for Conversation', *Language*, 50, pp. 696–735.

Schegloff, E. (1972a), 'Notes on a Conversational Practice: Formulating Place', in Sudnow (ed.), 1972, pp. 75–119.

Schegloff, E. (1972b), 'Sequencing in Conversational Openings', in Gumperz and Hymes (eds), 1972, pp. 325–45.

Schegloff, E. (forthcoming), 'On Some Questions and Ambiguities in Conversation', in Dressler (ed.).

Schegloff, E., Sacks, H. (1974), 'Opening up Closings', in Turner, R. (ed.) 1974, pp. 233–64.

Schegloff, E., Jefferson, G., Sacks, H. (1977), 'The Preference for Self-correction in the Organization of Repair in Conversation', *Language*, 53, pp. 361–82.

Schenkein, J. (ed.) (1978), *Studies in the Organization of Conversational Interaction*. New York: Academic Press.

Scott, M. B., Lyman, S. M. (1968), 'Accounts', *American Sociological Review*, 33, pp. 46–62.

Skolnick, J. (1966), *Justice Without Trial*. New York: John Wiley.

Sociology (1978), Special Issue on Language and Practical Reasoning, Vol. 12, No. 1.

Sudnow, D. (1965), 'Normal Crimes: Sociological Features of the Penal Code in a Public Defender's Office', *Social Problems*, 12, pp. 255–72.

Sudnow, D. (ed.) (1972), *Studies in Social Interaction*. New York: The Free Press.

Tribunals of Inquiry set up under the Tribunal of Inquiry (Evidence) Act, 1921. (1973) H.M.S.O., Cmnd. 5313.

Turner, R. (1971), 'Words, Utterances and Activities', in Douglas, J. D. (ed.), 1971, pp. 165–87.

Turner, R. (1972), 'Some Formal Properties of Therapy Talk', in Sudnow, D. (ed.), 1972, pp. 367–96.

Turner, R. (ed.) (1974), *Ethnomethodology*. Harmondsworth, Middlesex: Penguin.

Twining, W., Miers, D. (1977), *How to do Things with Rules*. London: Weidenfeld and Nicolson.

Waismann, F. (1951), 'Verifiability', in Flew, A. (ed.), *Logic and Language* (First Series). Oxford: Blackwell, pp. 117–44.

Watson, R. (1975), 'Calls for Help: a Sociological Analysis of Telephoned Communications to a Crisis Intervention Centre', unpublished Ph.D. dissertation, University of Warwick.

Wieder, D. L. (1974), *Language and Social Reality: The Case of Telling the Convict Code*. The Hague: Mouton.

Wittgenstein, L. (1972), *Philosophical Investigations*. Anscombe, G. E. M. (ed.) 1972.

Wootton, A. (1975), *Dilemmas of Discourse: Controversies about the Sociological Interpretation of Language*. London: Allen and Unwin.

Wootton, A. (forthcoming), 'The Management of Grantings and Rejections by Parents in Request Sequences', *Semiotica*.

Wootton, B. (1963), *Crime and Criminal Law*. London: Stevens.

Wright, F. (1973), 'Protestant Ideology and Politics in Ulster', *European Journal of Sociology*, 14, pp. 213–80.

Zimmerman, D. H. (1969a), 'Record Keeping and the Intake Process in a Public Welfare Agency'. In Wheeler, S. (ed.), 1969.

Zimmerman, D. H. (1969b), 'Tasks and Troubles: The Practical Bases of Work Activities in a Public Assistance Agency', in Hansen, D. A. (ed.), 1969.

Zimmerman, D. H., Pollner, M. (1971), 'The Everyday World as a Phenomenon', in Douglas, J. D. (ed.), 1971, pp. 80–103.

Index

Accounts, 58–60, 80, 138–40, 147, 160–70, 172–3, 177, 180–4, 187, 252n, 256n

Accusation, 31, 49–50, 55–9 passim, 66–81 passim, 106–7, 110–16, 131–4, 175, 184–7, 190, 195, 227, 241n, 247n

Adjacency pairs, 46–61, 64, 78, 86, 96, 98, 105–8, 112–14, 195, 197–8, 200, 227, 237n, 243n, 252n, 264n; conditional relevance of second pair part, 51–7, 59–60, 78, 197, 239n, 243n; noticeable absence of second pair part, 52–5, 57, 113, 115, 201, 203, 227; relative ordering of parts in, 49–51, 78, 136

Admission, 60, 140, 148, 157, 163, 186

Answers, qualified, 115–16, 120, 130–1, 136–7, 144–6, 158–9, 178

Apology, 49, 50, 57, 60, 98, 112, 185, 244n, 245n, 246n

Atkinson, J. M., 87, 96, 189, 243n, 244n

Audibility, 197–9, 202–4, 222

Austin, J. L., 140–1, 233n

Barnard, D., 9

Bittner, E., 23

Blame, allocation of, 60, 76, 79–80, 105, 107, 124, 129, 135–6, 142, 144, 147–54, 162, 168, 176–82, 187, 195, 230, 241n, 242n, 246n, 255n; avoidance of, 154, 156–9, 163, 173, 175, 177, 182, 187, 246n

Blumberg, A. S., 12

Bottomley, A. K., 12

Bruner, J., 261n

Campbell, C., 5

Carlen, P., 1, 2, 11–14, 17

Category, 7, 29, 84, 93, 117–21, 126–8, 196, 205, 235n; category bound activities, 93, 122–4, 127, 129, 249n; categorisation devices, 121–4, 126–8, 132–5, 249n–51n; see also Description, Identification

Challenge, 60, 69, 70–2, 76–9, 105–6, 126, 185–6, 238n, 252n

Cicourel, A. V., 2, 23

Classification, 56, 57, 64, 73, 237n, 239n, 240n, 260n

Classroom, organisation of talk in, 220–1, 263n

Closing, 182–4, 206–8

Complaint, 31, 49–50, 54–5, 59, 70–1, 74–5, 77, 79, 82, 184–5, 238n, 242n, 244n, 246n

Comte, A., 19

Confirmation, 116, 130–1, 161–2, 177–81, 198, 255n, 257n; disconfirmation, 80, 120, 154, 159, 178–81, 258n

Conversational analysis, 5, 6, 22–33, 190–2, 205, 216–19, 233n, 236n–7n, 242n

Correction, 51, 179–80, 258n

Courts, American, 2, 71, 192, 194, 236n; Coroner's, 87–92, 94–5, 100–4, 189, 236n, 243n, 244n, 259n; Juvenile, 2, 140, 225; Magistrate's, 2, 12; Swedish, 94, 223–5, 244n, 264n; U.S. Supreme, 97

Courts, hearings, 1–18 passim, 30, 31, 33, 61, 69, 75, 77, 82–6, 100, 104, 113, 184, 188–95, 197–9, 204, 215–18, 220–3, 227–31, 234n, 236n, 242n, 244n, 246n, 247n, 258n–60n, 263n, 264n; ecology of, 31, 92–3, 102, 222–6, 231, 244n; newspaper reporting of, 193, 259n; opening of hearing, 87–91; oppressive character of, 11–17, 34, 220, 222, 224, 228, 231, 236n, 264n; rules of procedure and evidence in, 6, 8–9, 34–5, 69, 84, 209–10, 214, 229–31, 241n–43n, 261n

Cross, R., 6, 8, 69, 241n

Defence, 60, 136–40, 142, 145, 148–51, 153–73, 181–7, 242n, 255n, 256n

Definition, 77–8, 241n, 242n, 248n

Delay, 56, 58–9, 96–7, 202, 205, 214, 216, 227, 239n, 240n, 245n

Dell, S., 12
Denial, 31, 60, 69, 70–1, 75–6, 78, 112, 114, 116, 120, 127, 132, 134–5, 140, 190
Description, 24–6, 28–33, 106–7, 118, 121–2, 125, 133–5, 139–40, 144–5, 155–9, 165, 170–1, 178, 180–3, 195, 235n, 255n, 256n; see also Categorisation, Identification

Emerson, R. M., 1, 2, 11, 12, 15–17, 34, 140, 252n
Ethnography, 2, 5, 17, 22–3, 201, 235n
Ethnomethodology, 5, 6, 18–23, 25, 28, 32–3, 189, 216–19, 233n, 236n–7n, 242n
Examination, turn-taking system for, 61–81, 190, 201, 241n
Excuses, 31, 49, 60, 112, 129, 136, 138, 140–1, 187, 190, 195

Filstead, W. J., 2
Frake, C. O., 233n, 242n

Garfinkel, H., 1, 12, 19, 21–4, 30–1, 233n–5n, 242n, 248n
Goffman, E., 2, 11, 15, 30

Hacker, P. M. S., 5
Hart, H. L. A., 5, 6, 233n, 241n
Heritage, J., 7, 241n, 247n, 248n, 258n
Hood, R., 12

Identification, of persons, 117–18, 126, 129–30, 196, 205, 222–3, 226, 248n, 249n, 264n; by naming, 38, 46–7, 196, 248n
Insertion sequence, 55–7, 64–5, 76, 210, 215, 239n
Interruption, 62–5, 76, 92, 94, 99, 237n, 238n
Invitation, 48–9, 51, 57–9, 70–2, 78, 138, 142–5, 253n

Jefferson, G., 36–8, 61, 65, 83–4, 216n, 237n, 240n, 258n
Jurisprudence, 5, 233n
Jury, 23, 68, 113–14, 184, 190, 197, 205, 243n, 262n; Chicago Jury Project, 23
Justifications, 31, 49, 57, 60, 69, 70–6, 79–80, 107, 112, 129, 136, 138, 140–1, 179, 187, 190, 195

King, M., 12

Linton, N. K., 1, 11, 240n

McBarnet, D. J., 1, 113
Miers, D., 5
Misunderstandings, 51
Multi-party settings, 35, 39, 81, 83–5, 90, 93, 104, 198, 202, 210, 220–2, 225–7, 262n, 263n

Napley, D., 9, 259n

Objections, 63–4, 209–16, 240n, 261n, 262n
Overlaps (between speakers), 38, 40–6, 58, 66–7, 99, 191–2, 199, 213–14, 238n, 261n; simultaneous starts, 40, 43, 238n; see also Turn transition

Parliamentary proceedings, 225–6, 264n
Participant observation, see Ethnography
Pauses, 38, 40–6, 52–5, 57, 67–8, 87, 191–2, 195, 198–205, 208–9, 213–16, 230, 238n, 241n, 260n–2n
Phillips, J., 233n
Place names, 106–7, 111, 117–21, 125–6, 134, 248n
Police witnesses, 107, 136, 140, 242n, 247n
Pollner, M., 234n
Pomerantz, A., 59, 240n, 255n
Positivism, 19–20
Preference organisation, 57–60, 112, 139, 143, 154, 185–6, 195, 227, 239n, 246n, 252n, 253n, 254n, 255n
Pre-sequences, 141–8, 173, 252n, 253n

Questioning, line of, 138, 141–2, 148, 173–81, 262n

Rape, 105, 240n, 246n, 258n, 260n, 262n
Raz, J., 5
Rebuttal, 160–3, 165, 170, 176, 184, 187, 242n, 252n, 256n
Recipient design, 92, 197, 199, 202, 204, 210, 248n
Reflexivity, 25, 122, 126, 249n
Religion, 107, 118, 120–1, 124, 250n; religious geography, 111, 119, 126; religious services, 100
Remedial/repair, 41, 45–6, 56, 64, 67, 196, 198–9, 202–3, 210, 215, 259n, 260n, 261n (see also Clarification, Correction, Insertion sequence, and Repeats)
Repeats, 45–6, 52, 54, 57, 67, 72, 88, 96, 148, 255n, 258n

Requests, 31, 48–9, 56–7, 71, 78, 99, 138–9, 142–3, 146–7, 174, 244n, 253n
Ross, H. L., 2
Rules, 5, 7, 15–17, 21–2; legal rules (laws), 8, 14, 229, 234n; see also Courts, rules of procedure in

Sacks, H., 23, 31–2, 36–8, 49, 61, 65, 83–4, 93, 121–4, 128, 205–6, 208, 216, 233n–8n, 240n, 242n, 245n, 248n–50n, 252n
Salmon Commission, 106, 246n–7n
Scarman Tribunal, 3, 71, 81, 106, 117–21, 136, 138, 144, 148–9, 151, 174, 182, 184, 241n, 242n, 247n, 251n, 257n
Schegloff, E., 32, 36–8, 61, 65, 83–4, 93, 205–6, 208, 216, 235n, 237n–40n, 245n, 248n, 252n, 261n
Schenkein, J., 233n, 258n
Sectarian groups, 124, 126, 127, 250n; sectarian bias, 74, 134, 242n
Silence, 95–101, 103, 113, 206, 263n
Skolnick, J., 2
Sudnow, D., 2, 23
Summons, 47–9, 94–5, 238n, 244n
Symbolic interactionism, 2, 3, 11, 18, 28
Syntactic form, 49, 50, 60, 72, 78, 92, 93, 98, 244n

Tanzania, village meetings in, 226, 264n

Tape recordings, limited availability of recording of court proceedings, 3, 188, 191–3, 215–16, 259n
Therapy sessions, 53, 77, 90, 94, 185, 193, 242n, 257n
Tribunals, 49, 106, 189, 191, 236n, 246n, 247n; see also Salmon Commission, Scarman Tribunal
Turn allocation, 37–9, 41, 43, 46–50, 53, 61, 78, 98–100, 238n; pre-allocation, 61–8, 75–81, 84, 104, 148, 181–2, 187, 190–1, 194, 197–8, 200, 204–5, 242n, 261n, 263n
Turner, R., 27, 90, 94, 233n
Turn-taking, 31, 36–61 passim, 83–5, 197, 220–1, 237n; see also Examination, Turn allocation, Turn transition
Turn transition, 38–46, 66, 199–202; see also Overlaps, Pauses
Twining, W., 5

Unspoken activity turn, 82–3, 85–7, 190, 194, 216, 223, 242n–6n

Watson, R., 247n, 249n, 250n, 258n
Weider, D. L., 23
Wilkins, N., 69, 241n
Wootton, A., 240n, 248n
Wootton, B., 10, 11

Zimmerman, D., 23, 234n